T0287008

## PRAISE FOR *THE INNOVATIVE PARENT*:

"With this wonderful guide you will find a fun and effective way to make your connections with your kids more fulfilling, while cultivating resilience and joy in their lives. Erica Curtis and Ping Ho provide artistic activities involving music, visual images, and dance for deep enrichment and enhancing our relationships with our children as they grow—with innovation, collaboration, and resilience front and center. Bravo, and thank you!"

> —Dr. Daniel J. Siegel, University of California, Los Angeles
> (*New York Times* bestselling author of *The Whole-Brain Child*,
> *Parenting from the Inside Out*, and *Brainstorm*)

"In crafting *The Innovative Parent*, Erica Curtis and Ping Ho have condensed decades of experience, both academically and on the front lines of their own lives, into a lively must-read for anyone invested in the self-awareness, success, and health of future generations. It provides compelling and easily digestible instruction for any parent, but also for educators, clinicians, researchers, program administrators, and community health practitioners, who will join parents in benefiting from this book's combination of witty observations and practical guidance. Designed for use by both novice and expert, the book's deep insights into the child-learner's mind and heart provide a beckoning path forward for anyone intrigued by the ability of the arts to engage, activate, inspire, and teach."

> —Dr. Jeremy Nobel, Harvard University (founder, The Foundation
> for Art and Healing)

"What adult wouldn't benefit from a creative approach to connecting with and engaging kids—theirs or not? Parents and professionals will find ways to promote cooperation, further social-emotional growth, and facilitate fun in the process. Grounded in studies from a variety of disciplines, as well as arts therapy practice, this book will introduce readers to practical techniques for use with people of all ages and challenges, also making it a guide to self-parenting."

> — Barry M. Cohen, board-certified art therapist and coauthor of
> *Managing Traumatic Stress through Art*

"*The Innovative Parent* manages to avoid the pitfalls of countless parenting books and tools. It offers sensitive, creative, and mindful parenting techniques that are specific yet flexible. While no child comes with an instruction manual, this book is the closest I've found to one in anchoring me—both as a parent and as a creative person—in what I know."

> —Dr. Einat Metzl, board-certified art therapist and Chair, Loyola Marymount
> University Department of Marital and Family Therapy

THE INNOVATIVE PARENT

# The Innovative Parent

## Raising Connected, Happy, Successful

## Kids through Art

# Erica Curtis and Ping Ho

SWALLOW PRESS
OHIO UNIVERSITY PRESS
ATHENS

Swallow Press
An imprint of Ohio University Press, Athens, Ohio 45701
ohioswallow.com

To obtain permission to quote, reprint, or otherwise reproduce or distribute material
from Swallow Press / Ohio University Press publications, please contact our rights and
permissions department at (740) 593-1154 or (740) 593-4536 (fax).

Printed in the United States of America
Swallow Press / Ohio University Press books are printed on acid-free paper ⊗™

29 28 27 26 25 24 23 22 21 20 19        5 4 3 2 1

Library of Congress Cataloging-in-Publication Data
Names: Curtis, Erica (Licensed marriage and family therapist), author. | Ho,
  Ping (Integrative medicine specialist), author.
Title: The innovative parent : raising connected, happy, successful kids
  through art / Erica Curtis and Ping Ho.
Description: Athens, Ohio : Swallow Press/Ohio University Press, [2019] |
  Includes bibliographical references and index.
Identifiers: LCCN 2018061234 | ISBN 9780804012140 (hbk : alk. paper) | ISBN
  9780804012157 (pbk) | ISBN 9780804040983 (pdf)
Subjects: LCSH: Parenting. | Arts and children.
Classification: LCC HQ755.8 .C88 2019 | DDC 306.874--dc23
LC record available at https://lccn.loc.gov/2018061234

To Corbyn, Isla, and Darian
My steady sources of innovation, inspiration, and joy.

—E.C.


To Eve and Halle
With whom I sing, dance, drum, and laugh.

—P.H.


. . . And to a world full of connected, happy, and successful children.

# Contents

# Preface

The task of parenting is like passing a baton from one generation to the next.

We all inherited a baton from our parents, which they inherited from theirs, and so on. Our parents did the best they could with whatever baton they were dealt. Perhaps they added decorative ribbons. Or made some cracks of their own in it. We were handed that baton—varnish, barbed wire, splinters, colorful paint, and all. We start with this.

When we parent, we pass the baton to our children. What we hand to them, in part, is what we have inherited. But we can improve upon what we pass on to them. We can remove tattered ribbons. Sand down splinters. Polish it. Attach embellishments of our own. It won't be perfect, but it can be better than before. And our children will have the same chance to make it better yet, for their children.

This process of change requires innovation—creative thinking, experimentation, and learning from mistakes for improvement. Innovative parenting is a state of mind. It requires stretching yourself as a person. It means trying something different so that your children will do the same.

Drawing, painting, cutting, taping, tearing, building, destroying, mixing, scraping, attaching, tracing, smearing, pounding, scratching, stamping, sticking, bending, sewing, dripping. Making art not only reflects what is going on inside but also has the capacity to transform it. As such, it holds a wealth of potential for enriching the lives of our children, as well as our own. I see this regularly in my art therapy practice and workshops, and at home with my own children. The experience of making, observing, and talking about art nurtures developing minds, emotional worlds, and relationships.

What's more, research supports this.

This book pulls together anecdotal experience from years of clinical art therapy practice with children, teens, and parents, along with research from the fields of psychology, child development, creativity, anthropology, and neuroscience. It offers insight into children's art as something more than refrigerator decor. We will explore how making and talking about art can help children make sense of emotions, build connections with others, cultivate empathy, develop critical thinking and problem-solving skills, process and retain information, and more. These are complex aspirations for something as seemingly simple as making art, yet therein lies the beauty of art for furthering the goals of parenting. It is wonderfully simple and do-able. And fun. Good news for not-so-artsy folks: this book is for you, too.

Far from being an arts and crafts book, *The Innovative Parent* is about breaking the conventional mold of parenting by applying creative thinking and exercises to raising children. At its essence, it's about becoming an innovative parent. It not only offers creative tools for raising connected, happy, and successful kids but also empowers you to find your own creativity to survive tough times during the day and access parenting skills that you possess but lose in the moment—when stressed, tired, or overwhelmed.

While this book is written for parents, it is also for anyone who cares for or works with children or adolescents: grandparents, caregivers, mentors, and professionals in education, mental health, community arts, health care, recreation, social services, spiritual care, and more. It empowers all to nurture kids with art, whether by opening communication, building tolerance for frustration, or teaching limits and responsi-bility. After all, the skills that children master when making and talking about art will last well beyond the activity itself and apply to other facets of their lives. Like-wise, the skills that we adults master, when facilitating projects and commenting on art, will seep into other interactions with our children, helping us become more versatile, attuned, and resourceful as parents.

This book focuses primarily on the use of visual arts to help you achieve your parenting goals. However, you will also find research and techniques involving movement, music, storytelling, theater, and writing. The undeniable benefits and ease with which you can apply these other art forms will provide you with additional tools and inspiration for your parenting adventure. You may even find yourself shift-ing from surviving to thriving in this creative process called parenting.

Here's to happy, healthy, and successful children, for generations to come. And here's to you, the innovative parent.

# Acknowledgments

We would like to offer a special thank-you to the young artists who filled this book with images: Darian (2), Isla (5), Corbyn (8), Maxine (14).

Thank you, also, to our esteemed colleagues Einat Metzl and Pat Allen for your thoughtful and enthusiastic critique of the original manuscript. Your input has helped shape this book.

To Ricky Huard, Sally Welch, Gillian Berchowitz, Jeff Kallet, Samara Rafert, Nancy Basmajian, Beth Pratt, and the others at Ohio University Press / Swallow Press for embracing our project wholeheartedly and bringing it to print.

Our heartfelt gratitude to the many children, teens, parents, and families with whom we have worked, some of whose experiences have inspired stories in this book. It is an honor to partner with you and to bear witness to the creative and healing potential within.

Finally, we offer gratitude to the countless friends, family, and colleagues who have provided sounding boards, encouragement, and guidance. Thank you.

# How to Use This Book

While this book breaks down theories and research behind arts-based parenting tools and techniques, ultimately *The Innovative Parent* is a practical guide. The chapters are written to stand alone, so that you have the option to read whichever ones are of most interest or relevance at the moment. Chapters are also conveniently organized into subsections to allow you to read short bursts of information. After all, parents rarely have the luxury of sitting down for long.

Each chapter contains practical tips, activities, and language to use with children and teenagers at home or in the community, individually or in groups. Activities best suited for children are designated by the symbol **Ⓒ**, and those adaptable for both children and teens are marked with the symbol **Ⓒ/Ⓣ**. Activities for parents and professionals are indicated by the symbol **Ⓟ**; however, many of these can also be done by teens and children. It's up to you. You need not worry about following the instructions precisely. As you become more comfortable using the visual arts, music, and movement in parenting, you may discover your own innovative and creative approaches to raising children. Every child is different. Every parent is different. Adapt the practical tips to meet your and your children's needs.

Abundant anecdotes are sprinkled throughout. Where examples from our professional work are used, names and identifying information have been changed. We have chosen to alternate "she" and "he" pronouns for readability and balance; however, we recognize that there are those who do not identify with either pronoun.

As you read, please keep in mind that the information contained in this book is not meant as a substitute for therapy. If you are caring for a child who exhibits behaviors of concern, such as developmental delays or a traumatic reaction to an event, we encourage you to seek support from a trained professional.

# 1

~~~~~~~~

## Talk Less. Draw, Dance, and Sing More

WHY ART?

I need to get ready for work. My daughter needs my attention. I need a
shower. She needs a snack. A cuddle. A book. A round of, "Let's pretend
we're mermaids running away from the shark." I need to be out the door in
30 minutes, and I need a plan. Redirecting her to look at a book or play with
her toys by herself isn't working. She wants time with me, and those won't
satisfy. Television would work. No question. It's tempting. I resist. "I know!
How about you draw a picture of us being mermaids running away from the
shark, and when I get out of the shower you can show it to me!" She's elated
and runs off to draw.

There are many options for responding to children. Experts generally agree that
some approaches are better than others; however, there are still many "best practices" from which to choose. More often than not, parenting is an exercise in trial
and error. Because of this, it's important to be versatile. Parenting with the arts in
mind allows you to be that versatile parent.

In the example above, there were many options for getting my needs met: distracting, reasoning, firmness, bribery. But this scenario (as with most all scenarios
involving children) was not just about *my* needs. It was also about *hers*. A parenting
moment like this is as much about nurturing connection, emotional health, and
cognitive development as it is about getting out the door. I was leaving for work. She
needed connection (probably *because* I was leaving for work). Neither reasoning,

bribery, firmness, or distraction would have addressed her need. Art, on the other hand, could.

### Art expresses and addresses internal needs

Inviting my daughter to draw us as mermaids wasn't just about keeping her occupied (as television would). Drawing allowed her to express something about our relationship through drawing us together. It allowed her to symbolically "play" with me on paper, as mermaids. It bonded us in our escape from the shark. It also gave her something to create that she could look forward to sharing with me when I was available again. On these many levels, it addressed her need for connection.

### Art has high nutritional value

Art is a nutritionally dense activity that imparts skills leading to greater social, emotional, and cognitive health (Catterall 2005). It involves imagination, creativity, problem solving, self-expression, risk taking, self-worth, and the making of meaning. It can develop fine and gross motor skills. It can promote focus, critical thinking skills, and tolerance of differences (Curva et al. 2005). It can even help us learn and remember information as well as perform better in a variety of academic subjects (Asbury and Rich 2008). Joint creative activities promote skills necessary for cooperation and communication (Burton, Horowitz, and Abeles 2000).

### Art is a child's home turf

I entered my daughter's world by inviting her to draw about us instead of trying to explain for the nth time why I couldn't play with her. Art is a language that makes sense to kids and teens. In fact, it has been said that art is our *first* language. Babies scribble and clap or bounce to music before they can talk. They recognize words more readily if paired with a melody than when spoken (Thiessen and Saffran 2009). Children will often create art simply because some stimulus is in their view that provokes interest, whether markers and paper, a drum, or natural objects and string. Kids learn best through hands-on experiences of the world, which the arts provide (UNICEF 1994), and will naturally explore, express, take in, and process more through play and the creative arts than they will through talking. Creative arts therapists and play therapists have been on to this for a while.

Lawrence Cohen (2002), author of *Playful Parenting*, describes play as a magical place where children can truly be themselves. Art is much the same. I've heard children describe their experience of making art as a place where they can feel free to express their own ideas and feel better. The respected anthropologist Ellen Dissanayake (1992) asserts that art has supported our survival as a species because it helps us make meaning, self-express, and bond as a community during difficult times. Indeed, art is much more than a pretty picture or a song well played. It is fundamental to who we are.

For our purposes, we will define art as the use of some tool or medium (be it paint in the visual arts, instruments in music, or the body in dance) and a creative or imaginative process. Together, these invite expression of one's internal world, exploration of the external world, or an investigation of the relationship between the two. Art may intend to communicate to another or be entirely self-exploratory. It may be functional or not. Art always involves a process and often, though not always, creates a product. So, rather than thinking about art as an equation where Paint + Canvas = A Painting, or Flute + Breath = Music, we will explore how art is integral to our lives and well-being.

Tool + Creative Expression = Exploration, Making Meaning, and Communication

This is an equation that has everything to do with parenting. And this is why it makes sense that we should all talk a little less, and draw, dance, and sing a little more.

## WHEN WORDS AREN'T ENOUGH

"Can we talk, sweetheart?"

"Yeah," grunts my son.

"When you don't like what someone is doing, don't do it back to them . . . [pause] . . . It doesn't solve anything . . . [he nods] . . . If a kid is bothering you, you can say 'Stop' or 'I don't like that' but calling names back just makes the situation worse . . . [pause] . . . Do you understand what I'm saying?". . . [he nods] . . . Or you can walk away . . . [pause] . . . Come tell us if there's a problem."

"Okay," he says.

"Do you understand?" I double-check.

"Yes," he affirms. "Next time I'll just annoy them back."

Cue: deep breath. Clearly, my words were not enough. Or, perhaps, they were too much. I grab a piece of paper and draw a stop sign. "When someone calls you a name, tell them to 'Stop.' And then stop yourself from saying anything else, and walk away . . . [pause] . . . What will you do next time someone calls you a name?" Now I hold my breath.

"Say 'Stop.' Then stop and walk away."

Bingo!

Talking to children is crucial to their development. Groundbreaking research by Hart and Risley (1995) connects higher IQ and academic performance to greater numbers of words spoken by caregivers to children from birth to age three. As children get older, talk remains important for developing vocabulary, communicating interest, setting limits, teaching problem solving, connecting, and more. But more talk is not always better, as the example above shows. Adults tend to overtalk to children, particularly when it comes to problem solving, addressing uncomfortable

**4**     feelings, and setting limits. Whether or not we care to admit it, our words of wisdom can be ineffective, if not irritating.

### TRY THIS:

In a moment you will read a short sentence. As you read it, pretend that someone is saying it to you. Take a minute to notice any thoughts, emotions, or sensations that arise. Close your eyes if you'd like to do so, and repeat the sentence in your mind. Ready? Here it is:

"Can I talk to you?"

What did you notice?

Now, let's do this exercise again. You will read a different sentence this time. Again, imagine someone saying this to you and notice any thoughts, emotions, or sensations that arise. Here it is:

"Can I show you something?"

What did you notice this time?

Many people experience anxiety or defensiveness in response to the first question, while the second produces curiosity and openness. I see this with couples in my practice. Although intended as an invitation to connect, "Can we talk?" is often met with resistance or defensiveness. Many have learned (starting in childhood) that talking indicates a problem (in other words: "Uh oh. I'm in trouble."). Even before children learn to tune out talking for self-preservation, they may tune out because it's difficult for them to absorb too much verbal information at once. Kids can also feel emotionally overloaded. A heart-to-heart can feel intense and leave kids feeling vulnerable. When we talk, we're playing on our home turf, not theirs.

Then there are times when we remind our kids to do something, over and over again. When it comes to multiple reminders, children aren't necessarily tuning out because they are overwhelmed. They don't listen because, frankly, it's pointless—more reminders are coming, so why bother now?

Of course, there are ways to talk effectively to kids and break the cycle of non-productive communication. There are many worthwhile books that give practical tips on how to listen and talk to children. Yet even with these talk-based approaches, talking as a means of nurturing children—socially, emotionally, and cognitively—still has inherent limitations. Even in my best therapist-mommy moments when I am entirely present and empathic, if one of my children is upset, my verbal attempts are often met with grunts or with running and hiding.

### Words aren't enough to build connection

Talking does not guarantee connection. Just as people have different learning styles, they also have preferred ways of connecting. While some people connect through a chat, others prefer physical proximity, a shared activity, or a symbolic gesture, such as an offering of food or a gift. For most children, play and art are the primary ways of developing connection with others. Art making buffers the discomfort that can accompany difficult conversations. It offers a language of metaphor and fantasy to which children can relate. It provides for symbolic acts of connection through gift giving. Art making can be a shared activity. Unlike talking, the creative arts provide limitless ways to build connection and communication with children. (Chapter 4: "Connect First" explores building connection and communication through art.)

## Words aren't enough to build emotional health

When it comes to nurturing emotional health, talking also has limits. We've all had the experience of not being able to communicate clearly what we are feeling with words alone. Even if we can find the words, we may not feel comfortable sharing them. Other times, we're not at all aware of how we are feeling. Feelings can elude us. This makes it difficult to communicate them, let alone to understand and work through them.

Words are also limiting in that they can easily lead to misassumptions of someone else's experience. While we all have a general sense of what feeling "down" means, my feeling "down" and your feeling "down" may in fact feel quite different to each of us. What if my "down" looked like an overcast day, and your "down" looked like a hurricane? As the saying goes, a picture is worth a thousand words. The creative arts can allow kids to express much more about their emotional experiences than words alone can. (For more on maximizing emotional health through the creative arts, see chapter 5: "Raise Happy Kids.")

## Words aren't enough to build a foundation of success

Finally, talking is also a limited tool for educating children, whether we are teaching academics or important lessons of life. The brain is wired more for active engagement than for passive absorption of information (Bransford, Brown, and Cocking 2000). When we talk and expect children to listen and learn, we're missing a big piece of how they absorb information. There are different learning styles to consider when we think about the best way to teach a child (seeing, hearing, or doing). While some have a specific preference, many children benefit from a combination of all three approaches (e.g., Brown et al. 2003; Dunn et al. 2009). The creative arts provide this. Whether it's the tactile experience of certain art materials, the physical experience of movement, or the auditory experience of making or listening to music, the creative arts engage the senses to sustain attention, build associations for learning and retention, and develop observation and problem-solving skills in a way that talking and listening cannot. (For more on enhancing cognitive and academic performance through art, see chapter 6: "Raise Successful Kids.")

Before we look more specifically at how the creative arts can address our goals of connection, emotional health, and academic success, let's first consider your personal short- and long-term parenting goals.

"Who wants to do a special project?" my husband, Mathew, inquires. He is in charge of the kids for the afternoon and is taking stock of his short-term goals: 1) keep the two older kids from killing each other, 2) attend to the youngest, 3) make dinner, and 4) maybe, just maybe, get some work done.

Mathew doesn't like art much. He doesn't understand it and feels that he isn't very good at it. To him, art + kids = mess. And yet, he brings out the markers and paper, on which he has printed each child's name in block letters vertically down the left side of a page. On another sheet of paper are lists of traits and strengths, all starting with letters from their respective names. They are going to make name poems.

"Here's what you get to do. Decorate each letter of your name. Then, choose one word for each letter of your name from this list. Pick words that describe you. We will write that word next to the letter." The kids rush to the table to begin.

(We'll return to this story in a moment.)

Short-term goals involve shaping behaviors, avoiding problems, or de-escalating situations that have already gotten out of hand. Getting your kids out the door in the morning, resolving sibling conflicts, and avoiding power struggles over bedtime are common short-term goals. Long-term goals, on the other hand, involve nurturing qualities that you believe are important to the development of character, such as self-motivation (getting out the door), thoughtfulness toward others (sibling squabbles), and problem solving and collaboration (conflicts over bedtime). These goals facilitate long-term social, emotional, and cognitive health.

Our methods for achieving our short-term goals need not be out of alignment with our long-term goals—yet often they are. While few, if any of us, would say that our long-term goals are to nurture compliant adults, the fact is that, in the moment, compliance is what we want. As a result, we intervene in ways to achieve quick resolution, order, or agreement. This can put short-term goals of behavior management at odds with long-term goals of character development.

Luckily, the arts can facilitate both short- and long-term parenting goals simultaneously.

Returning to the story above:

Later that evening, I ask my husband, "So, what inspired you to do an art project with the kids?"

"To impress you," he jokes. "Actually, I thought learning the different words for characteristics would help expand their vocabulary. But more importantly, I hoped it would help them think about their strengths. I thought it would be good for their self-esteem."

My husband's short-term goals (entertaining the kids) and longer-term values (education and positive sense of self) could be met simultaneously through this creative activity. Here are some other examples: Dancing to the car together (instead of cajoling your child to leave the park, pretending to leave her, or carrying her out kicking and screaming), gets your child to the car (short-term goal) while teaching her that she is capable of positively transitioning from a preferred activity to a less-preferred activity (long-term goal). Making a collage about going to a new school, rather than offering bribes for going or laying down the law, can help decrease morning meltdowns (short-term goal) while providing an opportunity to process difficult feelings about change (long-term goal). It takes some creativity on our part, which can feel time-consuming, but it's far less tiring than fighting the same battles over and over again. And it allows us to parent today in a manner that is consistent with our hopes for tomorrow.

While it may feel foreign at first to use creative arts strategies in parenting, these approaches to parenting will come more readily to mind with practice. Even I forget, at times, to turn to the creative arts to help my children (and myself) work through difficult moments. But one thing is for sure: there *will* be a next time to do a parenting moment better. Make a plan for how to approach a challenging interaction more creatively when it comes around again. This can be easier than finding a creative response in the heat of the moment.

〜〜〜〜〜〜〜〜〜〜〜〜〜〜〜〜〜〜〜〜〜〜〜〜〜〜〜〜〜〜〜〜〜〜〜

💡 Ⓟ TRY THIS:

Take a moment now to write down three short-term parenting goals:

_____

_____

_____

Now write down three long-term parenting goals:

_____

_____

_____

〜〜〜〜〜〜〜〜〜〜〜〜〜〜〜〜〜〜〜〜〜〜〜〜〜〜〜〜〜〜〜〜〜〜〜

As you read this book, keep your short- and long-term parenting goals in mind. This will make it easier to apply the tools with your own unique child.

## FIND THE FUN

Ping arrives to lend a hand after the birth of her second granddaughter and finds that two-year-old big sister is not a happy camper. Routine activities

**8**  like nose wiping, hair washing, and changing clothes now provoke tantrums. Previously effective consequences and rewards for behavior management are backfiring. This is clearly not sustainable for anyone. Ping concocts a creative plan to address each scenario that leads to resistance. The next day the "boogey monster" (a flying tissue) gets a meal from her nose. The bathtub washcloth becomes a soaking wet hat that they take turns wearing. The pop-up tent contains a magic blanket, under which pajamas are removed and play clothes are put on. Big sister changes her clothes gleefully without incident and proudly shows her parents what she can do. Eventually, she dresses her little sister, too. Fun is exchanged for fuss. Laughter replaces tears.

Every moment with our children has the potential for being fun—if not memorable—if we don't take ourselves too seriously, and if we develop a creative mindset. (See the section entitled "Develop a creative mindset" at the beginning of chapter 7: "Tap Into Your Own Inner Artist"). While it's important to parent with social, emotional, and cognitive goals in mind, it's also important to simply have fun with our children. Unfortunately, a hyperfocus on achievement from early ages has become prevalent as a result of increasing competition for admission to schools from pre-K to college and fewer employment opportunities, even for those with bachelor's degrees. As one Harvard study reveals, kids believe that their parents value achievement much more than happiness and kindness (Weissbourd and Jones 2014). And those same kids, taking a note from their parents, agree that achievement is the most important value. While there are numerous social, emotional, and cognitive benefits of incorporating the creative arts into parenting, one of the most fundamental assets of the creative arts is the opportunity they provide for fun and relaxation.

Like play, the arts can offer both serious rehearsal for life and pure fun. And like play, the creative arts don't always have to serve a purpose (at least not an obvious one). There's already so much that consumes the attention and energy of parents that it's nice to have a creative way to let go. Singing along to the radio, redecorating a room, or bouncing to a beat can simply feel good. As the saying "art for art's sake" suggests, art sometimes needs no justification. It is enjoyment. It is downtime. It is valuable in and of itself. And because it is valuable for these non-achievement-based reasons, incorporating more creative arts into your home may have some added, unexpected benefits.

We all need time to de-stress and to unconsciously process information or emotions from the day. Engaging in the creative arts can allow us to do that. When we make art, we can lose our sense of self and time, as we focus intently on the present moment while simultaneously being energized and fully engaged. This experience of "flow," a term coined by positive psychology expert Mihaly Csikszentmihalyi (2013), is associated with increased long-term happiness. What's more, engaging in the creative arts can simply put a smile on our faces—an often taken-for-granted act with enormous positive mental and physical health benefits (Beres et al. 2011; Kraft and Pressman 2012). Oh, and fun time is also bonding time. We all need more of that, especially in this digital age.

Specific parenting goals aside, simply introducing, encouraging, and modeling engagement in the creative arts at home fosters happier, healthier, and better-connected kids. I've prescribed snapping pictures of eye-catching scenes to shift a teen's focus from the negative to the positive. I've encouraged knitting breaks during homework to curtail anxiety-driven meltdowns. I've invited a mother and child to scribble together in order to disrupt their roles as the punisher and the punished. All experienced positive results.

Simple creative activities that result in laughter (whether scribbling together or dancing around the living room in last-year's Halloween costumes) can not only bring more joy to family life—they may even boost immunity (Bennett et al. 2003; Christie and Moore 2005). Art that invites judgment-free self-expression, connection, and discovery naturally reduces stress and anxiety and improves vital signs (Stuckey and Nobel 2010). An analysis of 146 studies concluded that expressive writing improves not only immune function but also self-reported health, psychological health, and general functioning (Frattaroli 2006). Art for the sake of fun, relaxation, and leisure is actually art for the sake of health and well-being—for kids *and* parents.

## THE NOT-SO-ARTSY PARENT

When I invite adult clients to make art in therapy sessions, it's not uncommon for them to feel ambivalent or even negative about it. They may approach art with skepticism or discomfort. They decided long ago that they're not artistic. They haven't made art since childhood. They had a negative experience with it in school and didn't learn how to enjoy it. It's unfamiliar territory for them.

At home, plenty of parents encourage their kids to color independently, but if it becomes more involved or requires parent participation, they divert the activity to something else. It's not necessarily because they don't want to help their children or spend time with them. It's because they don't feel comfortable in the realm of the creative arts, they find other activities "easier" or less messy, they don't see the point, or they simply don't enjoy arts activities.

The most highly regarded theory of typical artistic development in children, created by academic Viktor Lowenfeld in the late 1940s but still widely referenced today, identifies the last stage of development as ages thirteen to sixteen. He called this stage the "Period of Decision/Crisis." In this stage, teens decide whether art is worth pursuing. They decide (or are often told) whether they are good at it or not. At this stage, many people stop making art. How, then, can the not-so-artsy folks among us begin to access the arts to enrich our children and further our parenting goals?

**10**    Using the creative arts to further your parenting goals *isn't* about becoming a skilled artist or devoted scrapbooker. It doesn't matter if you're good at it or not. It doesn't matter if you sing off-key or can't draw a straight line. It really doesn't even matter if you like it. After all, there are plenty of parts of parenting that we don't like but do anyway because it works or it's good for our kids. I don't particularly like to read the same book over and over again to my preschooler, but I do it because I know that 1) she enjoys it, 2) research supports that repetition helps with mastery of language and vocabulary (Horst, Parsons, and Bryan 2011), and 3) repetition is comforting to a child. So I do it and find enjoyment, instead, in watching her delight in her favorite book of the moment (even for the hundredth time).

If you are a not-so-artsy parent, congratulate yourself for picking up this book (and turn to chapter 2: "Why We Love to Hate Glitter Glue (and Other Struggles with Art)"). This is an opportunity for you to challenge preconceived ideas that you may have about art making and to stretch yourself as a parent. Kids challenge us daily, and approaching those challenges with creativity will help us become more skillful and versatile as parents—and people.

# 2

## Why We Love to Hate Glitter Glue
## (and Other Struggles with Art)

As a child, my wooden blocks become buildings and cars, with windows and wheels meticulously drawn using crayons and markers. Under my bed, I am Michelangelo drawing on the bed frame—my personal Sistine Chapel. In the dark corner of my closet, I am making ritual cave drawings on the walls. My little creative juices are flowing, and I am thrilled about my ideas. My parents are not. "No," they say. "No. No. No." My face falls. I feel my creative voice being stifled. Into adulthood, I secretly question their wisdom in those moments . . . until I become a parent myself. "We draw on paper, not on furniture. No, not on your toys either. Not walls. Paper. No. No. No." As I hear my words, my own childhood experience returns to me. I feel conflicted. Where do freedom of expression and limits intersect?

It's messy. It creates frustrations. It will likely get on clothes. It could ruin the furniture, the floors, the walls. Frankly, there are easier things to do with your kids than art. Blocks, trains, and video games don't require hosing your kids down afterward. They won't drive your child to tears because something got spilt or doesn't look right. Other activities don't make us hold our breath as we anticipate a rogue scribble spree on the walls or an entire bottle of glitter glue squeezed directly onto the table. There are a lot of good reasons we love to hate art. Art materials can challenge both kids and parents. And yet, these very situations that test us can provide some of the most powerful opportunities for personal growth.

Art gets messy, and so does life. What better place than the untidy world of art to practice ways of dealing with the messiness of life. Art offers the important

**12**  opportunity to explore boundaries between personal freedom and the needs of others; between self-expression and self-containment. It allows us to consider where we can loosen up as parents, distinguishing between necessary limits and unnecessary preoccupations. In this chapter, we will not only explore these themes but also offer practical strategies for setting limits, containing messes, and rethinking our struggles with the unpleasant parts of art making as a metaphor for parenting in general.

## WHERE LIMITS MEET FREEDOM OF EXPRESSION

"Can I pour my orange juice into my oatmeal?" My son asks. "No," is my husband's immediate response. (He feels strongly about kids not playing with food.) I get it. Nevertheless, I check in to see if he is okay with me stepping in. He gives me the green light.

"What's your plan?" I ask my son. "Are you done eating? Are you curious about how it would taste? Do you want to experiment to see what happens?"

"I want to make a new recipe," my son replies.

"Sure," I say. "Let's get a separate bowl and put a little oatmeal in it and add a little orange juice. If you like it, you can mix it all together. If you don't, then you won't have ruined your breakfast." He gets a separate bowl and tests out his innovative recipe. He likes it, mixes up the rest of his breakfast, and licks the bowl clean.

Kids need a balance between freedom of expression and containment. With too many demands and restrictions (authoritarian parenting) or too much freedom and indulgence (permissive parenting), kids will tend to display more behavioral, social, and emotional difficulties. Research on parenting styles from the 1960s until now has consistently revealed that children raised with a balance of high expectations and responsiveness to their needs, as well as a balance between clear limits and flexibility, do better socially, emotionally, and academically (Baumrind 1966; Suldo and Huebner 2004). This is called authoritative parenting, and the creative arts offer a rich arena for parents and professionals to rehearse and fine-tune this balancing act.

### Expression and experimentation

Many of us have a knee-jerk "No" reaction to creative expression and exploration either because we were taught in the past that it was not okay or because we determine in the present that this is going to be a hassle. When we think consciously about it, we can begin to clarify *why* it's not okay. We may even be surprised that we are okay with the activity after all and come to see these moments of spontaneous creativity as something upon which we can capitalize. Here's how:

Pause first. Instead of "Yes" or "No," try saying: "I'm not sure. Tell me what you're doing here." Or, as in the example above: "What's your plan?" Asking thought-provoking questions like these will help you and your child pause to consider the situation, without cutting off the creative potential that's brewing. Inquiring about your child's plan prompts the executive functioning part of his brain (responsible for planning, organizing, problem solving, and thinking before taking action) to come online and consider: "What *am* I actually doing here?" In the above example, it allowed my son to consider his intention and develop a deliberate, creative idea. Learning more about your child's intention also allows you, the adult, to help shape the direction of the activity as needed (e.g., "Let's get a separate bowl and mix just a little bit together first.").

Next, ask yourself the following three, simple questions (see fig. 2.1):

2.1 Three steps for deciding to give the go-ahead

1. Is it safe?

2. Is it respectful of the rights or property of others?

3. Does it align with family values?

If the answer to each of these questions is "Yes," then it's probably okay for your children to go ahead expressing and exploring. For my husband, playing with food was a violation of number three, a conflict with his values: We don't play with our food. However, he forgot to consider the intention behind the behavior. Our son was playing chef (or at least that's what he decided he was doing after I asked him to pause and consider his actions). He wasn't just interested in smooshing and squishing his food together. In our family, creating new recipes is acceptable for mealtime.

*Why We Love to Hate Glitter Glue*

Smooshing and squishing for the sake of smooshing and squishing would have needed to wait until later.

Let's look at another example:

When my son first draws on himself with a marker, my "No" reflex kicks in: "We don't draw on ourselves, we draw on paper." I ask myself: But why? Because it's not okay? Because my parents didn't let me draw on myself? Hmmm. Not a good enough reason. So, why? Because it violates our family value of looking presentable? But for what? For whom? He's a kid. We're not going for family photos. Why then? Because it's toxic! Safety is a good reason. But the markers are nontoxic. Hmmm. Back to the drawing board. It doesn't violate any property or person. It is safe. I value self-expression more than I value a marker-free body. I decide that I don't care after all. Instead of "No," I exclaim joyfully (and nonjudgmentally), "Look at you!" My son beams.

But this is not the end of the story. As things go with kids, he takes his experimentation a step further. Thrilled by the go-ahead to draw on his body, he begins to color his face. I decide to set the limit there. Despite being "washable," marker ink takes days to remove, and I prefer for him not to have a green face for the better part of the week. I buy him a set of face paints instead. "You can draw on your body, just not on your face. If you want to decorate your face, use the face paint." My son is excited about the face paint, but corrects me: "I wasn't decorating my face, Mom." (Insert "Duh!" look here.) "I was making a mask!" I chuckle to myself as I realize I had forgotten to ask about his plan in the first place. "Of course you were! Would you like to make a mask together?" I get out the construction paper, a less messy option for mask making. "What color do you want it to be?"

There are no absolutes when it comes to deciding when to cut our kids some slack and when to rein them in. It's okay for you not to allow your children to draw on themselves. Perhaps one of your family values is to have clean, marker-free bodies. Perhaps you're concerned about toxicity or possible classroom distraction and disapproval. You can decide on a case-by-case basis whether or not there is more room for creative expression and exploration than you may have initially thought. A "No" conclusion also doesn't have to mean putting the kibosh on creative expression altogether. It may simply mean providing a bit more guidance and containment, as the next section explores.

### Containment

I present a box of markers to the members of my art therapy group at a school for teens with emotional and behavioral difficulties. I don't even have the chance to share my activity idea before the markers start flying across the room as the kids take aim at one another. It is chaos. "Stop" will not work. Reminding them of expectations will not work either. They are full of energy and feeling rambunctious (aka defiant). Removing the markers altogether would stop the playful battle but with a counterproductive message: "You're not capable of handling yourselves." They are capable of managing themselves; they just need a little more containment.

I quickly tape a large piece of butcher paper on the wall and draw a bull's-eye. Several feet back from the wall, I stick a strip of masking tape on the floor. "Line up here!" I call. Then, pointing to the bull's-eye, I challenge them: "Let's see who can score the most points." In an instant, the markers stop rocketing through the air. The teens all line up with their marker "darts" in hand. They wait patiently. They take turns aiming at the makeshift dartboard. They keep score and even root for each other. They enjoy themselves and, importantly, contain themselves.

When we think about containing children's behavior, we often cut our options short, relying either on verbal limits (stop, don't, not okay) or removing them from the activity. While, indeed, removal is sometimes the only option, these common strategies significantly reduce our opportunities to teach children how to stay engaged and expressive in a manner that is safe, respectful, and in line with our values. Containment comes in many different forms. It may include clarifying expectations, offering alternative choices, or providing boundaries, as in the example above. For any of these to be effective, however, the choice of containment must be informed by needs underlying the behavior.

A single behavior can represent any number of needs, feelings, thoughts, concerns, or curiosities, depending upon the child and the situation. An adult may insist, "Stop drawing on the furniture." However, changing a child's behavior requires addressing the underlying reasons for the action: Did she not know the rule? Is she testing a limit? Is she curious about how the marker looks on the sofa? Is it part of her play? Did she run out of paper and not know what to do? Is she angry? If the child was never taught the rule, or needs reminding, a simple reminder and redirection to a piece of paper may be sufficient. However, if the child is angry, reminders alone will not address the issue. She'll likely scribble on the wall or table next, just to make her point known. In such a case, the anger needs to be addressed also.

Sometimes we can take an educated guess as to the need behind the action. With the marker-throwing teens in the example above, I had a good hunch that their needs included fun and energy release. They were also testing my limits. The containment of a large piece of paper, a piece of tape on the floor, and a simple set of directions responded to each of these needs: 1) yes, we can have fun, 2) yes, we can get our energy out without throwing things at each other, and 3) yes, I can handle whatever you throw at me (literally).

If you're uncertain of the need behind the behavior, try these steps (see fig. 2.2):

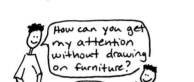

2.2 Identify and address underlying needs

| Steps to Identifying and Addressing Underlying Needs | Examples |
|---|---|
| 1. State what you see (start with "I see" or "I notice"): | "I see you drawing on the table." *This nonjudgmental observation, when spoken neutrally or with curiosity, minimizes defensiveness and keeps lines of communication open.* |
| 2. Inquire about underlying needs (start with "I wonder"): | "I wonder what made you decide to draw on the table?" *"I wonder" orients the child toward curiosity about her own behavior. It promotes self-reflection.* |
| 3. Suggest possible underlying needs: | Curiosity: "Did you wonder what it would look like?" Attention: "Did you need my attention?" Upset: "Did something happen?" *Younger children may need help identifying underlying needs. While older children and teens may find it easier to identify what they need, they may still benefit from assistance.* |

| Steps to Identifying and Addressing Underlying Needs *(cont.)* | Examples *(cont.)* |
|---|---|
| 4. Find alternatives that respect limits (start with "What" or "How"): | Curiosity: "How can we experiment without drawing on furniture?"<br><br>Attention: "How can you get my attention without drawing on furniture?"<br><br>Upset: "What are some ways to express your feelings or feel better without drawing on furniture?"<br><br>*If ideas are not forthcoming, then offer alternatives:*<br><br>Curiosity: "What about gathering different materials to experiment with?"<br><br>Attention: "How about asking me to stop what I'm doing so we can spend time together?"<br><br>Upset: "What if we tape a large piece of paper to the door for expressing your feelings?"<br><br>*Help your child put the alternative into action to meet his need.* |
| 5. Teach responsibility taking and natural consequences (start with "Let's"): | "Let's use this sponge to clean off the marker. *Then* we can experiment with drawing on other materials."<br><br>"Let's clean this up. *Then* you can do something else."<br><br>*If there is resistance or refusal to help:*<br><br>"I see you're not ready to clean it yet. Let me know when you're ready. When the table is clean, you can play."<br><br>*So as not to initiate a power struggle, remember the formula for staying positive: When X, then Y. ("When the table is clean, you can play.")* |

If the same behavior persists, consider providing containment by making the items in question available only under supervision. The scissors in my house have fallen into that category several times. Over the years my three kids have, at various times, cut their own hair, a pillow, window blinds, the rug, each other's belongings, and more. The needs behind the actions have varied from "my bangs were too long" to "I was mad" or "I wanted to see if the scissors were sharp enough to cut this . . . and they were!" For repeat offenses, regardless of the underlying reason, you can explain, "I'm going to put the scissors away. When you need to use them, if I'm available, I will get them and sit with you while you use them." This applies to other materials as well.

### Paint and pencil yield different powers

"Using markers and paper, draw something from nature," I announce to a group of teens with autism spectrum disorder (ASD). We are generating images for a mural they will later paint in the school courtyard. They set to work at their desks and voilà! Drawings of trees, flowers, a pond, a volcano, a forest, butterflies, and more. The next week, we brainstorm further. They are given paint and work in pairs to create images of nature again. We get muddy mess, frustration, conflict, and shutdown. What happened?

Materials have different properties and thus evoke different experiences in the user. Structured materials such as markers, pencils and erasers, rulers, collage materials, and glue sticks tend to be containing. They are less tactile and easier to control. On the other hand, looser materials like paint, wet clay, runny glue, and glitter are harder to control. They tend to be oozy and gooey, sticky, or messy and, like their sensory qualities, can loosen up emotions and impulses as well. Because of this, sometimes the key to balancing self-expression and containment resides within the properties of the art materials themselves.

Returning to the example above, there are several ways to explain what may have gone awry during the painting activity: lack of interest in the activity, lack of technical skill, inability to collaborate. But none of these fit. The students *were* invested. They *were* able to draw images from nature. They *were* capable of collaborating . . . they just needed more containment to be successful at it. As is typical for individuals on the autism spectrum, social interactions were not only difficult but also distressing. Offering a loose material, when these teens were already feeling challenged socially and emotionally, was not a recipe for success. They needed more structure and containment, and we could provide that through a simple change in materials.

We swap paints and brushes for materials that provide significantly more containment and structure. By shrinking and photocopying their original nature drawings onto transparencies, our students are able to overlap their images with those of their classmates, thus creating a single, combined image. A tree on one transparency can now find a home next to an ocean from another transparency. Using an overhead projector to project and trace their combined images onto a single piece of paper, they successfully work together to create a collaborative landscape.

Thinking about the materials that you offer and how they might affect emotions and behavior can make all the difference in helping your child explore the balance between freedom of expression and self-containment. If she is playing with looser material, it's important to think about how to help contain the energy that the material creates. In the face of a more challenging task, your child may benefit from more structured materials. Here are some more examples of ways to use materials to help children from getting too carried away, overwhelmed, or overstimulated by an art activity:

- Put a paper plate or tray under clay, glitter, or beading activities.

- Offer a smaller piece of paper instead of an overwhelmingly large one. Or place a larger piece of paper beneath the smaller one. The larger piece of paper can essentially "frame" the smaller one, providing clearer visual boundaries for art making. If a child is working with paint or a similarly loose material, the larger piece will also catch the overflow and prevent it from ending up on the table.

- Make hand wipes accessible.

- Place finger paints and paper inside a shallow box.

Conversely, looser materials may be useful for children who could use a little loosening up. For children who become easily frustrated, don't like messes, or tend to be hard on themselves, you may want to slowly challenge them to have fun with looser materials:

- Offer paints and the task to "make the ugliest painting possible."

- Provide larger paper, paintbrushes, and sponges. Put paper on a floor, wall, or easel instead of on the confinements of a table.

- Experiment with process-based activities without any expectations for the outcome. For example, attach crayons to the top of a canvas with hot glue. Then use a hair dryer to melt the crayons and watch them drip down the canvas.

Keeping the properties of materials in mind isn't only about containing messes and behavior with which we prefer not to deal. When we provide support for children to practice the balance of self-expression and self-management, we are helping them prepare for life (see fig. 2.3). From peer relationships to classroom and workplace demands, the more opportunities that children have to practice impulse control, persistence, collaboration, focus, and breaking down large tasks into manageable parts—to name a few—the more connected, happier, and successful they will be.

2.3 Balance containment and self-expression

🗲 Ⓒ/Ⓣ  **TRY THIS:**

Experiment with how different materials feel not only to the touch but also in terms of sensations, impulses, or thoughts that they provoke in mind and body. Set out a variety of materials, both structured and unstructured. Try each one out with your children in turn. What thoughts and feelings, if any, do they evoke? Do you or your children feel challenged by any of the materials? Loosened up? Contained? Which materials do you dislike? Why? Of what do they remind you? If you are doing this experiment with younger children, ask which they like best and least. Which are easy or hard to work with? Which make them feel messy, silly, happy, or frustrated?

We can use information generated from this exercise to inform what materials to use with our children to loosen them up or rein them in. What's more, the exercise itself helps children begin to pay attention to the impact of different experiences on how they feel and respond, as well as how they can shift their feeling state by changing sensory input.

## MESSY, LOUD, AND OFF-KEY

"Da Da Da da-da Da da-da Da," My son starts singing the Darth Vader theme from Star Wars. After a few bars, my daughter starts in with her favorite princess song. My son gets louder. My daughter tries to outdo him. They're enjoying themselves as they sing over each other, louder and louder. My nerves are shot. We're in the car. I'm driving. The cacophony is compelling me to shout: "Stop!" I resist. They're not doing anything wrong, per se. I want to want to let them carry on, but I'm tired and want them to cease.

Kids are told "No" a lot during the day, which is why it's important to use creative moments to say "Yes" as much as possible. Encouraging creativity, exploration, and self-expression indeed requires tolerating scraps of paper on the floor, loud banging on pots and pans, and off-key singing of the same annoying song over and over again. But it doesn't have to mean a free-for-all either. It's equally important to teach kids how and when to be messy, loud, and off-key in a way that considers the needs of others and teaches responsibility.

### Nope, that doesn't work for me

"Can we add glitter?!" my daughter asks as we work on her brother's birthday banner. Ugh. I want to say "No." I go through my checklist. Is it a safety issue? No. Does it violate the rights or property of others? No. Is it in opposition to our family values? Nope. So, then, why not? The answer comes, clear as day: because I'm tired, and I have a million other things to do, and it's just plain inconvenient for me right now. And then I realize that's okay, too.

It's okay to say "No" to our children, even when it's for entirely selfish reasons. In fact, it's important to do so. For starters, we parents need breaks now and again. We're happier and more balanced as parents when we take them. We need opportunities to meet our own needs, instead of stretching ourselves so thin that we resent the continual demands of others.

Saying "No" also provides the opportunity to teach valuable lessons, such as consideration of others and time constraints. As Robin Berman points out in *Permission to Parent* (2014), many well-meaning parents overindulge their children for fear of hurting their feelings. What results, she emphasizes, is a generation of children unable to handle setbacks and disappointments. They struggle to consider the needs of others. As important as it is to open the doors to creative expression (and to stretch our tolerance for loud, messy, and off-key activities), we can also support our children's growth when we say "No" once in a while. It matters how we do this, though (see fig. 2.4).

Step 1: Affirm the activity—Find something positive about the activity: "I notice you came up with a new idea" or "I see you really rockin' out on those drums."

Step 2: Take responsibility—Clearly state whose needs are not being met: "Unfortunately, it doesn't work for me (your brother, the family, us, our classroom) right now." Together, steps 1 and 2 communicate clearly that you are open to the creative expression, *and* something about it isn't working right now for other reasons.

Step 3: Give your reason—Explain why it doesn't work right now. Be concise. Explanations are not invitations for negotiation. Nor are they attempts to convince. Rather, an explanation helps children learn to consider factors such as time management or the needs of others.

Step 4: Explore alternatives—Offer an alternative time or place to do the activity, a different activity altogether, or an adaptation of the activity that addresses the issue. You might even ask your child to come up with suggestions.

Here are some examples of how to put this into practice:

2.4 Four steps for saying "No"

Scenario 1: Your child is pulling out the paints, and you both need to leave soon.

| Steps to Setting Limits | Examples |
|---|---|
| 1. Affirm the activity: | "I see you have a creative idea." |
| 2. Take responsibility: | "Unfortunately, painting doesn't work for me right now." |
| 3. Give your reason: | "It takes a lot of cleanup, and we need to be out the door in ten minutes." |
| 4. Explore alternatives: | Encourage problem solving: "What can we do to solve this?"<br><br>Offer an alternative time or place: "You can paint as soon as we get home. Let's leave this all set up so it's ready for you when we get back."<br><br>Offer a different activity: "You can draw until we leave, instead."<br><br>Adapt the activity: "You have five minutes to paint before we need to clean up, so let's start with one color and one brush right now." |

Scenario 2: Your child is singing loudly in the car.

| Steps to Setting Limits | Examples |
|---|---|
| 1. Affirm the activity: | "It sounds like you've learned a new song." |
| 2. Take responsibility: | "Unfortunately, singing loudly in the car doesn't work for me right now." |
| 3. Give your reason: | "I'm tired and need to concentrate on my driving." |
| 4. Explore alternatives: | Encourage problem solving: "What can we do to solve this?"<br><br>Offer an alternative time or place: "You can sing as loudly as you want as soon as we get home."<br><br>Offer a different activity: "How about finding shapes in the clouds instead?"<br><br>Adapt the activity: "Maybe you can sing more quietly or sing it in your head." |

"Here," I say, as I hand my client a piece of paper. "Rip this up." He has come into my office angry, and my aim is to give him an outlet. And rip he does. He tears that piece of paper, and several more, into tiny bits. Then he throws them all over the couch and floor like confetti.

"Wow! It's a lot, isn't it? . . . And all over the place," I comment about the paper (and his anger). He has expressed his anger, discharged some of his emotional energy, and demonstrated the magnitude of his feelings. We sit amid the resulting mess. Now what?

"Okay, now what should we do with all of this?" I pose the question to him. He looks at me quizzically. Was I really suggesting that he clean it all up?!

"Do you want to keep it in an envelope or get rid of it?" I ask.

"Let's get rid of it," he says definitively.

"Okay, let's do it!" I say. I have a hunch that, while he's not too keen on tidying up the room, he is ready to throw out the anger. Together, we put hundreds of paper scraps into the recycling bin and, in the process, his mood returns to baseline. Addressing the mess is as important as expressing anger in the first place.

Addressing the aftermath of an art experience can feel tedious for parents and kids alike, but inherent in the process are valuable opportunities. Cleaning up helps kids take responsibility, teaches problem solving, and promotes a sense of family citizenship. As in the example above, it also helps kids feel more contained after an energetic or emotional art session. Many parents avoid art activities due to the mess factor. However, when we consider cleanup as a valuable experience in itself, rather than just a tiresome means to an end, we may be willing to let our kids get down and dirty more often.

Of course, it also helps to minimize the mess to begin with. We do, after all, have other things to do in our day. Here are some practical tips to minimize mess:

- Designate a craft table and make it accessible—My kids had a craft table but they never used it. Instead, they staked claim on the dining room table for projects; thus, mealtimes began with the added inconvenience of tidying it up (or at least shoving things to the side). Why didn't they use the craft table? I surmised that the problem was twofold: 1) it wasn't big enough for both of them to use at the same time (I believe they secretly like to be near each other *all* the time, despite a façade to the contrary) and 2) it was in their bedroom, away from the main activity of the house where they like to be. We got a larger table for them to work on and moved it to a more central location. While we still needed to tidy it from time to time (lest they revert to the dining room table), we were able to do so at our own convenience rather than at every mealtime.

- Use drop cloths, newspaper, or paper bags—As obvious as it may seem to suggest using such things as drop cloths or newspaper to catch a mess, you wouldn't believe the number of times I've found myself scrubbing the coffee table while muttering to myself: "Next time I *have* to put down wax paper before they start clay projects." Throw a sheet over the dining room table or onto the floor. Afterward, toss it into the washing machine. Or, use old newspapers. For smaller, drippy, gooey, or glittery projects, provide a paper plate on which to work. Not only will this protect the work surface and contain the mess, but also it will make the project easier to move.

- Invest in bins or baskets—Bins, craft containers, folders, or baskets into which to throw materials make cleanup much easier. It's easier for the kids to help if you don't worry about organizing the bins themselves. Throw all the paints and brushes into one. Put all the stickers, glue, and scissors in another. Markers and pencils in yet another. Snap, stack, and done.

- Bring out the vacuum!—The vacuum cleaner can be your best friend.

My kids think that they hit the jackpot when they discover colored sand in the craft cupboard. I let out an audible groan. I don't want to deal with the mess that I know it will make. I am about to say "No" when I realize . . . there actually couldn't be an easier mess to clean up. "No problem!" I say, delighted by my revelation. "When you're done, here's the vacuum." Weeks later, they want to break up Styrofoam. No problem! "When you're done, vacuum it up." Another day, it was cutting tiny pieces of felt for no apparent reason. "Looks like fun! There's the vacuum for when you're done."

- Move the project outside—While moving a project outside can make it more expansive and messier, by the same token it doesn't matter quite as much. Hosing down grass, sidewalks, or your kids is a lot easier (and more fun) than scrubbing floors and tables. Alternatively, move the project to the bathroom. Painting, shaving foam, and other ooey-gooey activities that are safe to wash down the drain can be done right in the bath or shower.

- Make available only those materials that you want to deal with at a moment's notice—My kids have access to most art materials. I like them to be inspired by what they find, and I also like them to be relatively self-sufficient with their projects. It promotes independence and saves me from having to find whatever they need. That said, I also keep certain materials out of reach. Paint and loose glitter, for example, are accessible only to grown-up hands. Because of their mess factor, potential for overuse, and labor intensiveness, these are projects that I want to know about before my kids start them.

Make cleanup and care for materials a habit. We all fall into the bad habit of cleaning up messes for our kids. It gets too late. It's easier (and faster) if we just do it ourselves. You know the reasons. I use them, too. Making cleanup a habit (even for children as young as two or three years old), however, sets up a healthy habit for years to come. Here are some tips:

- Help your kids clean up—Shouting "Make sure to clean up!" from the other room is rarely effective. I know. I've tried. Working together is not only motivating. It also reinforces the important feeling of being a team.

- Think small, specific tasks—Kids (even teens) need large tasks to be broken into small, specific tasks. "Clean up" is a confusing and overwhelming concept. "Put all the stickers in this box, first" is doable. Think of it as running a marathon. It's much easier to run from the end of one block to the next until you've finished the distance than it is to set out focusing on the entire, overwhelmingly large distance ahead.

- Make it fun—Sing. Race the clock. Race each other. Let them do the spraying and vacuuming. For younger children, encourage them to load up materials in their toy trucks and drive them where they need to go. For teens, turn up their favorite energizing tunes. Cleanup need not be a chore.

- Teach natural consequences—Let them know that leaving the lid off clay or caps off markers will dry out those materials. Point out that unwashed brushes will get too hard to use again and will need to be tossed. Papers left on the floor will accidently get stepped on and crumpled.

- Involve your child in problem solving—Instead of "time to clean up," ask your child specific questions that require putting on his thinking cap: "Okay, where should we put your picture to dry? What should we do about these brushes? Where should we put these strips of fabric?" and so forth.

## DESTRUCTION

Just a few weeks before our final session together, Christopher begins dismantling the structure on which he has worked so hard during his year in therapy with me. He tears off the toilet paper roll chimney, detaches the cardboard roof, and rips off the button and string that serve as a secure latch for the door. As he removes each piece, he places it back in the supply bin from where he originally got it. A colleague surmises either that the destruction represents his anger about the upcoming goodbye or that he doesn't trust me to keep his structure safe after he leaves. Another hypothesizes that he wants to destroy the memory of our time together, to make goodbye more tolerable. The following week, I watch and narrate as the destruction continues. I comment only on what I see, rather than making assumptions or judgments (see also appendix 1: "Guidelines for Talking about Art and Life"). I remark: "I see you're taking it all apart and then putting the pieces back from where you got them." He looks up at me, "Yes. That way you have them to help the next child, just like you helped me." Christopher isn't angry. In fact, he isn't destroying anything at all. He is acknowledging his own healing and paying it forward.

When we think about art, we think about *making* stuff. Rarely do we think about dismantling or destruction. We smile at the thought of our children drawing pictures (not scribbling over them), manipulating pipe cleaners into flowers (not chopping them into hundreds of pieces), and playing rhythms (not banging as loud and hard as possible). When we get handed an "I love you" drawing, we respond with: "Ahhhh." Drawings of buildings exploding get an: "Ohhhh." When we see something that looks like destruction, either during or after the creative process, we may jump to negative conclusions and unnecessarily cut the expression short. We may also miss the opportunity to explore the meaning behind the action.

Sometimes what looks like destruction isn't at all destructive. It is productive. This section examines the productive nature of destruction in children's art. We'll look at how we can better understand, discuss, and embrace the scribbles, scrunches, and explosions that are part of art and, metaphorically speaking, life.

### Mess-ups and meltdowns

My son expects a lot of himself. He hates it when he forms his numbers and letters "wrong." He likes his drawings to look "just so" and berates himself when they don't. When he's not satisfied, he scribbles over his art or writing, scrunches it up, and gets stuck in a funk. While I want to reassure him, I don't try to convince him that his mistakes "look fine" because that approach won't work. On many occasions, I try to problem-solve with him about how he can change mistakes into something new. I encourage him to think about how to fix what he doesn't like. For inspiration, I read him the book "Beautiful Oops" by Barney Saltzberg (2010). Sometimes my strategies work. On many occasions, they don't . . .

One day my son is drawing, and he "messes up." I try to comfort him. He shouts, "I'm so stupid at this!" I try to encourage him to fix it. His agitation grows. I remind him he can start over. He begins taking it out on everyone around him. I look at the scrunched-up paper in front of him—his little wad of frustration, disappointment, and anger. In a flash of insight, I try an entirely different approach. "Look what you made!" I exclaim, pointing to the crumpled paper. He stops and looks at me. I have his attention. "You made a sculpture of your mad brain. Can we title it and put your name on it?" He smiles. We write "Mad Brain" on his sculpture along with his name. Then we photograph it.

Weeks later, I find my son drawing at his table. In front of him are a couple of drawings and three wads of scrunched-up paper. "Look, Mommy!" he announces cheerfully. "I made three mini-mad brains!" He smooths out the wads of paper, shows me his mistakes, and then scrunches them up again. "You can tell I've been working hard this morning, can't you?" he says with a grin. I smile back. "You sure have."

Sometimes when kids destroy their art, they want it gone—forever—but just as plants grow from fertile soil after fire, dismantling or destroying what was originally there can make room for new creation to emerge. Our adult impulse may be to fix or repair (whether it be art, homework, or feelings), but when we embrace what is present, rather than trying to make it better, sometimes it resolves on its own. In this example, rather than trying to alter my son's experience, I simply acknowledged it without judgment or expecting it to be different. It was from this mindset that I was able to respond more creatively. It was from this place that my son could be okay with his mistakes.

Helping kids embrace their mistakes may be even more important than we realize. According to Sir Ken Robinson (2011), internationally acclaimed author and expert in arts education and business innovation, innate creativity is destroyed when we stigmatize mistakes. He asserts that those who are not prepared to be wrong will never come up with anything original.

Embracing mistakes is also characteristic of a growth mindset that supports learning and creativity. Carol Dweck (2006), professor of psychology at Stanford University, defines a growth mindset as one that embraces mistakes as part of the learning process, which enables positive risk-taking and greater academic achievement. This contrasts with a fixed mindset that avoids challenges and making mistakes because of the belief that capabilities are fixed and limited. A fixed mindset may say, "I'm not good at this" and avoid engagement for fear of revealing deficiency; whereas, a growth mindset may say, "I can learn from this mistake" and pursue a challenge toward achieving mastery. Both behavioral observations and neuroimaging reveal vastly broader brain engagement in students with a growth versus fixed mindset when doing the same cognitive task (Moser et al. 2011). Not surprisingly, students whose brain scans showed greater engagement were more successful at learning from their mistakes, and at making fewer future errors, than their fixed mindset counterparts. The good news is that a fixed mindset can become a growth mindset under the right learning process that embraces mistakes and rewards effort.

Make a binder that celebrates oopses, errors, and unexpected surprises. Read Barney Saltzberg's *Beautiful Oops* or Peter Reynolds's *Ish* with your children for inspiration on ways to turn mistakes into opportunities. Keep a binder for each of your children, where they can celebrate their messes and mistakes whether in art, schoolwork, or other activities. Share an observation such as "I notice you didn't give up on this homework project" or "I heard you say you messed up, and yet you turned it into something new! Would you like to put it in our special place of honor?" So as not to embarrass them, make adding "oopses" to the binder optional. Alternatively, place a jar in a communal area where children and parents alike can place a colorful pom pom every time they make a mistake from which they learn (see fig. 2.5). Rather than something about which to be embarrassed or frustrated, this simple activity can transform mistakes into something to celebrate.

2.5 "Learning from mistakes" jar

As with all aspects of parenting, helping your children learn how to tolerate mistakes in life takes a little trial and error. In chapter 3: "Survive the Day" we will explore ways to talk to children about their art through "useful praise," such as reinforcing qualities that you want to develop, helping your child reflect on his own work, and being accurate while being encouraging. While many of these tools are useful when your child is feeling frustrated by his art, you may need some additional approaches in those especially tough moments. Here are some to try:

- Acknowledge feelings—With any fumble in life, art making or otherwise, try to acknowledge feelings (without interpreting them) before jumping in with solutions so children feel understood. A simple statement of inquiry, prefaced by what you literally see (without judging it), may suffice: "I see your paper scrunched up. I wonder how you're feeling?"

- Help them get specific—"I don't like it" or "I messed up" is too general to address a problem effectively. Helping children hone in on the specific part they don't like can reveal that the problem isn't as big as their brain makes it seem. This can make problem solving and coping with difficult feelings much easier.

- Problem-solve together—Invite your child to problem-solve with you or a peer: "Let's take a look together. You say you don't like this part here? What do you think it needs so that you'll like it better? Should we ask someone else for input?" Soliciting support from others may not only help in the moment but also impart a skill that will serve your children when dealing with other problems in life.

- Explore options (see fig. 2.6)—If your child has no idea how to proceed, you might offer some suggestions:

  - "Would you like me [or someone else] to help fix it?"

  - "Would you like to start over?"

  - "Do you want to take a break from this for a little while?"

  - "Should we turn this into something completely new and different?!"

- Admit you're stuck, too—If you don't know how to help, or your child has rejected all of your ideas, it's okay to say "I'm not sure how to help, but I really want to." Acknowledging that you're also stuck can normalize the child's experience and show that it's okay not to know what to do sometimes.

2.6 Explore options for addressing mistakes

*Why We Love to Hate Glitter Glue*

A child is drawing happily when she suddenly begins to scribble over her drawing. The grown-up cries, "Oh no! Don't scribble over it! It looked so pretty. Why did you ruin it?" The child replies, "I don't know." But she does.

Let's rewind and redo.

A child is drawing happily when she suddenly begins to scribble over her drawing. The grown-up calmly notes, "Wow. I see a lot going on with that drawing. I wonder if you can tell me about it." The child takes a deep breath and begins talking animatedly, "Well, there was a mermaid and a dolphin and they were swimming in the ocean and then this giant wave came splashing over them and they were riding in the wave and . . ."

She hasn't destroyed the drawing. She is bringing it to life.

Certainly, there will be times when your child will scribble, scrunch, or rip when upset or frustrated. And yet other times what looks like destruction isn't destruction at all. Young children will "scribble" over their drawings because they are doing their version of coloring it in. Slightly older children will scribble over their drawings or smoosh a sculpture as part of a story they've created in their imagination, as in the example above. At other times, a child may simply be inspired to change directions midstream. So, how do we know the difference?

Ask.

Rather than assuming something is wrong when scribbles and smooshes strike, approach your child with curiosity (see fig. 2.7):

1. Look for nonverbal clues—Your child may appear energized or animated, but does he look angry or frustrated?

2. Make nonjudgmental observations—"You're ruining your beautiful art" is not an observation. It is a judgment about the art (it's beautiful) and what you see happening to it (it's getting ruined). An observation is a neutral description of what you actually observe: "I see you covering the whole page with red paint" or "I see you ripping up your paper." Judgmental statements tend to stifle creativity, self-expression, and communication, while provoking resistance ("But I want to scribble on my art") or resentment ("They don't get it"). (For more about making nonjudgmental observations and preventing resistance, turn to appendix 1: "Guidelines for Talking about Art and Life" and chapter 4: "Connect First.")

3. Invite more discussion—"I wonder what made you decide to do that?" or simply "I wonder if you can tell me about that?" are open-ended ways to encourage your child to share more about her intention. "I wonder" invites dialogue in a nonthreatening way, as it suggests that conclusions have not been reached.

2.7 Remove judgment and approach with curiosity

## Guns, bombs, and other pictures we can't stand

I cautiously enter my son's room. I have just gotten frustrated with him and he with me. He doesn't look up. I notice he is drawing a picture of a figure holding a gun. I begin to talk to him about what just transpired. I'm not sure if he's listening. His only response is, "Uh huh. Uh huh." He draws another figure—the target of a bullet flying out of the gun. I know he's angry with me. I pause but continue. I acknowledge his anger and admit that I could have handled the situation better. He says nothing, but gives the targeted figure a hefty shield. I explain the reason for my frustration and tell him I love him. He adds a spaceship with two smiling figures inside. I ask him about his drawing. He says that he is fighting a bad guy, and then we escape together. He says he is sorry for what happened.

A lot of concern about angry, violent, and aggressive imagery comes from our fear of real violence. Although the National Center for Education Statistics reveals that school violence has actually decreased since the early 1990s (Musu-Gillette et al. 2018), tragic incidents like the 2012 shooting at Sandy Hook Elementary School, where twenty children and six adults were killed, and the 2018 shooting at Marjory Stoneman Douglas High School in Parkland, Florida, where fourteen students and three adults were killed, raise very real concerns. Adults are quick to respond to violent imagery and words with discouraging statements like "That's not nice" or "That's not appropriate." In some cases, children have been suspended from school or parents have been punished over the drawing of a gun. The American Psychological Association Zero Tolerance Task Force (2008) found that such punishment typically associated with "zero tolerance" policies is ineffective at reducing actual incidence of misbehavior, yet we misguidedly continue to respond nonconstructively to aggressive art in the hope of deterring actual threat.

Destructive or aggressive art often represents a healthy expression of children's feelings and may even prevent the likelihood of actual violence. A music therapist might invite a child to write lyrics that express angry feelings. An art therapist might encourage a teen to express his upset toward someone in imagery as a substitute for bottling it up or acting on those feelings. One teen I worked with spontaneously drew futuristic spaceships firing guns. Seeing this as an opening to communicate about his emotional world, I asked him at whom the ships were firing. He responded by adding a math book and a dismembered math teacher floating in space. Far from an actual threat, his drawing was an expression of frustration toward the academic subject. By showing curiosity in his drawing and permitting the spontaneous violent imagery to emerge, I created an opportunity for a heartfelt conversation about his struggles.

While aggressive art can communicate something that is bothering a child, at other times it signifies a normal developmental curiosity about power, good guys versus bad guys, or exposure to weapons through media. When my young son bites his pancake into the shape of a gun, he's not necessarily angry. When my daughter draws herself with a magical sword, she isn't necessarily expressing violent inclinations. At times they are simply fascinated, like many kids their age, by themes of conflict and power. Through make-believe games and art they are able to explore these ideas safely, at least in contexts where permitted.

But how can we be sure that violent imagery isn't a threat? How do we know whether it's an expression of anger or merely repetition of something seen? Here are some points to consider:

- Understand the context—Are you aware of something having happened recently to upset your child? In the example above, my son and I had just had a conflict. This helped me understand his drawing of one person shooting another as expressing feelings about this event. Did he recently come across something that introduced a new idea? When my child started school, peers introduced him to themes from television shows that he hadn't previously seen. When he started drawing ninjas, I knew that it was due to this influence. Have there been behaviors of concern or changes in your child's demeanor lately? Aggressive art along with concerning changes in behavior or mood could suggest underlying emotional turmoil. Explore this further using some of the tips below or seek help in understanding what's going on.

- Look for nonverbal cues—Consider your child's body language and facial expression. Notice her demeanor while she is drawing, when she shows art to you, and when she talks about it. These will give you clues about her emotional state.

- Ask open-ended questions—"I wonder if you can tell me about this?" and "I wonder what's going on here?" are good conversation starters. You can also encourage your child to tell a story about his art by saying, "I wonder what's going to happen next?" or asking questions like, "I wonder what are they shooting at each other?" Your child's answer can help you get a better sense of his intentions. If your child responds with, "They are shooting chocolate at each other," it's probable that he is being playful. If he answers, "This guy is shooting fire at his brother," it's possible that he is having feelings toward his brother that need further exploration.

- Reflect what you see—If a child won't respond to your questions (a good clue that she may be upset about something), try reflecting what you see: "Hmmm . . . I see a lot of teeth showing on that guy's face. I wonder what he is feeling?" or "I see this guy doing something to that guy." Literally stating what you see in the art is a noninterpretive and nonjudgmental approach that may help your child start talking about her art.

- Address the feelings—If your child expresses anger, frustration, or hurt feelings toward you or someone else, let him know that you appreciate that he shared how he feels. Also let him know that you're glad that he used drawing to feel better rather than saying or doing something hurtful to the other person.

- Teach empathy—While we want to validate art making as a good way to express difficult feelings, it's also important to teach children about the power of pictures and words to hurt the feelings of others: "I'm glad that you are dealing with your anger toward your sister with drawings. How do you think she might feel if she saw this, though? . . . Yeah, so it's a good way for you to get *your* feelings out and, at the same time, showing her would hurt *her* feelings and not solve the problem. Instead, when you're ready, we can go tell her that you didn't like what she did to you."

- Seek a second opinion—If you are concerned about a child (or find that you are trying to convince yourself not to be concerned), do not probe further than what feels comfortable to you. Instead, talk to someone about it. Seek the input of a teacher, school administrator, friend, or therapist. If you are not the parent, share your observations and concerns with the parents or others.

## LETTING GO

During a visit to the home of my in-laws, I introduce window crayons to my kids and their cousins. The crayons seem harmless enough. Draw on the window. Wipe it off. What fun! Unexpected condensation, however, spells disaster. The window drawings drip and smear and—worse—stain my mother-in-law's new, white window blinds. Yikes! My mother-in-law tries to convince me, "It's okay. Really. I'm really okay with it." But how can she be? It isn't going to come out. I feel terrible. She continues, "Whenever I look at it, now, it will remind me of the kids and what a nice time we all had together." I am in awe.

Change your thoughts and change your experience. Despite the number of times that I teach this in my therapy practice and workshops, I'm always amazed at its effectiveness when put into practice. My mother-in-law easily could have told herself that her blinds were "ruined." She could have lamented about the amount of money she had spent on them and how new they were. But she didn't. This moment held in it the potential for frustration, disappointment, and annoyance. And yet, it equally held the potential for understanding, nostalgia, and joy. It wasn't a given. It was a choice, and she chose the latter.

When we start to notice how we think and feel about daily events with our children, we begin to see how powerful our beliefs are about those events. Although changing how you think about spilled paint may not seem like a big deal, small creative moments that push your buttons are ideal opportunities to practice noticing your reactions and then shifting your thoughts and feelings to a more neutral, if not positive, framework. Stained blinds. Messy spills. Sticky fingerprints. Loud instruments. Scuffs on the floor from tap shoes. These are cringe-worthy moments that, if reframed, can not only strengthen our tolerance muscle but also help us experience parenting in a whole new light. Plus, they provide effective role modeling for our children.

Practice these four simple steps (see fig. 2.8):

1.  Notice your thoughts—Notice your knee-jerk responses by acknowledging your present thoughts. Is your thought a judgment ("Ugh—that sounds horrible!"), worry ("I'll never get the stain out"), or criticism ("How could he be so . . .")? Notice the thought and name it "judgment," "worry," "criticism," or whatever other label fits best.

2.  Notice your feelings—How do your present thoughts and narratives about the situation affect your feelings about what's going on?

3.  Accept that it's already done—We can't change the fact that paint spilled, so why resist it? Try telling yourself, "It's already done. It's okay." Or "It's already in the past. We can deal with it."

4.  Look for something to savor—Ask yourself: "In the grand scheme of things, how big of a setback is this mishap? Is there anything about this moment that I can appreciate? Might I someday look back on this and smile or laugh? Could this be a good story to tell?"

2.8 Shift from worry and judgment to acceptance and savoring

Try not to be discouraged if you don't feel blissful each time the violin shrieks, paint flies, or tears fall. Setbacks are an important part of an innovative life, and of parenting. Start by simply aiming to feel slightly less irritated than usual. Work up to letting go a little more. As when strengthening muscles, start lightly with lots of repetitions. Over time, small day-to-day shifts will add up to big changes. Through this creative process, you can build the strength you need for the heavy lifting of parenthood.

# 3

## Survive the Day

I'm cooking dinner and balancing on one foot, as my other foot bounces my six-week-old in his baby chair. My daughter is screaming, "I SAID stop it!" from the adjacent room. My older son continues to provoke her. I shout from the kitchen, "Something isn't working in there!" No good. It continues. I maintain my cool as I move to ineffective tactic number two: "Come into the kitchen!" I shout to my oldest. "I'm trying to cook dinner and take care of your baby brother, and I can't have you antagonizing your sister in there!" My son runs into his bedroom and slams the door before returning to bop me on the back with a wrapping-paper-roll-turned-light-saber. Laughing menacingly, he returns to his room and slams the door again. He's angry. I stand outside his door and invite him to talk. No good. I try empathy: "You're upset." He shouts, "Go away!" I offer a hug (that can sometimes disarm him). No response. I give him some space and then try to talk again. He yells, "I can't hear you!" Argh! But then I take a piece of paper, draw a sad face, and slip it under the door. He opens the door and lets me give him a hug. Then we talk about what happened.

Parenting is challenging, not only because our children can push our buttons but also because we're often stretched in many directions at once. Nine-to-five jobs notwithstanding, there are places to go, boo-boos to kiss, tantrums to de-escalate, feelings to repair, fights to break up, homework assignments to supervise, appointments to make, meals to prepare, rooms to clean, bills to pay, bottoms to wipe, and teeth to brush. We take "time-saving" shortcuts like shouting from the other room

While it's hard to image that drawing, singing, or dancing can help you with those grocery-store tantrums and homework protests, it's even harder to believe that the creative arts will save you precious time. But they can. This chapter explores how.

## CREATIVE CURES TO CONFLICTS

Art can give you access to your children when words don't. When emotions run high or your children feel miles away from you; when you're knocking but they're pretending that nobody's home, art gives you a key to get in through the back door. Even if you would describe your relationship with your child as generally positive, connected, and mutually respectful, everyone experiences times of rupture now and again. Day-to-day conflicts that arise from misunderstandings or a mismatch between your needs and your child's needs are inevitable. At these times, you can use the creative arts to reconnect with your child, resolve problems, and curtail future occurrences of the same conflict.

Art works to resolve day-to-day family conflicts for many reasons. With creative strategies, you're playing on your children's home turf where they feel more comfortable. Rather than approaching a conflict with explanations and reasoning, a creative approach is naturally more imaginative, metaphorical, and playful. That's not to say that conflicts should be turned into fun and games when kids need clear expectations, limits, and boundaries. Creative arts strategies are not intended to deflect from or minimize the problem at hand. Rather, they can allow us to go deeper into the issue by fostering authentic (re)connection before talking, by preempting defensive responses (my kids' favorite is "I ALREADY KNOW THAT!"), and by giving children a language in which they're comfortable communicating feelings and needs.

### Reconnect

One of the biggest mistakes we make when trying to end a conflict is attempting to resolve it before reconnecting with the other person. Art can first help lower defenses, reestablish connection, and open lines of communication. Just as in the example of the interaction between my son and me at the start of this chapter, sometimes even our best traditional efforts to make amends are met with anger or dismissal. In this case, art served as a sort of mediator or peace negotiator. It became a neutral third party that could carry a message to my son. Although he didn't want to listen to me, he was able to take in what the visual messenger had to say: "I'm sad. You're sad. I see you. I feel you." With that, he was able to reconnect with me so we could talk about what had happened and where things went wrong.

Reconnecting through art can take several forms. It's up to you (and maybe a little trial and error) to determine the most suitable approach. Sometimes kids need acknowledgment of their feelings. Sometimes they need to stew in their feelings for a bit. Sometimes kids need quiet. Sometimes they literally need to shake it off. Here are some ideas to try:

(C/T) Empathize with art (see fig. 3.1)—Let your child know that you see how upset she is by drawing a sad or angry face. You might write a simple message that goes along with it: "I'm sorry" or "We both got angry." Even if your child isn't a reader yet, written words may open up the conversation when she asks, "What does this say?" Alternatively, draw two circles and label them "me" and "you" (or your name and your child's name). Draw a simple sad or confused face in the "me" circle, then pass the paper and pen to your child. Without saying a word, you've just invited your child to share her feelings in a way that will be easier for her than telling you with words. If your child doesn't understand the cue, offer a little assistance by saying: "My guy is saying 'I'm sorry.' What does your guy say?" or "My person is sad. Show me what your person looks like."

3.1 Empathize with art

Ping's one-and-a-half-year-old daughter (not granddaughter) is scurrying through their home, systematically putting things into her mouth or throwing them—keys, toiletries, papers, and whatnot. She manages to keep one step ahead of Ping, who is chasing her around for hazard and damage control while futilely hollering variations on "No" and "Stop." Finally, her daughter grasps the oil-laden spokes of a bicycle. She looks back at Ping for a reaction before making the next move. Ping sighs, sits on the ground, and extends her arms out toward her little one as she says, "Do you need some love?" Immediately, her daughter runs into her arms for an embrace. Defiant behavior over.

**C/T** Show a little love (see fig. 3.2)—It is precisely when kids are acting their worst or pushing us away that they most need reassurance of our love for them. They may be unconsciously seeking love and attention, and a simple offer of love for a child of any age may do the trick, as in the example above. However, it may be difficult for some children to be receptive to caring words or a hug in the midst of a conflict. Defenses are already up. Show your kids how much you love them by drawing a symbol of your love and desire for reconciliation. For example, you may draw two stick figures, one sending a heart or rainbow toward the other.

3.2 Show a little love

**C/T** Let me hear how angry you are (see fig. 3.3)—Teach your kids that it's okay to let you know just how angry they are, without having to yell, slam doors, or ignore you in order for you to get the message. Grab a shaker or a drum, for example, and ask: "Just how angry are you right now? Are you this angry [shake lightly], this angry [shake harder], or THIS angry [shake really fast and hard]?" Pass the instrument to your child. You can take a turn, too: "I got this angry, didn't I [shake]? But now I'm feeling this sad/calm/happy [shake]."

If you don't have an instrument at hand, you can make your own or find an object that will suffice as one. Try the same idea with scribbling on a piece of paper, inviting your child to make a small, medium, or large scribble to show just how big the feeling is. Don't be surprised if he rips up the paper instead. That's just another way of showing you the magnitude of his feeling.

3.3 Let me hear how angry you are

Ⓒ Shake things up—Sometimes people need to move their bodies to discharge the energy or tension built up from a conflict. Many creatures in the animal kingdom do this instinctively following an attack from another animal. Their bodies literally shake until the energy from the "fight, flight, or freeze" encounter is released. Trauma experts, like Peter Levine (1997), have noted something similar with human beings. If we don't mobilize to discharge energy from a conflict, it can remain in our systems and make moving forward difficult. Try standing up and shaking your body. Jump around with your arms flopping loosely by your sides. If for no other reason than pure confusion about what you're doing, this might just get your child's attention enough to break her out of a stuck place. The element of surprise can be disarming (Kornblum 2002). As you jump around, share, "This makes me feel better . . . to shake off the angry feelings. Want to try, too?" Another way to get your child moving is by inviting her to stretch her arms as wide as she is angry at you, or jump as high as she feels frustrated. Movement like this has the added advantage of expanding breath, which engages the "relaxation response" and calms the body (Benson 2009).

Once you and your child have reconnected by acknowledging feelings, communicating care, or shaking off energy, you can move on to finding a solution to the problem at hand.

Naturally, a lot of talking happens while resolving a problem. If the conflict is between two children, we want to know what happened, when, why, and to whom. If the conflict involves us, we usually do most of the talking, explaining why a certain behavior, choice, or tone of voice doesn't work for us. All of this talking is to arrive at a solution, whether that means a relevant consequence, a compromise, or an understanding. Talk can be an efficient way to get to the heart of the matter, but it can also backfire. Frustration may seep out in our tone of voice. We may talk too much. And, thus, our children may tune us out—again.

Resolution time is not just a time for grown-ups to talk. If we want to maximize this teachable moment, it's a time for us to listen. The problem is, kids often don't know what to say. Basically, they want to say whatever will get them out of the situation as quickly as possible with as little consequence as possible. When asked "What's a solution to this problem?" your child may respond with "I don't know" (because they don't know) or "Sorry" (because that usually works to get things over with fast). Because words can be hard to grasp, it's even more difficult for children to listen and then come up with a solution on the spot. Kids benefit from concrete tools to flex their problem-solving muscles. Here's where an art approach can come in handy:

> I am making school lunches when my daughter screams, "I'm never going to play with you again!" I enter the room and ask what the problem is. She explains that her brother said "never mind," and she really wants to know what he said. I turn to my son and translate: "She's really interested in what you have to say." My son whines, "I just don't know how to explain it, though, so I said never mind." I offer two choices for assistance: "Would you like help explaining your idea, or would it be easier to draw it?" My son opts to draw it, which his sister enjoys watching. Once drawn, he finds it easier to explain. They have fun through the process, and I am able to get lunches made.

As this example shows, art making can help children develop their ideas. By literally seeing their idea on paper, they are better able to put it into words. Here are a couple of strategies for putting this principle into action when it comes time for children to identify a solution to a problem:

**C/T** Create a comic strip (see fig. 3.4)—Roughly map out the scenario frame by frame, like a comic strip. Keep it simple, with few frames. Don't worry about your artistic talent (or lack thereof). Invite your child or teen to tell you what goes in the next frame by simply asking, "And what should we draw here?" or "And then what happened?" Encourage him to fill in some of the frames. This will help him review what happened leading up to the conflict. Once the storyboard is created, tell your child, "Let's add a new ending to this story. What should we draw so that the people in this story feel better/ get done what they need to get done? What are they already good at doing that we could put into this story?" Referring to characters as generic people, rather than as your children, minimizes defensive reactions and will maximize your child's ability to think objectively.

3.4 Create a comic strip

Ⓒ/Ⓣ Choose your own adventure—The next time your child needs help coming up with a solution to a conflict or other problem, draw a few possible options. For younger children you might draw people giving a hug, picking up together, or arriving at some sort of compromise, for example. You might throw in some silly suggestions to keep it light (and to keep them engaged), such as taking off to outer space in a rocket ship. For older children or teens, sketch (or write) options, such as asking the other person what might make it better, finding a creative way to make amends (like offering to help out), taking care of personal tasks (e.g., homework or clearing dishes) within the next ten minutes without reminders, putting on music to make the task more fun. Explore together what might happen if each of the options were chosen. Ask your child to choose a resolution to put into action.

Another way to help children develop their ideas is through strategies from theater arts:

I'm working with a family of five. The children are in frequent conflict (at home and in the art therapy office). We use the framework of film production to help the sibling "actors" rehearse listening while the parent "directors" practice containing and redirecting their children's energy. We're not getting very far.

"No!" says a child. "But!" says another. Over and over, the make-believe scene gets stopped short by a sibling's insistence that the others are doing it wrong.

Then, "director" Dad has a flash of inspiration. "Let's play the 'Yes, and . . .' improv game. When actors work on their improvisation skills, they follow the rule that every sentence must begin with 'Yes, and. . .'"

He has his children's attention. "Roll camera and . . . action!"

A child begins: "Hey, do you want to play basketball?"

"No. . .uh, I mean . . . Yes, *and* . . . how about if we also play tag?"

"No, I don't . . . oh . . . I mean . . . Yes, and then we can go get ice cream."

Now we're moving!

**C/T** Act out the alternatives—Enactment, observation, and imagination build pathways for new behavior in the brain (Chartrand and Bargh 1999; Pineda 2009). Playacting conflicts can be done face-to-face, as above, or with puppets, stuffed animals, or figurines. Encourage children to ask the "audience" (or other characters) for suggestions on how to resolve the problem. Silly ideas for resolution, as well as serious ones, can be enacted to help hold the attention of children. Teens may like to write down ideas for conflict scenarios between two characters and put them into a grab bag. They can decide whether the scenario will result in a win-win, win-lose, or lose-lose situation for the two characters. Then, possible solutions can be enacted using movie-set phraseology ("Action!" and "Cut!") to rehearse alternatives.

## Make a plan

Making a plan for how to handle similar situations in the future is extremely useful. Not only does it engage the higher cortical functions of the brain that we want our children to exercise (such as planning, organizing, and impulse control), but also it gives you and your child concrete strategies on which you can agree next time. Whether it's making a plan for a smoother bedtime transition or starting homework, for example, you will be able to remind your child what *he* chose to do: "Remember your plan for this."

While you can simply talk about a plan, if you take the extra step of having your child *draw* her plan, you introduce a host of additional benefits. Drawing out a plan with your child, rather than just talking about it, helps make ideas more concrete. Your child can take more ownership of the plan when she's the one drawing it, which aids also in developing responsibility for future planning. Having a literal image hanging on the fridge or wall for reference is a powerful reminder of intentions. Rather than you as the parent having to remind your child, the image reminds her. In a sense, she is reminding herself to get back on track. This entire process helps with the development of self-regulation: the ability to notice and control one's own behaviors.

"Tools of the Mind" is an early education curriculum, inspired by the work of psychologist Lev Vygotsky and informed by neuroscience, that incorporates pre-play

**44**    image making for planning, self-regulation, and problem solving with striking results. Considered an "exemplary educational intervention" by UNESCO's International Bureau of Education (2001), one hallmark of the curriculum is the drawing and writing of "play plans," which are then enacted by the children (Bodrova and Leong 2006). Regardless of their age or drawing ability, each day children draw out plans for their day's activities. Along with visual and auditory cues for daily school expectations, the children are supported in following through on their own plans. For children participating in "Tools of the Mind," the most recent outcome studies have shown measurable improvements in memory, reasoning, attention, and behavior control (the ability to refrain from a habitual behavior in favor of a more appropriate or goal-oriented one) (Blair and Raver 2014). It seems that they are onto something.

 💡 **C/T**  TRY THIS:

Invite your child or teen to sketch out a plan that addresses how he would like to approach a situation differently next time (see fig. 3.5). Drawings can include a series of steps, like a storyboard, or be a singular drawing. They can be simple. If your child can only scribble or make basic shapes, ask him to describe the plan. You can write his words on the picture for him. A plan might represent an intention such as "I will ask for help when my sister hurts my feelings" or a series of specific steps such as "I will do two pages of homework at the dining room table. I will take a fifteen-minute break. Then I will do the next two pages of homework." Help your child frame language in the positive (that is, what he *will* do instead of what he *won't* do). Ask your child how you might be a part of the plan. Your child may wish to add a drawing that depicts your part in the plan, or your part may simply be to remind him of the plan by referring to the drawing at relevant times. Once the plan is drawn, with any accompanying words or explanations added, find a special place for it. He may wish to hang it up or store it in a special folder. You can bring it out and refer to it as needed.

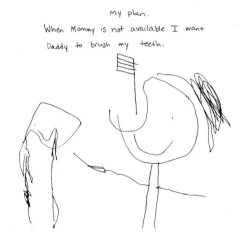

3.5 Sketch out a plan

By using creative approaches to conflicts, you are making a long-term invest- **45** ment. Naturally, at times we get tired and fed up. You may say to yourself, "But I don't want to have to bring out paper and a pen . . . I just want my kids to do what I tell them to do." I'm certain that some days our kids say something similar to themselves, "I wish my parents would just do what I tell them to do!" The creative arts offer valuable tools not only for solving conflicts but also for helping us feel generally less fed up. While it may seem more time-consuming and laborious in the moment, using art to reconnect, problem-solve, and plan ahead may ultimately lessen the frequency, intensity, and duration of conflicts.

## TIME TO BRUSH TEETH, DOO WOP, DOO WOP

My daughter says it best when it's time to stop reading books and move on to brushing teeth: "But it's booooorrrring!" I consider explaining that while it is boring, it is important for preventing cavities. I consider reminding her that the dentist says she has to brush. Instead, I opt for "Yes, it is boring, but we can make it more fun." Then I belt out, "Brush your teeth, brush your teeth" to the tune of her favorite song, "Let it Go," from the movie *Frozen.* While she protests me ruining her favorite song, she also giggles and opens her mouth.

Brushing teeth, getting dressed, coming to the dinner table, getting into the car, getting out of the car, sitting down to start homework—all of these tasks have one thing in common (that is, one thing other than their ability to start a minor war). They all involve a transition. If you think about it, many of the daily conflicts that happen with kids occur when they are asked to transition from one activity to an- other (particularly if they are being asked to shift gears from something that they like doing to something that isn't as fun or interesting). It's a common problem even for kids who tend to be more flexible.

There are plenty of well-known parenting tips on how to talk to your kids in order to make transitions easier. You are probably familiar with some of them: "In five minutes it'll be time to . . ." or "After dinner you will have more time to . . ." However, chances are that you will find yourself repeating these phrases ad nau- seam or cajoling, if not resorting to threats or bribes. Verbal cues can be helpful. Let's not get rid of them. But let's see what happens if you add some arts-based strategies, too.

Larry, an attendee at one of our recent workshops, shares a successful inno- vative parenting moment:

Larry oversees his three children, ages nine, seven, and five, setting the table for dinner. They bicker. It escalates. Meanwhile, the table is not getting set. The children are tired and "hangry" (hungry and angry). Although not generally artsy and never having before used a creative arts strategy to manage behavior, he takes a deep breath and initiates a rhythm by clapping to the syllables of "Pass the popcorn. Gimme some more." The children join in, smiling, and laughing. Moods are elevated. Table is set. Problem over.

There's a reason why teachers and kids sing cleanup and goodbye songs in preschool. They work. Using music, rhythm, movement, or visual cues to help kids move from one activity to another decreases behavioral issues during these times (Hemmeter et al. 2008). For starters, they capture attention; children will tune in to music more than to the sound of voices uttering repeated requests. Secondly, songs, movement, and visuals are fun. Transitioning from one activity to another is disruptive. It can be boring. Using creative tools when shifting gears can spice things up and keep kids engaged not only during the transition but also during the next, less preferred activity. What's more, the arts add an element of routine and ritual to transition times. Singing the same song when it's time for a certain activity, for example, makes the change predictable and less anxiety provoking.

Based on frequency of occurrence, think about daily transition moments that can be difficult for your child. Choose one or two to keep in mind as you read the creative arts ideas that follow. Consider how some of these ideas might apply to your situation or how you might adapt them to meet the needs of your unique child. Be creative. Invite your child to come up with ideas, too. But beware. You might end up getting requests for a "brush your teeth" rendition of your child's favorite song every night. It may verge on unbearable, but you'll likely agree that it's preferable to a standoff at the bathroom sink.

Get attention with music:

**C/T** Call and response—Used in classrooms, the military, and at sporting events, call and response songs and rhythms are a tried and true method for getting people engaged with an activity at hand. At a football game you might hear: "When I say Go! You say Tigers! Ready? Go! (Tigers!). Go! (Tigers!)." At home you might instead try: "When I say Time For! You say Dinner! Ready? Time For! (Dinner!)" Young children will get into it. Teens may think you've lost it, but even if they don't participate, at least you'll have gotten their attention, and they may respond a little more promptly.

**C/T** Sing the expectations—Music helps people remember information (Rubin 1995). Help your children remember routine expectations by putting them to a tune. For example, sing to the tune of "If You're Happy and You Know It": "When you're finished getting dressed, please brush your teeth (brush brush)."

**C/T** Use a song as a timer—There are many ways to use songs as creative timers: "When this song's done, it's time to start homework" . . . "Let's see if we can all get buckled in before the song is over" . . ."We will clean up for three songs and then you can go back to what you were doing." Smartphones have made it even easier to access music, wherever you are. Call up a tune at home, at the park, or in the parking lot to help move tasks along.

**C/T** Clap the rhythm of the task—Put a task, or a series of not more than three tasks, to a rhythm. For example: (clap, clap, clap) "Shoes, lunch, dog." Or for younger kids: (clap, clap, clap) "Potty, brush, floss." You may find your child clapping along and repeating the steps as they do them. I started using this to move my children through their "good nights" to each other when what should've been a simple hug, kiss, and "good night" turned into a ten-minute, free-for-all tackle and roundup. Clapping a rhythm has (mostly) eliminated this. They delight in trying to keep pace with my steady rhythm: "On my rhythm! Ready?! Hug. Kiss. Good night. Hug. Kiss. Good night!" It's done, and they're off to bed.

Move them along with movement:

Ping's three-year-old granddaughter loves her removable sticker scenes. So much so that getting her to stop playing with them before naptime guarantees a meltdown. One day, Ping invites her to scroll through sample sound options on the iPhone timer. They find a sappy tune that makes them both dance and laugh out loud. Now, as soon as the song timer goes off after an agreed-upon length of time, they immediately hop into dance mode and boogie away to naptime.

**C/T** Dance your way there—Practice dramatic leaps and twirls, or just boogie on down to the bathroom, car, dining room table, or location of the next task. Put on energizing music if you wish.

**C/T** Play with your speed—Get your child's attention by moving oh so slowly to the next task at hand. Talk ridiculously slowly to emphasize just . . . how . . . . slowly . . . you . . . are . . . moving. Invite them along: "We're . . . going . . . soooo . . . slowly." Once you have them engaged, speed things up with your body and voice: "We're walking fast. We're walking soooo fast! Now . . . we're . . . walking . . . slowly . . . again." Let them take a turn at controlling the speed. For teens, simply try racing them to the destination.

**C** Count the steps—Get kids curious about their movement. I used to say to a client of mine who had a hard time transitioning to my office from his class-room, "I wonder how many steps it will take to get there." Focusing attention on counting steps helped minimize his anxiety while keeping his feet moving in the right direction. You can mix it up by counting big steps versus little steps versus ginormous steps.

**C** Move like an animal—Ask your child, "What animal should we be when we go to the car?" Or give suggestions, such as "Should we be cheetahs going to the bathroom? Or turtles?" You can also move like robots, fighter jets, ninjas, or anything else of interest to your child at the time.

Let pictures do the talking:

**C/T** Use visual charts (see fig. 3.6)—Visual charts that illustrate morning or evening expectations can help children and teens develop more independence. Sure, they'll still need reminders, but instead of asking, "Did you brush? Pack your homework? How about taking your dishes to the sink?" you can simply point to the pictures or, for older kids and teens, suggest that they check their to-do list to make sure they've done everything. Get them involved in making the chart. Let them select images and decorate it.

3.6 Use visual charts

🅒🆃 Hold a photo shoot (see fig. 3.7)—Kids are good at showing their feelings about things they don't want to do, so why not memorialize it? Grab your smartphone and encourage them to ham it up: "Show me 'I looove brushing my teeth.' Okay, now show me 'I'm sooo bored brushing my teeth.' Good! Now how about 'I'm scared brushing my teeth!'" While busy acting for the camera, the acting out will diminish, and the task will be done before they realize it.

3.7 Hold a photo shoot

## Consider deeper emotional needs

Sometimes transitions are difficult for a more significant emotional reason. When a transition requires separating from you, like going to bed or leaving for school, for example, it's worth considering that your child may be having feelings beyond a struggle to shift gears to a boring task. While some kids simply don't want to stop playing, others may have a genuine fear of the dark or being away from you for the night. While some kids are hard to get out the door for school because they are easily distracted, others may be truly unhappy at school due to social or academic issues. In situations like these, it's important to identify and address your child's deeper emotional needs. Although it may help to make something together that your child can keep with him (a painted rock or a homemade book, for example), you may want to explore other creative options for addressing emotional needs that can be found in chapter 5: "Raise Happy Kids."

## BEHAVIOR IS COMMUNICATION (EVEN WITH SIBLINGS)

A father meets with me to discuss his son, Calvin, who is alternately loving and abusive toward his toddler brother—sneering, calling him names, and jeering "I hate you." Dad adds, "Even more intolerable is that he is rude, angry, and disrespectful toward us, his parents. It's bad. Really bad." Dad makes a safe assumption that Calvin's behavior communicates jealousy about not having as much time with his parents. As such, they have been taking Calvin special places, without his little brother in tow (when possible). It doesn't make any difference.

I agree that the behavior is likely communicating something about his feelings toward family members. Yet we haven't quite hit the nail on the head. "Offer him blank paper and pens," I suggest. "When he starts to act in a way that feels disrespectful to you, redirect him to make art about his feelings instead."

The following week, the father is eager to share what he learned through Calvin's art making and ensuing discussion: "It's not about having more time with us. He's afraid there isn't enough love for him *and* his brother inside our hearts."

We'll return to this story in a moment.

"Show me a sibling who experiences no sibling rivalry, and I'll show you an only child," jests George Howe Colt (2012), American journalist and one of four brothers. She's too close to me . . . I don't want to play that . . . stop looking at me . . . his music is too loud . . . that's my toy . . . he took the last (cookie, drumstick, piece of broccoli!—it doesn't really matter what it is). Children fight for all sorts of reasons. They fight when jealous or bored. They fight when they want more attention and don't know how else to get it. My son once eloquently explained this feeling, "I wish we had three moms, then we'd each have one to ourselves." And even if they each had their own (fill in the blank), they'd find something else about which to squabble because the fighting often isn't about the thing they think they want. Behavior communicates something more, even when they don't know what they are trying to say.

"Behavior is communication" is a generally agreed-upon tenet. A similarly well-accepted notion is that sibling squabbles communicate jealousy, desire for a fair share, or deep-rooted fear about limited resources; however, quickly labeling sibling conflict as "just jealousy" or "being competitive" may overlook the nuances of communication. Sure, Calvin was feeling jealous, but he was worried that there was literally insufficient love to go around. Understanding this, we could intervene more precisely.

Returning to the story from above:

I suggest that the parents invite Calvin to draw the heart where the love lives. "Ask him to show how much is reserved for him; how much is for his brother? Are they inside or outside the heart? Is there space for anyone else?" I encourage them to allow Calvin to respond in any way that he needs. "If he needs his brother to be outside the heart for now, that's okay, too." The following week I get the update: "He drew the heart with space for all of us inside! We taped it up in his room. He seems fine now. We didn't have any of the usual problems this week."

When we help kids learn how to get their deeper needs met, we enable them to get along better with others, including siblings. This is important because even when rivalry exists, positive and lasting relationships grow out of sharing more good times than bad or neutral times (Bronson and Merryman 2009). Yes, we can address behaviors with distraction, bribes, and consequences. However, to truly eradicate the problem, we need to understand why it's there in the first place. Just as with a headache, which can be diminished through medication, unless we identify the underlying reason for the discomfort it could reoccur, worsen, or take longer to resolve. Indeed, if your head throbs from dehydration, you may need to drink water; whereas, if you've hit your head on a low tree branch, you may need to apply ice. Like resolving a headache (and sibling conflict is often a headache!), knowing what conflict is actually communicating helps us meet needs rather than mask symptoms.

Here are a few examples of what behavior (aka antagonizing, opposing, putting-down, and bickering) can actually mean:

- "I need space"—When my sister and I were young, my parents would send us into separate rooms when we argued too much. While sentenced to our rooms, we would write secret notes and use sparkly batons to slide them across the hall to each other. We wanted to connect but needed space to do it. You can suggest something similar before escalating to "GO TO YOUR ROOMS!" Teach your kids how to build a telephone out of cups and string. Challenge them to see how long they can make the string and still be able to hear one another. Or suggest that they find something to do in separate rooms while sending notes or secret messages to each other (you can be the mail delivery person or they might want to set up a more elaborate system for delivering messages).

- "I want to play with you but don't like this game"—There was a period when a dance party was the solution to almost any conflict between my children. I kid you not. They could do their own thing while still doing it together, without rules or compromises. The upbeat music would lift our moods as we released pent-up energy through jumps, twirls, and rolling on the ground. Sometimes they'd start interacting more through the process, saying, "Look at me" or "Try this!" I'd join in often, too, filling their emotional cups with attention, energy, and love.

- "I really want to do it my way" (and don't yet have the skills to compromise)—Working on solo art projects at a table together gives kids enough autonomy to enable collaboration, problem solving, and compromise. It also offers structured opportunities to practice meeting their own needs while considering the needs of others. Something as simple as wanting the red crayon when someone else is using it is a rich moment to teach some of these skills. Prompt your child to say, "When you're done with the red crayon, may I please have a turn?" This simple question teaches your child self-advocacy, delayed gratification, and respect for the needs of others. At the same time, the other child learns that he can meet the needs of others without having to compromise his own needs entirely. When you think that they have the skills down, try stacking the deck against them by giving them only one of something that they both need to use. Point out that there is only one glue stick, for example, and ask for suggestions on how they might go about dealing with the situation. Then see if they can put their ideas into action!

- "I'm bored but can't think of anything to do with you" (see fig. 3.8)—On those days when kids are able to work more collaboratively, there are all sorts of creative activities they can work on together; they may just need a little spark. Sometimes, teaming kids up against you is a perfect way to realign them and get their collaborative juices flowing. Give them some yarn, boxes, or other materials, and challenge them to create the hardest obstacle course for you to negotiate when they are done.

3.8 Address what behavior is communicating
("I'm bored but can't think of anything to do with you")

- "I need love and attention"—When it seems that my kids just need attention (and arguing is a surefire way to get it), I hit the pause button for myself. I either stop what I am doing to play, dance, or make art with them, for example, or I make a plan with them for some uninterrupted special time later. I may even suggest that they switch gears to draw a plan for what they'd like to do with me later during their special time. Usually they stop fighting and get to work on their drawings, chatting away casually about what they plan to do with me later.

- "I like you but don't think you like me"—Kids sometimes think more highly of their peer or sibling counterparts than they let on, yet it's not easy for them to say so. They may even feel unliked by someone they secretly wish to emulate. As a birthday gift or for another special occasion, invite your child to cut out magazine pictures and words to make a collage about what he likes about a friend or sibling. Not only is this a chance to reflect on the positives in that friend or sibling, but also it's an opportunity for the recipient to learn what they mean to your child.

Remember, there are many possible needs that can be expressed by the same behavior and, thus, there is no one-size-fits-all solution to conflicts. There are days when I suggest a dance party, and my kids argue over what music to put on. There are days when one of them will hoard all of the markers, maybe to get back at the other for some previous wrongdoing. Often, when my go-to strategies aren't working, it's because I haven't actually understood the need behind the behavior in that moment. You may not always figure out the hidden needs on the first (or second or third) try. Innovative parenting requires trial and error. Dealing with conflict isn't easy, but when you translate it into needs that can be met, spiced with a little creativity in response, you will be able to bask more often in the sound of happy children.

## BUYERS BEWARE

"Brave woman," I hear someone murmur as I walk through the automatic, glass doors. Someone else wishes me luck. You'd think I was slaying dragons or setting sail with nothing but a compass and a shoestring. But I'm not. I'm walking into the grocery store with my three children. It doesn't take long before my daughter is whining for a cereal that has a favorite character on it. My oldest steps in with a big brother, I-know-better-than-you voice: "They're tricking you into buying that." He has her attention. "Yeah, they just put that picture on the box to try to get you to buy it. She's not even in the box." Phew. Saved.

Milk, butter, eggs, and something for dinner. Easy enough, right? Except that you have your kids with you. That complicates things. Even the calmest of kids can lose it the minute they enter a grocery store or hunger hits, turning a relatively mundane activity into an exercise in futility. Somehow "Stop that," "No, not that," and "Come back here" don't stand a chance in the face of towering displays of strategically placed goodies or colorful packages sporting favorite cartoon characters and superheroes. But if we approach the task like an arts education outing, we might have a fighting chance.

Art isn't just about drawing and painting. It's also about understanding the images that we see. We tend to assume understanding from images at-a-glance. However, just as we learn to read words for meaning, we can also learn to read images for meaning. In museums, visual literacy skills can significantly improve our enjoyment and appreciation of the art that we view. When we think critically about the meaning and messages behind images in stores, commercials, and other marketing arenas, they have less power to influence us. Instead of reacting to images, kids can begin to look for hidden visual messages.

When kids engage thoughtfully with images they see in stores, a shopping trip can turn into a game of "not being tricked into buying things," rather than a game of "who can sneak the sugar cereal into the cart without Mom noticing." Kids feel empowered when they are given tools to outsmart the grown-ups who put cartoons on boxes and colorful candies by the checkout counter. What's more, building visual literacy is advantageous in school, work, and life. It has been shown to increase cooperation and respect for others, improve reading and math achievement (Curva et al. 2005), and enhance critical thinking (Adams et al. 2006; Housen 2002). It also teaches the valuable lesson that things are not always as they appear at first. Oh, and it can make your shopping trip more tolerable, too.

Tuning up visual detective skills to tone down undesirable behavior during shopping trips can start at any age. In fact, the earlier you start the better. Kids are fascinated to learn about how pictures are used to trick them into thinking and acting certain ways and, in their never-ending quest for independence, they're often eager to show that they can't be controlled. Now instead of defying you, they become your ally in defying the artists and marketers whose job it is to control them. Sure, it takes a little time up front to point out what's going on with all these images. And it takes a little effort during shopping trips to ask the questions that will get their mental wheels turning. But ultimately the investment is worthwhile. The simple effort it takes to teach visual literacy is far more gratifying and less exhausting than the effort is takes to keep kids from pulling things off store shelves.

🄲🄣 Educate—Talking to your kids about images doesn't have to start in the store. It can start with billboards, commercials, junk mail, or the internet. Point out the images you see and what marketers are trying to achieve by using them:

○ "Look at how they put a picture of [character] on this box of cereal/diapers/yogurt to trick you into buying it."

○ "It's somebody's job to decide what pictures and colors to put on this package to make people want it, even though the picture has nothing to do with what's actually inside the box."

○ "Look at how colorful that candy is. You know what's interesting? Scientists figured out that people eat more of really colorful snacks. That's why they make them so colorful."

○ "Notice how much fun those kids look like they are having with that toy in the picture. Boy, the people selling that toy *really* want you to believe that it's a *lot* of fun."

**C/T** Share your weaknesses—Talk aloud about the products *you* want to buy and why you choose to buy them or not. Walking past a frozen yogurt shop, you might say, "Mmmmm . . . look at how they make that frozen yogurt poster really big and colorful so it catches your eye. They did a really good job of getting my attention. But I'd rather save my money for something else. Besides, my body would like it better if I gave it something healthy for lunch right now." Talking through your choices to buy or not to buy demonstrates that even if we really want something, we are ultimately in control of deciding to listen to those desires or not.

**C** Observe—Younger kids love to pretend to look through binoculars to find . . . anything. Really. Make circles using your hands and put them up to your eyes: "Let's put on our binoculars [or spy glasses] and look for pictures that are trying to get us to do/want/buy something."

**C/T** Ask thought-provoking questions—What really gets kids thinking critically about the images they see is asking them questions. Here are a few:

○ What do they want you to believe about the product by putting that image on it?

○ What do you think this movie is about by just looking at the picture on the poster?

○ Who are they trying to get to see this movie / buy this product?

○ Why did they use those colors?

○ Why did they put these by the checkout stand?

○ Whose attention are they trying to get?

○ How does it make you feel when you see this?

**C/T** Make it a game (see fig. 3.9)—When tasks or activities are framed as a game, kids are often keen to participate. It can be a game of "don't be tricked" or "count the number of cartoon characters on packages in the store." If you want to take it a step further, you can even assign points for every character spotted. Older children or teens can see how many different types of marketing techniques they can find, such as cartoon images, strategic placement of products in the store, images that create an emotional response (such as pictures of happy people), text that convinces the buyer of a product's importance, bright colors to grab attention, and so on.

3.9 Turn grocery shopping into a visual literacy game

## (USEFUL) PRAISE

I'm role playing with an adult student who is pretending to be a child. He says, "Look what I did. Do you like it?" To communicate genuine interest and learn more about his intentions and feelings about the piece, I reply, "Let me take a close look at what you did. I wonder if you can tell me about it?" (I'm modeling an alternative to "I love it. Good job.")

He states abruptly, still in character, "It's a tree, and this is a sun. So, do you like it?" He's laying it on thick to challenge me. I hold the piece at a comfortable viewing distance for him and say, "You really want to know if I like it. First tell me what you think about it."

He continues seeking affirmation, "Oh, I don't know. I guess it's okay. I just want to know if you like it."

Using his words, I reply, "Show me one part that you guess is okay." He does and, after several exchanges, he is smiling, sharing what he likes about his piece, and reflecting on what it reminds him of in his life. I still haven't said that I like it, or that it's good or beautiful. He concludes, "I guess I did a pretty good job."

"Now," I say, "let's play this out all over again. Go."

The same student restarts the role play: "Look what I did. Do you like it?" I say, "I do! That's great. Good job." He replies, "Thanks." The exchange is done.

I then ask, "What opportunities did we miss in that second role play?"

Surviving the day isn't just about thwarting meltdowns and de-escalating conflicts. Equally important (if not more important) is the positive reinforcement you give to your child to help her become an independent teeth-brushing, problem-solving, mess picker-upper who is capable of collaborating with others. While pats on the back like "You did it!" and "Look at you!" give kids a momentary feeling of accomplishment, *specific* praise can reinforce long-term qualities and skills, such as thoughtfulness, concentration, taking responsibility, and maintaining meaningful relationships; for example: "You're getting dressed all by yourself!" . . . "You were ready when I told you it was time to go." . . . "You are really taking care of your teeth!" . . . or "Look what you were able to do by working together!" When we give kids specific feedback throughout the day that names the very assets we want to encourage, we strengthen those qualities. We can reap the same benefits when we respond thoughtfully to their art.

The default reaction to art made by kids is often "I like it" or "It's beautiful!" But much like saying "Good job!" throughout the day for brushing, eating, getting home by curfew, or whatnot, it is too generic to make a significant, positive difference in our children's development. It teaches them to rely on us for kudos rather than developing their own internal motivation. Worse yet, repeatedly giving the same, generic praise can leave kids confused about their actual abilities and demotivate them. Well-meaning, generic comments like "Nice drawing!" and "That's so pretty!" may also start to sound as if we're not really paying attention. Frankly, sometimes we're not. Yet, other times, we simply don't know what to say instead.

Remarks about art often narrowly focus on how it looks rather than on how the project was approached or experienced. Responding to children's art with "What is it?" teaches kids that their art has to be something; self-expression isn't good enough as it is. This belief not only interferes with exploration, creativity, and self-expression, but also can build anxiety and self-judgment. Being able to embrace the creative *process*, mistakes included, fosters a growth mindset, which is associated with higher academic performance in the long run (Dweck 2012; Gunderson et al. 2013; Gunderson et al. 2018). The growth mindset believes that success comes from hard work and learning, not natural abilities or other fixed traits such as being a "good artist."

When we are thoughtful about how to respond, talking about art with kids becomes fertile ground for encouraging the types of behavior that we hope to see in other realms of life. Indeed, praise of effort, perseverance, and problem solving in children as young as 0–3 years old predicts higher motivation to learn and embrace challenges in second and third grade (Gunderson et al. 2013) and academic achievement in fourth grade (Gunderson et al. 2018). If you're not accustomed to giving specific praise such as this, art offers a relatively easy and stress-free place to practice. You're not typically battling anything in the moment (so it's easier to come up with something encouraging to say), and kids are generally in a receptive state when presenting their art to you. If you are someone who already points out positive behavior in your children during routine activities, notice whether or not you also take the opportunity to do so during moments of creative expression. Here are some tips on how.

**Highlight the qualities you want to encourage**

Remarking on what children have made can help them reflect on their self-expression, and encouraging them to talk about their creations can foster pride. However, highlighting *how* a child approached his art, rather than *what* he made, bolsters characteristics such as focus, initiative, and follow-through that can apply to other tasks in life as well. Here are some examples (see fig. 3.10):

- Effort—"I can see you worked on that for a long time! You put a lot of effort into it."

- Concentration—"You really had to concentrate on that in order to make all those details!"

- Planning/Organizing—"It took a lot of planning to put that routine together!"

- Perseverance—"You kept working at it!"

- Problem solving—"It wasn't turning out how you wanted, so you tried something different and made it work!"

- Taking initiative—"You came up with a new idea and ran with it!"

- Creativity—"You created those characters from your own imagination?!"

- Follow-through—"You started that project earlier, and now you've finished it!"

- Independence—"Look what you did all by yourself!"

3.10 Remark on qualities you want to encourage

### Encourage self-evaluation

No doubt, kids like to hear that you like their art, their singing, their acting, their dance routines. They'll ask you flat out and, if you evade their question, they'll insist that you answer it. Some will take a comment about their creativity or keen attention to detail as answer enough, but others will persist with "But do you *like* it? Is it beautiful?" Giving useful praise doesn't mean completely avoiding the L word. Go ahead and let them know how much you like it. But before you do, consider first saying, "I'll tell you, but first I want to know: Do *you* like it?"

We want children to have the opportunity to reflect on how they value their own creations, so they can feel proud of themselves when they make a work of art (or help set the table or pick up their pjs or finish their homework)—without requiring our validation. This is the difference between intrinsic motivation (I do it because I find it rewarding) and extrinsic motivation (I do it because I am rewarded or praised). Kids who are motivated intrinsically are more likely to perform even boring tasks more often than kids who are given external rewards. They may not like the task, but they do it because something inside tells them it's worthwhile.

Here are some ways to help your child or teen think about whether or not she likes her drawing, poem, or dance:

- "Do *you* like it?"

- "I see you smiling."

- "I wonder if you are feeling proud?"

Of course, there will be times when your child doesn't like what she's made. Chances are it'll be pretty clear: crumpled paper, grunts and whines, scribbles and cross-outs, walking away from the activity altogether, or perhaps a very tentative request for your opinion of it. If this is the case, you'll be approaching the situation differently by using empathy and helping your child problem-solve through the situation (for more about helping children cope with frustration, turn to chapter 5: "Raise Happy Kids").

### Be encouraging yet accurate

I am playing catch with my young son. He is capable of throwing the ball to me, but now and again it doesn't go much further than his own feet. Plop goes the ball. I say anyway, "Good throw!" He looks at me curiously and then remarks plainly, "No it wasn't." He is right. It wasn't actually a good throw— not even for him. I had reflexively tried to be encouraging or prevent him from becoming upset. At only three years old he taught me a valuable parenting lesson: be accurate while being encouraging. The same goes for how we respond to art.

Research shows that people generally have an inflated sense of their abilities (Dunning et al. 2003). They think they are better at tasks, academics, sports—even at being funny—than they actually are. Interestingly, this isn't because of arrogance. Rather, it's because they simply don't know. Growing up, kids tend to receive ambiguous or inflated feedback from adults (like trophies for everyone), often due to well-meaning but misguided attempts to promote healthy self-esteem. Instead of developing a positive sense of self, including a desire to improve and tackle challenges, kids grow into adults who don't really know how they measure up, and they feel confused or defeated when they don't.

Giving accurate feedback isn't about saying that you don't like your child's art or that it isn't very good. Even if your son's violin playing sounds like a tortured cat or your daughter's drawing of a lion looks like a frog, there are still ways to be encouraging. You'd be surprised how many people stopped making art as a child or teen, even if they truly enjoyed it, because someone told them they were not good at it. Likewise, telling a child he is lazy if he doesn't pick up his room or do his homework will only *discourage* him from picking up and doing homework. Instead, we want to provide feedback to children that is helpful, encouraging, and motivating. When your child or teen forgets her dance routine, presents you with a drawing into which she didn't put much effort, or sings off-key, here are some ways to be accurate yet encouraging:

- Focus on the fun—It's worthwhile to remind children that the enjoyment of drawing, dancing, or singing is at least as important as how it looks or sounds. Try: "I notice that you added more parts to the song. I wonder if you're having fun with it?" or "I notice that you really put your all into this project. I wonder if you enjoyed working on it?"

- Practice makes permanent—Let children know that the aim of practice is not perfection. Rather, that what they practice will become more ingrained and thus will come more easily. Encourage practice by using statements like "I noticed you didn't practice much this week. Maybe next week we can set some time aside to do it together" or "It sounds like you've been practicing. Do you notice the progress you've made this week?"

- Make comparisons—Invite your child to compare his art to his other work (not to the work of another child). When he asks, "Do you like it?" respond with, "Let's compare it to some other ones you've done." You can even suggest that he choose one drawing to frame and display, or one original song to record and send to Grandma. Discuss why he picked the one that he did.

- Encourage persistence—Sometimes a child will ask if you like her art when she's just gotten started. If this is the case, she's likely looking for encouragement to continue. Try these: "I see that you're just getting started! I can't wait to see it once you work on it a little more" or "I see it's coming along. Keep at it!"

- Oops—When a child misses a few steps of a dance, lines in a play, or notes in a song, the impulse can be to ignore that fact and tell her she did great. Instead, praise her ability to deal with the situation: "I noticed that you just kept going like nothing happened. That takes confidence and focus."

- Constructive criticism—If you have a younger child, constructive criticism isn't really necessary (or appropriate); however, an older child or teen who is committed to refining skills can benefit from constructive feedback. A good rule of thumb is to make one positive statement before offering constructive feedback. For example: "I understand your intention with these shapes down here. I wonder about this bit over here" or "I noticed that you really have all the notes down! The audience might be able to hear the melody more clearly if you take your time in the middle part."

- Avoid teasing and sarcasm—Even if you think it's good-natured, teasing and sarcasm can stifle creative expression.

You may find that giving encouraging yet accurate feedback to your children takes practice. That's okay. Use the arts as a realm to rehearse this parenting skill. When you do, you're honing your ability to give the same type of feedback in other daily situations, like getting out the door in the morning, starting homework, or taking care of hygiene. In addition, by highlighting the qualities you want to encourage and promoting self-evaluation, you will help your children discover their strengths and capabilities. The focus, persistence, and motivation that you point out when they are drawing or practicing an instrument, for example, will carry over to other areas of their lives when the stakes may be higher (such as taking a test, applying for college, or seeking a promotion). When you give your children useful praise about their creative undertakings, they have a greater chance of embracing and internalizing these qualities as part of who they are.

# 4

## Connect First

A mother and her teenage son sit in my office. He won't look at her. He won't talk to her. But he'll draw. He draws a water animal and an airborne creature, explaining the vast differences between the two. He's talking to her now. She tries to see that as a start but is frustrated at his inability to address the problems in their relationship. "Okay, but what about what's been going on at home? Tell Erica what you did yesterday when I asked you to turn off your video game."

I have a strong hunch that he IS talking about their relationship already.

I pursue the hunch. "I wonder which animal you might be?"

He indicates the creature in flight.

I point to the water creature. "And who would this be, then?"

He replies, "That's my mom." He goes on to explain how different they are. He looks at his mom for the first time since we've entered my office.

"I don't feel like you understand me," he says to her. And so begins a conversation. Lines of communication are once again open. A foundation of connection is established.

When children feel connected, homes tend to be more harmonious and children feel valued. In chapter 2, we learned the importance of reconnecting before trying to resolve problems. Connection allows the problem-solving part of the brain to come back online. Connection calms the lower brain (the area tasked with fight, flight, or freeze survival responses under conditions of stress), which enables engagement of the upper brain (tasked with learning, reasoning, and emotional regulation). As such, connection is essential to recovery from minor and major life disturbances and trauma (Szalavitz and Perry 2010). Moreover, the relationship we foster with children creates neural connections that support necessary brain development for emotional self-regulation, decision making, and meaningful relationships (Hambrick et al. 2018; Szalavitz and Perry 2010; Schore 2016; Siegel and Bryson 2016). Children may even experience the added benefit of improved physical health (Feeney 2000) and fewer health problems in adulthood (Stewart-Brown, Fletcher, and Wadsworth 2005). As in the story above, art can help us get there.

Staying connected and keeping lines of communication with children open, especially as they grow older and need us less, takes effort. We get busy with work and chores. They get busy with school and friends. We ask how school was. They say, "Good." Less communication and connection feels normal . . . until it becomes a problem. Susan Stiffelman (2012), parenting expert and author of *Parenting without Power Struggles*, points out that while it is true that children need to separate from us as they get older, it is not true that we need to be less connected with them. Rather, as children grow, we need *new* strategies for communication and connection.

What makes the arts unique is that they offer not only a road to many traditional forms of connection—shared activities, talks, empathy, and smiles—but also alternative ways to reach the same, desired destination when traditional routes are closed for repair.

## A HIDDEN LANGUAGE

A child and her father sit across from me—Mom has recently moved out. The child is bubbly and busies herself making silly faces at Dad, trying to get a laugh. Dad asks his daughter, "How have you been doing?"

"Good." She leans in closer to him, craning her neck and contorting her mouth into another funny face.

"How are things with your friends?"

"Good."

"School?"

"Good."

I place a small table in front of her with paper and markers. Tapping the paper, I ask, "I wonder what 'good' looks like? Would you like to draw it?"

She proceeds to draw a large rainbow, followed by thick, dark clouds. The weather turns stormy.

"I'm done!" she announces cheerfully.

"Would you like to tell me about your drawing?" I invite.

"It was all sunny, and there was a rainbow. But then it got dark and cloudy." She's a little less silly now.

I gently offer a reflection about her drawing and life. "It looks like a lot has changed. I wonder what that's like?"

"Sad."

Children need to share their thoughts and feelings, but are unlikely to say, "Hey, I really need to talk about this problem I'm having." Instead, children express their feelings and thoughts through behavior (some that we don't like), play, and the arts. If we "listen" closely with our eyes, we find that the arts often contain rich and meaningful messages about our children's internal lives. To understand these messages, we need to resist automatic tendencies to judge artistic expression based on beauty and instead become familiar with its unique way of communicating messages about self and relationships. By becoming more attuned to the language of the arts, we open doors to communication and connection with our children that can be difficult to access through talk alone.

### We see the world we feel

When I was nearing the end of pregnancy with my third child, my two other children started spontaneously drawing pictures of the family, including the new baby. At first glance, they look like typical family drawings made by a six-year-old (see fig. 4.1) and three-year-old (see fig. 4.2), respectively. A thoughtful inspection, however, reveals their unique emotional and relational take on the situation.

4.1 "Family Drawing" (six-year-old son)

4.2 "Family Drawing" (three-year-old daughter)

We do not see the world like a camera. Our brains selectively see what we feel **65** is important. What stands out as important is either essential to survival, or emotionally or relationally significant. In other words, how something *looks* to us is often related to how it *feels* to us. For this reason, when a child draws what he sees, the drawing will capture what is important to him. This holds true regardless of artistic talent or skill development.

Although both my son and daughter drew our growing family, the emotional and relational significance to each was different. My son placed himself in the center of the family with a large star on his shirt, positioning himself in close proximity to Mommy. He is holding hands with Mommy. And Mommy is holding hands with Daddy. Sister and baby brother are slightly off to the side, clearly part of the family but noticeably apart from the "eldest child, Mommy, and Daddy" trio. In this picture, his relationship to Mommy and Daddy is of the utmost importance. His central position and large star on his shirt may reflect his desire to feel important, even under changing family circumstances.

My daughter, on the other hand, focused on her relationship within the sibling unit. She grouped herself in the center of the three siblings, drawing herself larger than her two brothers and positioning herself sandwiched between them (truly, the position she would hold from now on as the middle child). She encircled the sibling trio in a shape that she explained was a rocket ship blasting off to outer space. Mommy (drawn with a prominent belly button, which had become of interest to my daughter during my pregnancy) was on the outside of the rocket ship. "Mommy's staying behind." Daddy was nowhere in the picture. "He's at work." In this drawing, her bond with siblings and role as middle child seem to be of utmost importance. It stands out to her that Mommy is more physically present than Daddy of late.

Noticing the unique ways that children express subject matter through art can give us hunches to use as springboards for conversation. The intention is never to psychoanalyze children or assume things that are not necessarily true to their experience. However, if we focus solely on *what* is drawn or its aesthetic beauty, as we frequently do, we miss the opportunity to obtain rich information about the child-as-artist. When we tune into messages conveyed through children's art, we have the opportunity to respond more thoughtfully to needs, interests, concerns, and emotions of which the child may be unaware or unable to communicate in words.

What follows are two very different ways to respond to children's art (using the examples of my own children's art described above). The first responds to *what* was drawn. The exchange is encouraging and positive, but it is brief and fails to consider the child's deeper experience, preoccupations, or needs. The second, alternative interaction uses observations about the child's unique depictions of the subject matter (*how* it was drawn). The results are quite different.

Interaction 1 (responding to *what* is drawn):

Adult: "You drew our family. Oh, and look! You included your new baby brother. That's so sweet. Nice job, sweetheart. That's really great."
   Child: "Thanks!"

Interaction 2 (responding to *how* it is drawn and possible hidden meaning):

Me (to my son): "I see you're standing next to me in this drawing." (I have a hunch he's showing me he likes to be close to me not only physically but also emotionally.)
   My son: "Yes, and we're holding hands, too." (He's reinforcing our bond by pointing out this detail. I wonder if he's concerned that this might change after the baby comes.)
   Me (responding to my hunch about his concerns): "Even after the baby comes we'll still be close to each other. It'll be a little different when the baby is here, but we'll make sure to spend special time together."
   My son hugs me.

Sometimes underlying meaning can be difficult to ascertain. Verbal and non-verbal cues from your child (including demeanor and behavior) can inform your hunches and guide your responses. Here is an exchange with my daughter about her family drawing:

Me (to my daughter): "I notice Daddy isn't in this picture. I wonder if you can tell me more about that?" (Here I avoid saying "Why?" If I had asked: "Why isn't Daddy in the picture?" she may have gotten the impression that he should be in the picture and then may have tried to "correct" that. Instead, I want to know her thoughts about the absence of Daddy. To do this, I merely make the observation and then invite her to tell me more.)
   My daughter: "He's at work."
   Me: "Daddy's been at work a lot lately, hasn't he? I've noticed that, too." Here I have options. I could: 1) wait and see how my daughter responds next, 2) probe further by asking, "How do you feel about that?" or 3) assume she's concerned about her father's absence and reassure her that soon Daddy won't have to go to work so often. I'm not getting many cues, so I opt for the second approach: probe further.
   Me: "How do you feel about Daddy being at work so much?"
   My daughter: "I miss Daddy."
   Me (aiming to meet her needs by validating her experience and reassuring her that this is temporary): "Me, too. Daddy's working extra hard right now so he can spend lots of time with all of us after your baby brother comes."

When looking at children's drawings, start by noticing what stands out most. What is central? What or who is included or omitted? What is large and what is small? Where are people or things positioned in relationship to the rest of the picture? What colors are prominent, and with what are those colors associated? These can all be clues about what stands out as important to them. The context within which the art is made and your existing knowledge about the child can provide further hunches about the meaning behind the art.

Next, share your observations about what stands out. While you may already have hunches about the meaning behind the image, keep them to yourself for now. Let the child tell you more, first. Then, respond to the needs, interests, concerns, or feelings being communicated through the art.

A literal drawing of a family, as in the examples above, may have obvious relational or emotional content, but even abstract paintings, smooshed clay, or drawings of aliens, sea creatures, or princesses can communicate something about a child's experience of the world. In these cases, thinking in terms of metaphors can help us translate their creative expression into meaningful communication that we can understand.

## The power of metaphor

A teen client of mine worked week after week creating small, clay animal families and their homes. There was the bear family, the squirrel family, the mouse family, the bird family. We talked some, but mostly didn't. Yet, she was communicating volumes through her art. Through each of her clay animal families—their personalities, needs, and struggles—emerged themes paralleling issues in her own family that were causing her unhappiness. It wasn't intentional on her part; she didn't realize how meaningful and personal her creations were until we were close to ending therapy. Yet, all along she had been "talking" through metaphor about herself and her world.

Images do not always communicate something deeply personal. Sometimes a mouse family is simply a mouse family. Or sometimes a mouse family reflects a subject from a book or television show to which a child has been recently exposed. Often, however, subject matter *does* reflect themes of importance to the creator, be they emotional, relational, or developmental. While my children's obsession with ninjas is a direct result of their recent exposure to "cool" popular characters in media, this creative world of good versus evil powers, hard work, discipline, and honor is much more than "cool." Ninjas have become their metaphor for exploring emotional themes (such as fear and defeat), relationships (such as when my eldest mentors the younger two in the ways of the ninja), and themes of developmental importance (such as who holds power and how power is cultivated).

Children are natural metaphor makers. Even before two years of age they begin to notice similarities between unrelated objects (Geary 2011). A stick is a gun. A climbing structure is a castle. Even a "lovey" or a "blankie" is essentially a stand-in for the comfort of the primary caregiver when she or he is not near. Metaphor helps children make sense of their world and allows them safe exploration of novel or difficult experiences because these experiences are essentially disguised as something else. In art, as in play, children can exert control over feelings and experiences when they, for example, draw superheroes blasting bad guys or scribble over a representation of something undesirable or frightening.

To begin understanding children's metaphoric expression, we need only to become more aware of how often we already use metaphor in our own lives. While most of us no longer spend much time engrossed in the metaphor-rich world of play and art, adults frequently compare one thing to another to explain unfamiliar ideas (e.g., "germs are like tiny bugs"), communicate hard-to-explain feelings (e.g., "a broken heart"), or paint a clearer picture of a situation (e.g., "my kid's room is a disaster zone"). Likewise, if someone shows you a picture of a clock with wings to represent time flying or a heart with a crack in it to communicate lost love, you'd understand the meaning behind these images, too. So, you see, you already know how to speak the language of metaphor. The trick is to intentionally use this knowledge when observing children's acts of art so as to respond to possible hidden meaning, rather than surface expression, as in the following story.

> My son draws a detailed picture including a house with a chimney. He adds smoke coming out of it. In a flash, his sister grabs a marker and scribbles over the picture. My son is understandably upset. I console him and turn to talk to my daughter about not drawing on other people's pictures when I realize what she has actually done. She has not scribbled haphazardly over his entire drawing. She has specifically obliterated the smoke. Metaphorically speaking, she put out the fire.
>
> Days before, there had been a small fire in our complex. My daughter was with me when we saw smoke pouring out of a window. I called 9-1-1. Our neighbor broke the fire extinguisher glass. Firefighters arrived. It was memorable. She seemed unaffected at first but started having trouble falling asleep at night. We talked about it. I reassured her. She continued to struggle with the event. Now, in one swell swoop of the marker, she has taken control of the situation, eliminated the smoke, and symbolically put out the fire. Instead of "Don't draw on your brother's art," I respond to the symbolic meaning of her scribble. "You took care of that, didn't you? You

got rid of the smoke. It's all gone." She had an easier time going to sleep at night after that.

It was possible that my daughter really was just scribbling on her brother's art as she had done several times before, either in an attempt to help him color it or perhaps to see what his reaction might be. But when I considered the possible metaphor at work in this particular instance, knowing about her recent worries, the scribble took on new meaning. In so doing, I was able to maximize the moment to meet her needs.

Look and listen for themes in the creative expression of your children. Themes of power, control, aggression, nurturance, family, friendships, or school may be of particular relevance and may reveal themselves within the metaphor of images. A family of rabbits may be the child's family. A battle scene might represent a child's desire to feel more powerful. A desolate planet might communicate a feeling of loneliness. Even a drawing of a favorite cartoon character might reveal something unique about your child. After all, your child chose that character, out of all the characters out there. What might it say about him? Use your hunches about metaphoric meaning as a springboard for exploration and discussion with your child. Whether talking with your child or teen, simple questions or theme-based observations such as those that follow can unlock a world of significance hiding right before your eyes (see fig. 4.3).

- Explore feelings:
    - I wonder what this animal / creature / person right here is feeling?
    - I wonder what made her feel like that?
    - I wonder if she needs anything?
- Explore relationships:
    - I wonder if you can tell me about these animals / creatures / people?
    - I wonder if they know each other? Are they friendly or not friendly?
    - I wonder what they are doing?
    - I notice this figure is separate from the others. I wonder if you can tell me about their relationship?
- Explore normal themes of childhood and growing up:
    - I notice that those guys have big muscles and are carrying a lot of things. I wonder if they are strong or powerful?
    - I see that they're taking good care of him.

4.3 Learn about a child's world through metaphor

When exploring metaphors, it's not necessary to make a direct comparison to your child or a real situation. You have the option to ask, "Do you ever feel like that, too?" but children mostly work through life experiences through metaphors without needing to relate them directly back to themselves. As in the example above, when my daughter obliterated the smoke image with her marker, it wasn't necessary to say, "That smoke coming out of our neighbor's window the other day was scary, wasn't it? You don't like seeing the drawing of the smoke." While it would not have been "wrong" to say this, it was more effective in this circumstance to speak her language of the scribble (rather than sharing my adult understanding of it). In her metaphorical world she had power and control. She needed to stay in that world, at least for the moment. All she needed from me was to affirm that power: "You got rid of the smoke. It's all gone."

### A visual conversation

Responding to art's underlying meaning need not always be done with words. Once we understand the language of art, we have the option to respond to our children's art with art. Some children may even be more responsive to an entirely visual dialogue than to verbal commentary. If the topic is particularly sensitive, if a child simply doesn't want to talk, or if it seems that communication breaks down when talking starts, you might try an entirely visual conversation.

My son awakes to find his goldfish, Lola, dead. He is sad. Really sad. He spontaneously draws a picture of her. He is quiet and contemplative. I surmise that he needs to be alone with his feelings, so I say nothing at the time. After acquiring a new fish, a beta (I hear they live longer—fingers crossed), I find him drawing a hybrid goldfish-beta. He entitles it "The mixed up fish" (see fig.

4.4a). "Wonderful. He's working through this," I think to myself. Then I notice a sharp-toothed, grinning shark swimming into the scene. Uh-oh. Death is knocking. My son is likely wondering if his new fish will meet the same fate as Lola (who lasted only four days). I sit down next to my son and, without saying a word, take a separate piece of paper and draw a cave. I write "CAVE" with an arrow (in case it isn't clear) and place it next to his drawing, in the path of the fish (see fig. 4.4b). I can't actually protect his new fish from Lola's fate, but I can communicate my intentions to help keep his fish healthy and alive as long as possible. Speaking the language of art, I offer these intentions through the cave image, a safe haven from the shark. He responds by drawing his own cave, complete with door and keyhole.

"Luckily the fish has the key to get inside," he says. "Here's the game. You have to guess if he'll unlock the door in time or if he'll get eaten."

I venture a guess. "I think he'll be okay."

My son agrees. "You're right. You win a prize, Mom."

4.4a "The mixed up fish"

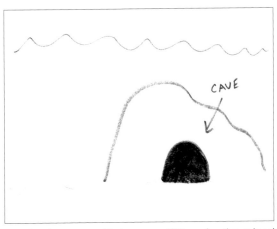

4.4b Respond to imagery with imagery ("Cave for the mixed up fish")

In this example, I had a sense of my child's needs (reassurance that his new fish would be okay). I communicated this by providing a cave to enable the fish to escape becoming the shark's next meal. How did I know that the cave was the right image? I didn't. I asked myself, "What does this fish need?" "Someplace safe" is the answer that came to me. I could have equally thought up a little fishy jet pack or a weapon for doing battle. But my son didn't seem to be in the fighting mood. He didn't seem like he needed to flee either. My son, not just the fish, needed a safe haven from his big, toothy feelings. My son took the bait (so to speak). The cave worked just as intended.

Sometimes in a visual exchange, just as in a verbal approach, a child isn't amenable to attempts to connect and communicate. Sometimes a visual conversation can be entirely about *not* wanting to have a conversation. As the following example demonstrates, visually conversing about not wanting to have a conversation can serve as a backdoor approach for connection, too.

> A client of mine is noticeably upset but unable (or unwilling) to talk about it. I draw a quick cartoon of him with an empty word bubble coming out of his mouth and pass it to him. He fills in the word bubble with random shapes, hash tags, stars, and exclamation marks. I draw a "translation machine" with buttons and levers. I pass it back. He draws a plug . . . out of the socket. I draw a power generator. He draws it blowing up. The conversation goes on like this for nearly an hour. He never says what is on his mind, but it doesn't really matter. We have had a full and fruitful conversation wherein I expressed my desire to connect with him, and he got to feel in control and powerful (perhaps something he needed in order to work through whatever was bugging him that day). It was a humorous conversation, lightening his mood by the end. And this conversation took place without a single word spoken.

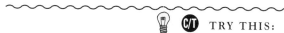

**TRY THIS:**

The next time your child is drawing or making something, spontaneously take another piece of paper or your own small piece of clay and make something that either responds to or adds to your child's art. If your child is making a pot, you can mold a small heart to place inside. If your child is drawing animals, you can draw food. If it's raining in your child's painting, you can paint an umbrella. Approach this activity in a playful and spontaneous manner, focusing on communicating messages of care, nurturance, or love to your child. Do not draw on your child's art or change her art unless you have been invited to do so. Instead, draw on a separate piece of paper and, if you'd like, cut it out and place it on top of or near your child's artwork.

If the idea of spontaneously responding to art with art leaves you feeling like a fish out of water, you may prefer to start a visual conversation through a structured game-like activity. If so, get playful with the following activity.

💡 🅒🆃 TRY THIS:

The Family Blueprint Activity (see fig. 4.5), designed by pioneering art therapist Helen Landgarten and published in *Family Art Psychotherapy* (1987), is a traditional art therapy activity that can be easily adapted for fun at home. It's an effective way to spend some concentrated time tuning in to your child. Initiate a joint drawing activity with your child or children (or the whole family!). Explain that the game is to create a picture together—the only rule is that there is no talking. The drawing is done when you both think it's done. While you do the activity, notice what your child does on the paper. Does he dive right in, or is he more hesitant to start? Does he take his cues from you, or is he oblivious to your part in the activity? Does he add onto or color inside what you draw, or does he maintain his own space? Consider what your part of this conversation is. Do you play a supportive role? Do you offer ideas on the paper? Do you add onto his ideas? Do you fill in his shapes? How does he respond? If siblings are participating, notice how they interact on the paper. What kind of nonverbal conversation are they having? How do you respond on the paper to their interactions there? Get curious and have fun!

4.5 The Family Blueprint

## A DOORWAY TO TALKING

A teen client is clearly not interested in attending therapy. Week after week he sits, slumped back on my couch, arms folded, eyes closed, headphones on with music blaring. Nothing I say is going to get through to him, and he is going to make sure of that. One day I casually bring out air-dry clay and start to sculpt a miniature replica of the portable music player he always brings with him. It doesn't take long before he is sneaking peeks at what I am doing. Next, he lifts up the music player so I can get a better look at it. Eventually, he is sitting up at the table with me, headphones off, pointing out details that I should include. He helps me paint the replica and, while he does, chats freely about his hopes for the future.

While art serves as a language in and of itself, it also serves as an effective doorway to a more traditional form of communication: talking. Talking to someone isn't always easy, especially when the topic is of a serious, personal, or emotional matter. This applies to everyone, not just kids. Talking can feel too intensely intimate. It can feel embarrassing. We may worry about what the other person is thinking, or we may be preoccupied trying to figure out what the other person wants to hear. While we may want to connect, we may simultaneously feel too vulnerable or threatened to expose ourselves. When we are busy doing something, however, talking becomes much easier.

In the example above, several important steps happened in the development of communication and eventual connection. First, I neither fought his resistance nor gave in to it. I could have insisted that he take off his headphones or just given up entirely, hoping that he might eventually come around in his own time. Instead, I honored his desire not to talk while at the same time continuing to attempt connection through a less threatening means: art. By sculpting a replica of his portable music player, I nonverbally communicated that I recognized the importance of this object to him. Soon, the very thing that he used to block me out (the music player) was transformed into the thing that brought us together. Once he was engaged in the process of making art, he was able to open up. Surely some of this opening up could be attributed to the fact that I had earned his trust, but something else was happening, too. The very act of molding clay and painting freed him up to talk. If we hadn't been making art, no doubt we would have continued to sit in silence.

Making art frees people up to talk for several reasons. To start with, when you make art, the attention is neither on you nor on the other person. It is on the material with which you are working. Focusing on art making, rather than looking at another person (or at the floor), decreases the discomfort that can come from face-to-face conversations. With art making as the focus, it becomes easier to move in and out of dialogue because talking feels secondary. Slipping into silence while making art feels more acceptable than silence during a verbal conversation, which often leaves people feeling awkward. It's much easier to talk when we feel in control of when and how much we talk.

Not only does art increase comfort during a person-to-person chat, but the physical experience of manipulating media itself can also free people up to talk. As long as the activity doesn't require too much concentration or technical attention, the process of art making itself can loosen people up enough to start a flow of thoughts. When another person is present, this can easily cross over into sharing those thoughts aloud. Process-based activities such as playing mindlessly with clay, watercolors, or doodling, for example, allow the mind to stay aware of the activity without requiring complete focus or quiet. Frequently in my work, I invite clients to play with a small ball of clay, during which they begin to spontaneously share their stream of thoughts. Repetitive activities such as making friendship bracelets, beading, or knitting provide a similar opportunity. Once proficiency is attained, the rhythm of the activity takes over. While the hands are busy, the mind can wander and, in the presence of another, conversations emerge.

If you want to talk to a child or teen about a difficult situation or if you simply want to create a space to learn more about what's generally on her mind, try starting with art:

- Initiate an activity—Invite your child to do an art or craft activity or just start it yourself to see if you can pique his interest. Once the activity is in process, share a thought casually or ask a question to see if it will spark conversation. Sometimes you don't need to say anything at all. A child may spontaneously begin sharing thoughts while occupied with the activity.

- Make nonjudgmental observations—A nonjudgmental observation remarks on something that is observable without interpretations, assumptions, or value judgments—whether positive or negative. These statements open communication, foster connection, encourage creativity, and prevent resistance. A judgment-free observation often begins with "I see" or "I notice," followed by a specific, observable action. For example:

| Recommended | Not Recommended |
|---|---|
| *Nonjudgmental or neutral statements about that which is literally observable, beginning with "I see" or "I notice."*<br><br>"I notice you're not touching the clay." | *Judgmental statements involving interpretation, assumptions, or value judgments—either positive or negative.*<br><br>"You don't want to do this activity?"<br><br>*This discourages participation and problem-solving.* |
| "I see you're drawing lots of circles." | "What's *that* supposed to be?"<br><br>"Is it a _____?"<br><br>*This communicates that art has to look like something and that self-expression itself is not enough. It discourages creativity.* |
| "I notice a lot of colors in this corner." | "I like it. That's beautiful."<br><br>*This inhibits further dialogue. It can set up performance expectations and anxiety, or disconnection if the artist does not agree. It can also be construed as meaningless if overused.* |
| "I see you ripping up your paper." | "You're ruining your beautiful art!"<br><br>*This is a judgment about the art (it's beautiful) and what is happening to it (it's getting ruined). Thus, it may stifle creativity, self-expression, and communication, while provoking resistance.* |

- Express curiosity—Sometimes a nonjudgmental observation is enough to spark a reply. At other times, you may want to follow up with a statement of curiosity beginning with "I wonder . . ." This is a nonthreatening way to make an inquiry because it does not suggest any conclusions have been reached. For example:

| Recommended |
| --- |
| "I wonder what you're going to do next?" |
| *This encourages independent decision-making and engagement.* |
| "I wonder what your plan was when you started?" |
| *This strengthens problem solving and planning.* |
| "I wonder if you would like to try that?" |
| *This invites participation, engagement, and creative risk taking.* |
| "I wonder if you can tell me more about this?" |
| *This encourages reflection and dialogue.* |
| "I wonder what happened?" |
| *This teaches that events precede feelings which, in turn, encourages problem solving and development of coping skills. Unlike statements like "I wonder why you're angry?" or "I wonder what's wrong?" it does not interpret how a child may be feeling or assume that anything is wrong.* |
| "I wonder what made you decide to do that?" |
| *This encourages reasoning skills.* |

(For more discussion and examples of nonjudgmental language, visit the section "Destruction" in chapter 2. See also appendix 1: "Guidelines for Talking about Art and Life.")

- Prevent power struggles—Simple shifts in our choice of words can help our children be more receptive to our communication. The use of "Let's," "AND," and "What's your plan?" removes the power differential in our language and encourages cooperation. For example:

| Recommended | Not Recommended |
| --- | --- |
| "Let's clean up now." | "I want you to clean up now." |
| *"Let's" is inclusive and nonthreatening.* | "I need you to clean up now." |
| | *"I want you to" and "I need you to" suggest a power differential that may invite resistance.* |
| *Context: Child has stated that an activity is boring.* | *Context: Child has stated that an activity is boring.* |
| "I hear that you find this activity boring AND how might you make it more meaningful to you?" | "I hear that you find this activity boring, BUT you have to do it." |
| *"And" validates the perspective of the other person. This response encourages engagement, creative thinking, problem solving, and connection.* | *"But" negates the perspective of the other person and has authoritarian overtones that may trigger resistance. Moreover, it discourages ownership of the decision to participate meaningfully.* |

| Recommended *(cont.)* | Not Recommended *(cont.)* |
|---|---|
| "What was your plan?" | "Why did you do that?!" |
| *"What" (and "How") elicit more information because questions starting with these words usually cannot be answered with a simple "Yes" or "No."* <br><br> *"What was your plan?" encourages engagement, critical thinking, problem solving, and connection.* | *"Why" implies disapproval, which might inhibit creative expression and may provoke anxiety, self-judgment, resentment, or resistance. Moreover, children (or adults) often don't know why they have done something. The question may be difficult to answer or lead to falsehoods.* |

- Be okay with quiet—If for some reason a conversation doesn't flow easily, know that simply sitting with your child while he makes art (or while you both make art) is still helping forge a connection. A father once shared that the most helpful thing he learned from his work with me was that his son still heard him, even when he didn't respond to any initiations of conversation. "It's not about what you say so much as it is about your gesture to connect," I told him. "Your son's silence doesn't necessarily mean 'stop trying.'" Understanding this encouraged the father enough to keep at it and, over time, his son began to share private thoughts with him.

## REBUILD LOST CONNECTION

Ruptures in relationships are inevitable. We all have them. A rupture can be as slight as a misinterpretation of your child's feelings or as large as a full-blown shouting match. You might feel a rupture when you hear "You never do anything for me!" after years of doing, doing, doing for them or when the dreaded "I hate you" comes from a child who, you thought, was much too young to hate you already. A child may experience a rupture when a parent is texting rather than fully listening or when he simply feels misunderstood. Ruptures can be minimized, but they cannot be avoided altogether. When ruptures occur, however, it is within our power to actively repair them.

When my oldest child and I have a disagreement or miscommunication of some sort, art often brings us back together. Sometimes he initiates the art making. Sometimes I do. After a conflict, my son might write "I HAT [*sic*] U" over and over again on a piece of paper before presenting it to me. He knows I'm not okay with him shouting out loud at me. ("You can feel angry," I tell him, "*and* you may not shout at me.") On paper, however, he is welcome to shout at me silently as much as he wants. Getting his anger out on paper in this way is more tolerable for us both. I can literally receive his anger as he hands it to me, which often enables him to spontaneously move on from it. The repair comes as I take the piece of paper without judgment or criticism, I squat down so I'm at his level, and I thank him for the note. If he's open to it, I'll offer a hug or ask if he wants to talk. If the rupture is still too big for that, I may get my own piece of paper and draw a heart on it or write "I love you" and pass it to him. Connection is reestablished.

Kathy feels worlds away from her preteen daughter. While she insists that she regularly offers praise, her daughter is unable to embrace her mother's occasional attempts at connection in the face of pervasive family discord. I suggest that Kathy start a sketchbook in which she can draw pictures and write messages, reflecting some of the positive things that she sees her daughter do each day. Making it visible through art, I suggest, would make it easier for her daughter to "see" her mother's attempts at connecting. Putting pen to paper would also help mother more consistently notice positives in her daughter. She gives it a try. Although her daughter is initially resistant to looking at the sketchbook entries, Kathy sticks with it. Eventually, her daughter shows interest, and slowly they begin to rebuild their connection.

It is never too late to rebuild, no matter how far gone you feel that your relationship is. Sometimes rebuilding connection needs to start with simply inhabiting the same space with a shared activity.

### The power of parallel play

It's not an unfamiliar scene today to see family members sitting side by side, yet completely disengaged with each other: one paying bills, another texting, another surfing the web. This is not a scene of connection. However, if we replaced bills and electronics with coloring pages or beads, we'd see a very different scenario. Even if family members are silently making art near one another, seedlings of connection are taking root. In the 1997 children's book *That's How It Is When We Draw*, author Ruth Bornstein begins: "You want to come over? But I need to be alone in a quiet place today and draw. You do? You want to draw, too? Okay! I guess when we draw we can be alone together." While being alone together is an important step toward connection, it matters *how* you are alone together.

My daughter is coloring an outer space scene. My son, a cheetah. I'm doodling. We're not exactly engaged with each other . . . but we're not disengaged either. Unlike people who are engrossed in electronics or paying bills, we are acutely aware of one another's presence. We share materials. We glance at each other's work from time to time. We're not talking, but we could be. It may not look like it, but we are connecting through this shared experience. It's a lot like parallel play, an important stage of social development that occurs between eighteen months and two years of age.

During parallel play, young children play next to other children who are engaged in their own play, but they do not attempt to be involved in one another's play. Because the play is solitary, it doesn't look like much is going on socially, but this is far from the truth. Children are extremely observant of those playing alongside them. They watch and listen to one another, mimicking behavior they observe. This normal stage can provoke anxiety in some grown-ups, who may wish to nudge their children toward more direct interaction. However, this experience of "being alone together" is a crucial step in learning how to be around others.

While the parallel play stage is commonly associated with very young children, the benefits of this type of interaction are applicable to all ages and stages of development.

Several teenage girls regularly refuse to attend their art therapy group. While the therapist could dismiss their behavior as defiant, she acknowledges the needs behind the behavior: the girls are so uncomfortable with the idea of forming relationships that they don't even want to set foot in the room (let alone participate in collaborative activities prepared for them). Friendships don't come easily, and trust is a rare commodity in the group home where they reside. Grasping this, the art therapist puts collaborative activities on hold and goes back to basics. She introduces coloring pages, an activity that requires little or no interaction. The girls enthusiastically begin to attend the group and color alone together. This is the first building block to developing relationships with each other. Little by little, the art therapist is able to encourage more interaction by setting up scenarios that require the girls to share materials (by limiting the number of scissors or glue sticks, for example) and by encouraging the girls to show each other what they have created. Eventually, collaborative projects that require direct interaction are reintroduced. Through this process, they are able to form connections.

Whether you're aiming to make amends after a clash with your child, you notice siblings struggling to occupy the same space, or it's simply been a while since you invited your teen to do something with you, apply the principles of parallel play to create a foundation for connection.

**TRY THIS:**

Set up an activity at home that you believe your child may have interest in: coloring, beading, making cards, a holiday-related craft, experimenting with a new or unusual material, or anything else you think of. Casually invite your child (or teen) to join you, "I'm going to make some cards. There's more paper here if you want to make some, too." Then start the activity. Even if your child doesn't join in, she will notice what you are doing and will sense your desire to connect. Maybe make something for your child. Depending on how distant you and your child feel from one another, it may take a long time before she is willing to join in. Keep at it.

## Sync up

It's late morning, the time of day when I typically squeeze in a workout and quick shower before running out the door for work. My six-month-old is happily chewing on something that he shouldn't be and my oldest, who would typically be at school right now, has just started summer break. He has plenty with which to entertain himself, but he wants to play with me. Even though I know it's not true, his words: "But you NEVER play with me" go straight to the heart. I want to meet his needs *and* mine. I know that when he feels connected with me, he is happier and healthier (Carter 2008). I also know that if I don't take care of myself, I'll get testy later. (Argh, and now my baby is chewing on something else that he shouldn't be.) No time for a board game, cards, or Legos. "Okay," I say. "Grab a piece of paper and marker. I will teach you a quick game." I explain the rules, "It's like tag. First you're 'it.' You chase my marker around the paper with your marker and try to tag me." We play it, our markers scribbling around the paper. In less than ten seconds, he's tagged me. We switch roles and play again, laughing as we go. Then we play "follow the leader" on a piece of paper, this time with me moving my marker more slowly so he can keep up. He spontaneously embellishes the resulting scribble, turning it into a silly, smiling character. He titles it: "The Big Blob Hug" (see fig. 4.6).

4.6 "The big blob hug"

This simple art activity took less than five minutes. In that short time, we regained our connection not only through laughing and enjoying time together but also by maximizing art's ability to help us sync up. We played out, on paper, the real-life situation unfolding that morning: my son trying to catch me while I ran to and fro. By matching each other's pace and movements on the paper, our connection came back to the forefront. It seems (based on the title of the scribble and his willingness to play with his baby brother afterward, while I did my workout) that this brief activity felt like a big, satisfying hug.

Synchrony has been found to be an important part of connecting with others in many realms of life. For our purposes, synchrony means matching the behavior of another. This can literally mean doing the same thing at the same time (mirroring) or responding back in a similar way (echoing). For example, our brains are hardwired to mirror people subconsciously; we assume a similar posture, voice, gesture, or facial expression because it helps us to learn and bond (Chartrand and Bargh 1999; Pineda 2009). A concrete example of the effectiveness of echoing can be seen when a waitress takes an order: she's likely to get a bigger tip if she repeats the order back to her customer (Van Baaren et al. 2003). Not only do echoed customers feel reassured that they have been understood, but also they experience a sense of sameness and, thus, increased rapport. In addition to fostering perceptions of similarity and connectedness, synchrony also increases cooperation, as measured by how efficiently a team completes a task (Valdesolo, Ouyang, and DeSteno 2010). Synchrony is a form of empathy; it's like having a voice and being heard.

While there are many ways to experience shared activities with our kids (from family dinners to playing games, shooting hoops, or reading books together), the creative arts offer unique possibilities for syncing up. For example, research demonstrates that when people sing in groups (even off-key) a sense of connection and belonging develops (Anshel and Kipper 1988; Gridley et al. 2011). A 2013 study by Vickhoff and colleagues revealed that even the heart rates of singers may align. Moreover, researchers have discovered that singing releases oxytocin, a hormone released in nursing mothers that is associated with developing social bonds and empathy (Grape et al. 2003). People who play rhythms in sync with someone else show more helpful, compassionate, and altruistic behavior (Kokal et al. 2011; Valdesolo and DeSteno 2011). Studies have also found that synchronized movement, as experienced when dancing with a partner, promotes feelings of trust, liking, and a desire to help the other person (Reddish, Fischer, and Bulbulia 2013; Tarr et al. 2015).

There are several creative activities that maximize synchrony to build connection. These types of activities are commonly used as icebreakers when building rapport with children in therapy or in classrooms because they require tuning in to one another in a fun way that builds and reinforces connection.

- Chase the Scribble—This activity, described earlier in this chapter and as shown in figure 4.6, allows your child to take the lead as you follow him around the paper. The speed is up to him. As he "runs" around the paper with a pen, you follow him with yours. The goal is not to tag the other pen. If he pauses, you pause. When he starts up again, you're off and running around the paper again, following your child's trail. Then switch roles with each other or invite siblings to try it together.

- Mirror Mirror—Invite your child to play a new game with you. Stand facing each other, and invite your child to move in any way that she would like. The goal is for you to mimic her movements as precisely as possible, as if you were her reflection in a mirror. She can move slowly so that you can keep up, or she can challenge you by making faster movements. Switch roles or experiment with siblings playing this game together.

Syncing up for connection is not limited to special movement and art activities. It can happen anytime throughout the day.

**C/T** Let your body do the talking (see fig. 4.7)—You may already notice how much more effective it is to talk to a child when you physically get down to her level. This decreases the power differential and helps her feel safer, while allowing her to feel more seen and heard. Don't stop there. Pay attention to what the rest of your body is doing, too. Even if you're kneeling down, you may not be communicating connection and empathy if your posture is upright with your arms crossed over your chest, while your child's posture is slouched with her arms hanging loosely by her sides. If her shoulders are slumped, try slumping yours. This doesn't mean throwing yourself on the floor flailing your arms and legs, if that's what your child is doing. But if your child is on the couch, try sitting next to her. If she is on the floor, try lying down there with her.

4.7 Let your body do the talking

**C/T** Match your tone—Making subtle changes to align your tone of voice with your child's emotions is as important as your body posture. Tone is an important communication tool that often speaks louder than words. When you empathize with your upset child by saying "You really want another cookie. It just doesn't feel fair," don't just say it with that normal tone that you'd use to order a coffee. Say it with a little feeling. Your child is upset. Connect by mirroring a little of that upset in your tone of voice. You're more likely to get through to him. Keep in mind that mockery sounds different from synchrony. If you try to mimic your child's emotional tone while you are angry or frustrated with your child, it may unintentionally sound like mockery. The point is not to imitate in order to "show your child how ridiculous his whining sounds." The intention is to show your child that you can feel a little bit of what he's feeling in that moment.

Making something for your child (or receiving a piece of art from your child) is another way to strengthen your connection. Hearing the words "I made this for you" is a lot like hearing "I was thinking of you" or "I appreciate you." Making something requires time and thought. Even if the giving is an afterthought, it communicates that the receiver is important. We give our kids a lot: snacks that they love, shoes that they need, sports classes that they want. But making something for them is different. Even a pipe-cleaner wand, a quick sketch of something, or a made-up song shows that you've spent your time and energy making something that communicates "You're special to me" in a way that buying toys, treats, and clothes doesn't.

Even if you don't consider yourself an artist, kids are often in awe of what grown-ups can do with a small hunk of clay or a couple of pipe cleaners. Younger kids marvel at a pinch pot (you know, those pots you make by pressing your thumbs into a little ball of clay and then pinching the edges to form the sides) or seeing how you twist two pipe cleaners together to make a candy-cane pattern. Older kids and teens may value a hand-drawn "just because" card with silly stick figure doodles. Making a gift need not be labor intensive; giving a gift need not be an ordeal. It can be done anytime and not just as a gesture of apology after a conflict. Oftentimes, when I give my kids a piece of art, it's when we're making art together. "This is for you," I'll say as I pass to them whatever I've been creating. And a lot of times my kids will reciprocate, "Here, Mom, I made this for *you*." Translation of the interaction: "I love you." "I love you, too."

How you receive art is as important as giving art now and again. Whether the gift is presented with the words "I made this for you" or "Here, Dad, I don't want it. You can have it," it's important that we welcome each opportunity as a chance to reinforce our connection with our children. When art is thrust at us casually (as often it is) with an abrupt "Here," it's difficult to receive it as you would a wrapped gift. Instead, we often barely pause from whatever we're doing and say, "Thanks, honey. I'll put it up on the fridge." While this seems reasonable enough ("thanks" and "put it up" seem to cover all the bases), consider what it would feel like if someone responded to *your* handmade gift with, "Thanks, it's great. I'm sure I'll use that," while absentmindedly putting it aside and going back to whatever she was doing. It's not *what* you say; it's *how* you say it that matters. Taking the time to make a specific, nonjudgmental remark about what you actually observe in the gift, such as "You made this with a lot of bright colors" will automatically slow down your response time and help your child feel seen and heard.

When your child hands you art, you don't have to drop everything immediately to look at it. If you're in the middle of something, it's okay to say, "Hold on just a minute. I'm in the middle of something right now, and I want to really be able to look

**84**   at this without feeling distracted." Then follow through. Finish up what you're doing (or find a good place to pause) and give your child undivided attention (see fig. 4.8). This also goes for watching his new dance moves or listening to song lyrics he has mastered. Receive the moment as you would a wrapped gift.

4.8 Receive art like a gift

Not only does giving your child undivided attention communicate caring but also showing heartfelt gratitude reinforces for your child that she is capable of spreading joy with her gestures. Research supports that giving promotes happiness (Dunn, Aknin, and Norton 2008), health (Piferi and Lawler 2006), and cooperation (Simpson and Willer 2015). Moreover, when we show gratitude for the art that our children give us, we're modeling a socially appropriate response as well as a grateful frame of mind which, in itself, promotes such qualities as optimism (Froh, Sefick, and Emmons 2007), feeling close to others (Lambert et al. 2010), and general happiness (Froh et al. 2009; Watkins et al. 2003; Wood, Froh, and Geraghty 2010). When we give thanks, kids are more likely to give thanks for the things in their life, too.

## THE TIES THAT BIND

I'm working on a birthday banner for my mother's milestone birthday. My kids are distracted by their own activities. I know exactly how I want it to look and can quickly get this done. And then . . . "Can we help?!" they shriek, running over and grabbing the glue bottle. Darn. "Of course!" (I grit my teeth). This wasn't supposed to become a big project. Now it's definitely not going to turn out how I wanted. "I'll get the treasures!" hollers my son, as he runs off to his room to retrieve them. My daughter squeals, "What can I do?!" I'm reminded of what really matters. My kids feel important. They're working together. They're connected to something bigger than themselves. These jewels, paper scraps, and glue aren't just embellishing the banner. They are reinforcing the social ties that bind. I relax and embrace this moment.

Nurturing ties between your children and their extended family, friends, and community matters greatly not only to their immediate happiness but also to their future health and well-being. Health risks associated with social isolation are right up there with the dangers of smoking and obesity (Holt-Lunstad, Smith, and Layton 2010; House 2001). From poorer immune function to increased stress and mental health problems, those who are lonely have a 30 percent increased risk of death. Loneliness negatively affects blood pressure (Yang et al. 2015) as well as the body's production of virus- and bacteria-fighting white blood cells (Cole et al. 2015). Conversely, support from others strengthens the functioning of bodily systems (Uchino 2006), and a sense of belonging reduces depression (Cruwys et al. 2014).

Loneliness may not seem like an immediate concern for your sandbox-playing youngster or phone-obsessed teen. However, national surveys reveal that loneliness is a growing epidemic (Cigna 2018; Wilson and Moulton 2010), with the youngest adults (ages 18–22) being the most affected (Cigna 2018). Just as with any family value or healthy routine, it is important to instill meaningful bond-building practices early. According to Harvard-affiliated doctor Jeremy Nobel, president of The Foundation for Art and Healing, bonds may be simply built by using the arts to tell your story (Nobel 2015). The British government adopted an innovative public health strategy, offering "social prescriptions" for participation in the arts to combat loneliness (Her Majesty's Government 2018).

By tapping into art's inherently collaborative, expressive, and meaning-rich nature, we can help our children feel connected and valued, building habits of connection that can last a lifetime. Here's how.

## Commemorating family moments

> When my son was nearing graduation from preschool, the school gave a large, empty scrapbook to each parent. Our task was to create a "grad book" by gluing photos, our child's art, and anything else that we wanted inside. It would be presented to our child on graduation day. However, the process of making the scrapbooks also offered the parents an opportunity to come together during this bittersweet transition to reflect on our growing children and the close of a chapter of their lives and ours. It was as much for us as it was for them.

The creative arts have traditionally been used across cultures to mark events. You have likely already used them to commemorate important times in your own home, whether celebrating life or mourning loss. The arts can help us make special moments even more special. They can become part of traditions that connect us to something larger than ourselves: recent family history, culture, ancestry.

Reflect on the ways that your family already commemorates events through dance, music, stories, photos, crafting, or decorations. Consider making some of them annual traditions. Introduce new creative ways to mark milestones in your lives. Here are some ideas:

**C/T** Invite your kids to select their favorite songs from the past year. Make a new mix each birthday or at the start of each year.

**C/T** Start a sketchbook in which your child can make a drawing or collage each year to commemorate a birthday, the first day of school, a trip, or another important event.

**C** Start a "dance party in your jammies" tradition for your family on Sunday mornings.

**C** Design and decorate a countdown calendar for an exciting event or the return of a family member who is away. It can be as simple as writing numbers on Post-it notes, letting your kids decorate them, and then sticking them on the wall.

**C/T** Make an altar or poster for a lost loved one. Commemorate pets or family members who pass by collaging photos, letters, drawings, or other memorabilia on a poster board or by placing them in a small box that you decorate. Even simpler, give your child a smooth rock to decorate in memory of a lost loved one. (Sharpies work well—just be sure to put down a brown paper bag, newspaper, or other protective surface first.) Invite your child to place the stone in the yard or, if you used paint or another material that will not hold up in weather, keep the stone someplace special in the house.

## Fitting in

My family moves to a new city, and my children are excited to find several children living in our neighborhood. As eager as they are to make friends, they are also tentative about doing so. There are days when my children are included in the group . . . and many days when they are not. I want to help my children join this new community without having to negotiate every step of the way. I set up a small table in our front yard with coloring sheets and a large box of markers and crayons. Like bees to honey, the children who often play outside come over and ask my kids if they can color, too. "Yes," is the reply. The kids get along and continue to enjoy each other as they branch out into other games. Many months later, the kids in the neighborhood still request, "Can we color again like we did that time when you first moved in?"

Making art brings people together for a common purpose without teams or sides, winners or losers. Even in neighborhoods torn apart by crime and poverty, people will come together to build parks, paint murals, or sing in a choir. According to the National Crime Prevention Council (2000), art making reduces conflict and crime by improving overall community belonging, happiness, well-being, and pride. Art is a powerful unifier. Look into arts-based activities that your community already offers, such as coloring contests at the local grocery store, sidewalk chalk festivals, or holiday sing-alongs. However, you need not wait for an organized event to help connect your children to their community through art. Here are some ideas to get you started:

- **C/T** The gift of art—Invite your children to make cards, design bookmarks, draw a picture, or create some other token of appreciation to pass out to the postal worker, garbage truck driver, or other valued service providers in your community.

- **C/T** Secret acts of art—My oldest son spontaneously made drawings one day, put them in his bike basket, and then rode around the neighborhood playing "mail carrier" by covertly dropping them off at neighbors' houses. He didn't write from whom the drawings came. He loved the idea that people would be confused, surprised, and happy when they found the drawings from an unidentified sender. Invite older children or teens to engage in secret acts of art by taking an evening stroll around the neighborhood writing positive messages on the sidewalk with chalk, such as "You make someone happy." Passersby will discover them in the morning.

- **C/T** Park art—Take a bucket of sidewalk chalk outside your home or to the park. Invite other children to join in decorating a sidewalk, basketball court, or other surface. You can even come up with a unifying theme such as "deep sea" or "outer space," "friendship" or "what makes me happy." Encourage your kids to tell other kids and parents about the activity: "We're making a big outer space scene! We need as many people to help as possible. Do you want to help?" Older youth may find meaningful bonding by illustrating and captioning something for which they stand as a group, like "Support Our Schools: Vote Yes on Measure A!"

- **C/T** World art—There are many online programs that can help children connect with other children in their community or around the world through art. From designing and sending dolls abroad to participating in worldwide art shows, the internet is teeming with organizations that can help your child begin to develop his identity as a world citizen. Be sure to talk to children about internet safety and screen any websites for legitimacy before they get started. On a simpler scale, you can help your child start an art pen-pal relationship with a cousin or family friend in another state or country. Get the other parent on board first, then invite your child to draw a picture to mail or send electronically to the other child, who will respond by sending back a drawing of his own.

## WHEN KIDS STRUGGLE TO CONNECT

One teenage client diagnosed with autism wants to connect with others, but is anxious doing so. He becomes easily distracted by his own thoughts, frequently retreating into his mind. Our work together begins outdoors where I invite him to draw anything of interest. He chooses the street gutter. He takes one look at the gutter and then proceeds to draw without lifting his eyes from the paper again. I encourage him to look back at the gutter to gather more information as he draws, challenging him to stay connected to the external world. I am building his ability to have a two-way interaction without retreating entirely into his own thoughts. Giving his attention to the gutter is a safer place to start than a face-to-face interaction. I am meeting him where he is. Over time, through this process, his ability to maintain attention to the external world grows. One day he decides to draw me. The back-and-forth process of looking at me to gather visual information before drawing the details he observes is a pivotal step toward connecting and communicating with me and others around him.

### Meet kids where they are

Kids may struggle to connect for a variety of reasons. Some children may have difficulties connecting because they are naturally shy or anxious in social settings. Some may struggle with situational adjustments, like living with a new stepparent or stepsiblings. Still others may be dealing with significant impairment from early childhood trauma or developmental delays, such as those related to learning disabilities or autism spectrum disorders. With the prevalence and convenience of technology nowadays, these children may seem even harder to reach, as they may hide in the realm of cyberspace, chat rooms, video games, or social media platforms.

According to Lawrence Cohen in his book *Playful Parenting*, when kids struggle to connect, parents need to insist on connection, but children get to decide on the terms. If you attempt more connection than a child is ready to handle, or a type of connection that a child doesn't want, the distance will likely increase. Instead, meet children where they are, and go from there.

A high school client of mine is graduating, but anger toward the teachers and principal makes it difficult for him to say a healthy goodbye. He has gotten into a lot of trouble at school, and he resents them. As he gets closer to graduation, he starts acting out fears about leaving school through increased conflict with school staff. Insisting that he make amends isn't going to work. He does not see the point. Instead, I suggest that I help him make a personal yearbook. We start where he is comfortable. I agree that we'll include only what he wants to include. We make a simple book out of construction paper and set off to capture his experience of school together with a digital camera. He works on it for several weeks, eventually taking pictures of the teachers with whom he has had conflicts. He even poses with the principal for a friendly picture. As he works on this project, he works through feelings about leaving and builds bridges with the staff with whom he has struggled so much.

One way to meet children where they are is to reach out through the medium with which they are most comfortable. Earlier in this chapter, we explored how children are natural metaphor makers; they learn and communicate more about the world through art and play than through talking. Another form of communication with which kids are intimately familiar is technology. It seems counterintuitive, but even children whose isolation is magnified by technology may be most easily accessed through the very thing that keeps them disconnected.

> Jonathan likely spends more time on electronics than on any other activity outside of school (including sleeping). His mother tries talking about responsibility. She invites him to go on bike rides with her. She tries getting angry. He isn't interested. In our work together, I print out pictures of characters from his favorite video games and encourage him to make up visual stories. Over time, we integrate themes from his personal life, gently bridging his tech world of fun and adventure with his real-world struggles. As much as his mom hates the technology that has distanced her from her son, I encourage her to show interest in his video games. "Ask him about them," I suggest. "Instead of doing laundry or returning phone calls, sit next to him. Cheer him on. Maybe ask if you can have a try. Make it a shared activity." I explain that while he plays video games because he likes them, excessive playing stems from the need to retreat from worries and preoccupations, including conflicts with her. If he feels more connected, he won't need to retreat as far and for as long. Indeed, on the days that his mother shows interest in his games, he is more open to unplugging and connecting with her.

Technology and parenting is a complicated matter. On the one hand, when our kids are "plugged in," life can be a little easier for us. They demand less, argue less, and are more self-entertained (and they may occasionally actually learn something useful). Yet, more technology can also mean less attention to homework and chores, increased impulsivity and aggression (The American Psychological Association Task Force on Violent Media 2017), as well as decreased communication skills (Turkle 2015), self-esteem (Anxiety UK 2012), and emotional intelligence (Uhls et al. 2014). Thus, connecting through technology requires a thoughtful balance between love and limits. It's important to establish clear guidelines for the use of technology, such as restricting content, times, and zones (limits); it's equally important to find creative ways to communicate and connect within that world (love).

In the example above, Jonathan needed more consistent limits regarding technology use. But that wasn't enough. In order not to fight the limits so vehemently, he also needed to feel understood. Like metaphor in children's art, video graphics and characters often reflect meaningful themes, such as power, love, conflict, teamwork,

**90**　or quests. Exploring the significance of themes like these with your child will give you a glimpse into her internal life. And she may begin to feel more understood and connected as a result.

TRY THIS:

Notice what characters your child or teen chooses to be when playing video games. Explore these animated graphics just as you would images that your child creates himself. Get curious about the themes that you see: "Which one is the leader? What's it like to be the leader?" or "So, this character has to go on a quest all by herself? What's that like?" Listen for stories that may relate to your child's own life. This may be the start of an interesting conversation.

Like other mediums for creativity, technology is versatile. Beyond showing interest in our children's video games, social media profiles, or other online activities, the creative use of technology can connect an isolated child with those around her. Even those of us who identify as technologically challenged can take advantage of the accessibility of technology as well as its ability to draw the interest of kids.

> After my third child is born, there are naturally times when the older two feel distant, left out, and unimportant, despite my best efforts to communicate otherwise. I try redirecting them to play on their own. I try simultaneously juggling feedings with playing board games. I feel overwhelmed and pulled in opposite directions. One day when I am feeling at the end of my rope, I have a creative flash. "Hey, do you guys want to be in charge of documenting this?!" As I hand them my phone to take photos, they immediately feel more important and in control of the situation. For many months, they continue to delight in artistically documenting diaper changes, feedings, burpings, and more.

In this situation, the convenient camera function on my phone served as an effective, creative tool in a pinch. My kids needed more than an activity to occupy them. With a new baby usurping a lot of my time and energy, they wanted not only my attention but also to feel important. Being responsible for documenting this time *and* getting to use my phone to do so met this dual need. Here are even more ways to use technology to connect with children and teens when they are particularly difficult to reach:

**C/T** What emoji are you?—An emoji cannot substitute for actual emotional expression, empathy, or conflict resolution; however, young people can relate to those little funny faces and other icons that you send electronically. Experiment with emoji images to help children get in touch with and express feelings. If a child is down and won't talk, bring up a menu of emojis on your smartphone and invite him to tap on one that shows how he feels. Wonder aloud about what words he might include with the image if he were to send that emoji to someone. Want to get really creative? Help older kids design an emoji-inspired T-shirt, cap, or cover for a notebook, based on the ones they like or can relate to. Add a motto. For younger kids, make an emoji-inspired mask or stick puppet. If your child refuses, have a go at it yourself, and then share what you made with him, inviting him to offer suggestions. Ask him to give the mask or puppet a name and tell you what it is saying. The use of puppets and masks can provide a comfortable way for children to dialogue with adults about what they are thinking and feeling (Reid-Searle et al. 2016).

**C/T** Snap, then chat—Encourage your kids to snap pictures of people, pets, objects, and environments that are important to them. As in the example above, taking pictures can help kids engage with others when it's difficult to connect (or when they don't want to let on that they want to connect). Cameras give kids a sense of distance and control over interactions. They're also a potential doorway to conversation. Ask if you can see the photos your child has taken, or follow your teen on popular photo-sharing social media apps. Ask which one is her favorite picture or online post and what title she would give it. Art therapist Robert Wolf (2007) offers additional photography exercises for emotional self-expression and social connection.

**C/T** Art apps—There are plenty of online applications that encourage creativity. Bridge the gap by inviting your child to join you in playing around with an art app. There are even apps that will animate your creations. One colleague of mine shared that her preteen used an art app to create a portrait of herself with her mother. She animated the image with silly voices, showing her mother nagging. It was not only humorous but also brought up an important dynamic that the child would not have been able to broach through talking alone. Creating it and then sharing it in this way made it more comfortable for both mother and daughter.

**C** Be a faux social media influencer—Children may not want to open up to you, but they may be willing to talk to a make-believe online audience of millions. Play a make-believe game wherein you are the producer and your child is the social media influencer. Invite your child to invent a name for his pretend channel. Using the video function on your phone, film your child commenting for his "audience" on benign topics like "What I want for my birthday" interspersed with more personal topics like "Something you're struggling with and how you'll overcome it." Encourage participation with prompting, such as: "I imagine your viewers would like to know of a time you had to deal with something difficult. I bet it would help all those other kids out there who are struggling with something similar."

While there are many ways to connect with children through the arts at home, sometimes it can be useful (or even necessary) to seek support from a trusted professional. If you feel disconnected from your child more often than not, if your child struggles to make friends, if sibling rivalry has turned into sibling bullying, or if your child regularly uses technology to escape from the world, you may want to seek the assistance of a trained therapist.

# 5

## Raise Happy Kids

"I don't know what happened," I say to my son who is in a bad mood and taking it out on me, "but I'm pretty sure it doesn't actually have anything to do with me. Why don't you go draw about it instead." I'm slightly surprised, but he takes the suggestion to heart. He goes to his desk and starts to draw, page after page after page—scribbles at first, then sad faces, and eventually drawings of aliens, princesses, and sea creatures. His energy has shifted. The wave of anger has passed.

I never found out what upset my son. I don't even think he knew. But through art, he was able to do something with those feelings. He redirected his anger toward the paper, rather than toward me. His furious scribbling and discharging of energy gave way to more tender feelings of sadness underneath. Drawing sad faces allowed him, in his own five-year-old way, to acknowledge his feelings yet see them as separate from himself. Through this simple process, he was able to cope with his feelings and experience enough relief to relax into a more playful world of aliens and princesses.

There are many explanations as to how art helps us feel better. It can help us relax. A review of thirty-seven studies has shown the effectiveness of making art, listening to music, and dancing for managing and preventing stress (Martin et al. 2018). Actively engaging in the arts occupies so much of the brain that it crowds out room for stress (Tramo 2001). The arts can provide a safe outlet for intense emotions. The physical experience of kneading clay, scribbling, or drumming can help discharge energy held in the body when we experience strong feelings. The arts in general offer a place where we can make choices and feel in control of things that might otherwise feel out of control. They can make us feel good about ourselves when we accomplish something creative about which we feel proud. They also give us a new language with which to express experiences that may be hard to put into words. Because children primarily understand the world through sensory and hands-on experiences (rather than through talking and listening), the arts can be a life preserver when children are in turmoil.

The arts are useful not only for helping kids feel better but also for helping develop emotional intelligence (Brouillette and Fitzgerald 2009; Whalley 2009), or the capacity to understand and manage emotions. For example, the arts help children learn how to identify their own feelings as well as those of others. When describing the emotions portrayed in a painting or evoked through a piece of music, kids learn how to recognize feelings within themselves and the artist. This aids in developing empathy. The arts also help kids think through their own emotional problems more tangibly by giving them something that can be seen and even manipulated. These abilities are crucial. Many researchers believe that emotional intelligence leads to improved job performance, quality of social interactions, and leadership (Bradberry and Greaves 2009; Jiwen Song et al. 2010). In these ways, and more, the arts can contribute to raising emotionally healthy, resilient, and happy kids. Let's take a closer look.

## TOLERATING CHALLENGING FEELINGS

Ping's extremely overtired and inconsolable, not-quite-two-year-old granddaughter is kicking and screaming in her arms in the rocking chair. Trying to hold her is like trying to hold a large and unwilling cat. There is no sign of slowing down in wailing, flailing, and contortions, let alone sleeping. No amount of rocking, consoling, patting, or bouncing is making a difference. With a rambling made-up melody (think: faux opera), Ping finally begins to sing a review of all the day's events that they had experienced together. The song captures her granddaughter's attention; she immediately stops crying, listens intently, and falls asleep. In this case, song enabled focus on positive things that had occurred during the day—an emotional coping tool. It's never too early to teach tools for emotional intelligence.

I enter my son's room to say goodnight. He is in bed, body tense, breath quick and shallow, fists and teeth clenched. He hasn't cleaned his room as requested. He has lost a privilege. He's mad at me. He's mad at himself. And for good measure, he's mad at his siblings, too. Everyone hates him. He hates everyone. The feelings are big.

I begin to sing a loving rendition of "Twinkle, Twinkle, Little Star," making up words as I go: "Be kind to yourself. Feelings are like waves. You may feel really bad right now, but feelings never ever stay." He begins to relax his body. "Sometimes being human means feeling kind of sad. Please know we love you lots and lots even when you're mad." His breathing slows and deepens. "You forget to flush the toilet," (he's laughing now because I said toilet) "and throw snotty tissues on your floor, still remember every feeling eventually comes to shore." He's relaxed now. Indeed, his feelings have come to shore. "Thank you, Mommy." He smiles.

It's hard on everyone in the household when a child is cranky, moody, chaotic, or rigid; yet, children need to experience and work through their feelings in order to prepare for the future and grow. Although most people would assert that they want to raise happy kids, what they probably want in actuality is to raise emotionally healthy kids. And that doesn't mean always being happy.

When our goal for our children is happiness, we run the risk of encouraging unhealthy emotional habits, such as denying or bottling up not-so-happy feelings. John Gottman (1997), author of *Raising an Emotionally Intelligent Child*, points out that even the most difficult-to-tolerate feelings, like jealousy or fear, are opportunities for children to understand themselves better and grow as people. They prompt us to pay attention to important moments and evaluate our experience (Adler and Hershfield 2012). Challenging feelings are part of life, so we may as well welcome them into our house rather than shut them out.

Like an annoying guest, unwanted feelings will likely keep banging on the door until they are acknowledged and their needs are met. In real terms, ignoring difficult feelings can equate to increased stress and health problems (Pennebaker, Kiecolt-Glaser, and Glaser 1988), which is why expressing them even in writing can have positive health benefits (Frattaroli 2006). Raising emotionally healthy kids means making it safe to experience all feelings through tools to deal with them when they visit. When we do this, our kids will grow up to be *generally* happy and content, but perhaps more importantly they will be resilient through life's tough times.

As the old proverb goes, necessity is the mother of invention, and there is hardly a more necessary time to get innovative than when kids are expressing large feelings (aka acting out, throwing tantrums, whining, being defiant, or sulking). Those feelings are important growth opportunities not only for children but also for parents. This is the time to experiment with creative approaches to help your kids tolerate feelings that come knocking. After all, kids won't say: "Hey Dad, the reason I stomp my feet and cross my arms when you say it's time to go to bed is because I'm lonely in my room. I miss you. But feeling lonely and scared makes me feel too vulnerable. So, anger comes along to help me out. It helps me feel more in control and powerful. Anger also seems to help me get more time with you because then you talk to me about my behavior." No. Kids will just stomp around the house.

## When feelings come knocking

Imagine this: You've just gotten home. You're about to prepare dinner and get the kids started on homework. You're looking forward to watching your favorite show later. You need to return some calls, too. You go to throw in a load of laundry, and you hear someone at the front door. Knock, knock, knock. Who could it be at this inconvenient hour? Knock, knock, knockety, knock. This is not a good time. BANG, BANG, BANG! You peer out the window. It's your irate neighbor, your emotionally needy cousin, or an irritating salesperson. Whoever it is, you don't want the person here at the best of times, let alone right now. Take a deep breath and get ready to think creatively.

To address challenging feelings, imagine that you're dealing with an undesirable visitor at the door. When we reimagine feelings as visitors, stopping by briefly before they leave, we may feel less overwhelmed by their presence. This metaphor gives us something tangible with which to work. It's difficult to understand and deal with feelings that can be neither seen nor touched. It's easier to imagine dealing with them as an unwanted guest.

To understand your children's underlying needs, as expressed through challenging feelings, partner with your children to get to know their emotional visitors. Find out what those visitors need before they return with a vengeance, as feelings (and unwanted guests) tend to do. Try these creative strategies:

C/T Be our guest—Rather than saying: "Why are you so angry?" try a nonjudgmental observation and inquiry: "I noticed a door was slammed shut and see books all over the floor. I wonder if anger is visiting you? I wonder what it wants?" This puts feelings in perspective as temporary, only visiting for a little while. It also separates the child from his feelings, so he doesn't over-identify with them. (We are not our feelings. We just experience them.) In addition, it helps him name his feelings, which calms the emotional center of the brain and stimulates the part that governs thought, emotion, and behavior (Torrisi et al. 2013; Siegel and Bryson 2012). This can make it easier for the child to make sense of and address his feelings. (For more information on and examples of nonjudgmental observations, see appendix 1: "Guidelines for Talking about Art and Life," and chapter 4: "Connect First.")

C/T Visualize the visitor (see fig. 5.1)—Invite your child to draw a picture of the visitor either with paper and pens, or in her mind's eye. Help her envision it by getting curious: "What does it look like? What color is it? How big is it? Does it look scary or friendly?" You also have the option of drawing it while your child describes it. For teens, use Google Images to find pictures of, say, "angry animals" or simply "angry." Then wonder aloud, "So, if your anger was a picture, would it look like any of these?"

C/T Get to know the visitor—Ask your child to give the visitor human characteristics. Doing so offers a comfortable way to reveal innermost thoughts and concerns: "What does it eat or drink? Where does it live? What does it wear? With whom or what does it hang out? To whom is it related? What things does it have in its room? What does it like to do? What does it not like to do?" Answers can be literal (e.g., disappointment eats cold eggs and melted ice cream) or figurative (e.g., anger eats its words or anger eats jet fuel and matches). There is no right or wrong way to answer the questions, and the more outlandish the answers, the merrier. You can help scribe for children who are unable to write for themselves or for whom speaking aloud would enable a freer flow of ideas. Teens may enjoy creating their own questions as well.

5.1 Visualize the visitor ("Frustration visits me.")

**C/T** Explore the visitor's needs—Saying to a child, "You're tired" (even if you know this to be true) will only be met with "NO I'M NOT!" Instead, invite him to ask his feeling what it needs: "If you asked anger what it needs right now, what would it say?" or "What does it want to say?" or "What does it want *you* to say?" You can also use humor: "Is it here to eat all of my laundry?! Steal the chocolate cake?! No? . . . What do you think it's doing here? Can we help it in some way?"

**C/T** Thank-you letter (see fig. 5.2)—Once you both have a hunch as to what emotion is visiting and why, you'll be better equipped to attend to it with compassion and kindness. This is your child's opportunity to tell the visitor what *she* wants to say. Together, try writing a note to the visiting emotion acknowledging 1) its intention, 2) that you both understand it is trying to help, and 3) that there may be a better way to resolve the situation. For example: "Dear Ms. Jealous, Thanks for letting me know how much I miss the way things were before I got my new baby sister. I know you were just trying to help me out when you thought I should hide the pacifier. But I'll just ask Dad if we can spend some special time together instead. Thanks anyway." For teens, you may write a letter to the feeling on behalf of your teen. For example: "Dear Anger, I know you really wanted Jessica to go out with her friends today. You might even be protecting her from feeling too sad about missing out. Thanks for trying to help her out. I hope you'll take a step back to give her a chance to talk to us about it calmly. Love, Jessica's Dad."

> Dear Sad,
>     Thank you for coming to visit me. You helped me run and hide away from my sister. I'm o.k. if you leave now. Thanks for being there when I needed you.
>                     Love,
>                         C.
>
>
> Dear C.,
>     Thank you for the letter. I will be here when you need me. Glad you're feeling better.
>                     Love,
>                         Sad

5.2 Thank-you letter to a feeling

**C/T** Stand up to big feelings—Welcoming an undesirable visitor into your home doesn't mean a free-for-all. Difficult visitors need clear limits, too. Just as you can tell your children: "You can feel angry. You may not slam doors. It's not safe," you can also teach children to stand up to their own feelings. Invite your child to draw a helpful feeling (or animal or character) that can stand up to the challenging feeling. Add a word bubble and ask: "What would she say to Angry?" Perhaps it might be: "Thanks, but I choose not to listen to your idea." A teenager might write: "Hey Disappointed, I am not going to let you ruin my weekend. I am going to make plans with my best friend!" If a child is unable to write, scribe for her.

**C/T** Reflect back—If your child isn't responsive to creative approaches in the midst of big feelings, casually bring up the moment later in the day. For example: "Remember when anger visited this morning, and we couldn't figure out what it wanted? And then we figured out that you wanted to finish reading that chapter before leaving for school, and anger told us that it didn't feel fair that you couldn't. What do you think helped anger to feel better?" For teens, you might say nonchalantly, "Hey, did you ever figure out why anger showed up this morning before school? What helped?"

Of course, there are times when you can't do anything to appease a difficult guest. As you'll see in the next section, sometimes kids are out of sorts simply because of cognitive leaps they are making at that point. Don't drive yourself crazy trying to analyze your child's behavior. You might not always be able to put your finger on the problem, let alone solve it. At those times, we must accept the unwelcome guest and provide it with a comfortable place and safe boundaries until it's ready to leave of its own accord. Ask your child to draw what the feeling needs in order to be comfortable while it is visiting. Maybe it's a cozy place to rest. Maybe it's a hug. When we tolerate our children's big feelings in this way, they will learn to tolerate them as well.

## Growing pains

Every year around springtime, my children seem to fall apart. One day my children are calm and cheerful and the next day—POW!—they are fussy, whiny, and rigid. And each year, around that time, I shake my head, at a loss, wondering: "What is going on?! Is it a full moon? Did they all get together and decide to give me a run for my money?" And then I remember: "Ahhhh, yes, it's disequilibrium time." Because of when their birthdays fall, my children all hit new developmental stages at around the same time annually.

Social and emotional development is not a steady one-foot-in-front-of-the-other progression but rather a one-step-forward-two-steps-back process, followed by a huge leap forward. In the seminal series *Your One-Year-Old* through *Your Ten- to Fourteen-Year-Old*, Louise Bates Ames points out that although there is variation in when these steps and leaps occur, there is striking consistency across children (Ames and Ilg 1989). Up until age five, the whole ages (two, three, four, and five) are characterized by increased confidence, emotional ease, and calmer behavior. Kids are easier to parent during these times of what specialists call *equilibrium*. On the flip side, the half ages (eighteen months, two and a half, three and a half, four and a half, and five and a half) are characterized by *disequilibrium*: more sensitivity, rigidity, uneasiness, stress, and anxiety (which typically equate to more difficult behavior). After five and a half, ages of equilibrium tend to be six and a half, eight, and ten; disequilibrium tends to fall around ages seven, nine, and eleven.

Periods of disequilibrium are times of rapid growth and change when children learn new skills and take cognitive leaps. Rather than swimming fluidly through mastered skills, they struggle to stay afloat through new developmental tasks. They understand more than they can handle emotionally; they want to do things physically that their bodies are not ready to do; they're learning about fairness and unfairness; and their imaginations are on fire, convincing them that they really *should* worry about monsters under the bed or (as in the case of my son) gophers in the closet. No wonder these times are more difficult. It's tough growing up.

As children generally can be discontented during times of disequilibrium, it may be more difficult to identify specific needs behind feelings expressed. The good news is, you don't necessarily need to know *why* a child is upset in order to help him with his feelings. At these times, relaxing activities, a comfortable refuge, or physical activities to shift energy may help.

**C/T** Relax—Certain creative activities tend to have a relaxing effect. Painting, doodling, coloring, playing with clay, knitting, or crocheting may help your child relax. Try pairing any of these with soothing or enjoyable music. Activities to help children relax will be explored in more depth later in this chapter, in the section "De-stress."

**C/T** Connect with nature (see fig. 5.3)—Studies suggest that a sense of connection to nature promotes happiness and a general sense of well-being (Capaldi, Dopko, and Zelenski 2014). Invite your children to paint on rocks or leaves, create an outdoor sculpture from fallen branches, make leaf imprints in clay, or sketch pictures of nature. There are many ideas for crafts involving nature available online. Search online for "nature crafts," "nature crafts for kids and teens," or "nature-inspired crafts."

5.3 Connect with nature ("My tree")

**C/T** A cozy place—Invite your child to create a cozy place where he can go to be comfortable or find some space while having big feelings. Use blankets, pillows, furniture, or cardboard boxes. If you use cardboard boxes, give your child crayons or markers to decorate the "walls" of his cozy place. Get your child involved by saying: "I'd like to make you a special, cozy place where you can go if you want to when you need some space or quiet time. Where should we put it? What do we need to make it?" For teens, you may invite them to fill a corner of their room with meaningful pictures, relaxing activities (such as a book, art supplies, or music), and a comfy place to lounge.

**C/T** Hum a tune—Research supports physical and emotional benefits to humming. Humming slows down your breathing rate and reduces blood pressure, which can promote a general sense of calm (Pramanik, Pudasaini, and Prajapati 2010). It also reduces thoughts rattling around in your mind and appears to decrease activation in the part of the brain associated with depression (Kalyani et al. 2011). When my youngest would cry in the car as a baby, I'd hum "Don't Worry, Be Happy" by Bobby McFerrin. My other two kids would join in, and we would all find some relief. You can model humming during stressful times, explaining the science behind it to older children and teens.

**C/T** Dance, drum, scribble, knead—Physical movement can shift emotional energy. Dancing, drumming, scribbling, or kneading clay, for example, can help a child or teen literally move from her current emotional state to a more balanced state. We will explore the benefits of using physical movement to shift emotions later in this chapter, in the section "Release."

You can also use the arts to help your child explore enjoyable and difficult parts of growing up.

〰〰〰〰〰〰〰〰〰〰〰〰〰〰〰〰〰〰〰〰〰〰〰〰〰〰〰〰〰〰〰〰〰〰〰〰

💡 **C/T** TRY THIS:

Have your child write his age as a large numeral in the center of a piece of paper. Next, help him select magazine pictures or online clip art that represents themes of "I can" and "stuff that's tough." Invite your child to arrange the pictures on the paper. And keep the collage someplace handy. When your child is struggling or having big feelings about something, you can ask: "I wonder if this is a 'stuff that's tough' time. Should we add another picture?" When your child solves a problem, copes well with disappointment, shows flexibility, or does something more tangible like completing a difficult puzzle for the first time, you can invite your child to add an "I can" picture to the collage. Through this process, you will reinforce that, with every age, there are tough times and easier times. Later, you can reflect together on all the things that *used* to be tough but now come more easily. Try adapting this activity for hallmark birthdays like thirteen, a Quinceañera, or a sweet sixteen.

〰〰〰〰〰〰〰〰〰〰〰〰〰〰〰〰〰〰〰〰〰〰〰〰〰〰〰〰〰〰〰〰〰〰〰〰

A teenage girl sits across from me, working on a self-portrait. I ask her to show me what happens when she bottles up her feelings (see fig. 5.4). She draws a match being lit by negative and overwhelming thoughts. She adds a line from that match leading down to her body where feelings explode like fireworks inside. She shows the fire of emotions raging up into her throat, in turn fueling negative thoughts. The intensified thoughts cycle back to stoke the fire of feelings. Beneath all of this activity, trapped deep in her body, are rain clouds. She says they symbolize sadness.

Most of the time at home and at school she keeps it together (good grades, good daughter, good friend), but for the past year she has become depressed and rageful. She goes off like fireworks and is inconsolable when she cries. Her feelings, having been stuffed down and bottled up for too long, are making themselves heard. They are seeking a way out.

5.4 Bottled-up feelings

Children, just like adults, attempt to suppress feelings because it feels safer than letting them out. We may feel overwhelmed by big feelings or afraid that we will overwhelm others by expressing them. But ignoring feelings can backfire. Unexpressed feelings manifest themselves in unhealthy ways: headaches or stomachaches, erratic behavior, avoidance of people or places, difficulty sleeping, conflict with others, lethargy or loss of interest in otherwise pleasurable activities, irritability, preoccupation and inability to focus, emotional volatility, and more.

Talking with children about their feelings helps. Merely naming a feeling decreases activity in the emotional center of the brain, the amygdala, and reduces distress (Burkland et al. 2014; Torrisi et al. 2013). It also increases activity in the prefrontal cortex, which governs executive functions such as decision making and social behavior (Torrisi et al. 2013). Psychiatrist Daniel Siegel describes this integration of the feeling and thinking parts of the brain as the "name it to tame it" principle of emotion regulation, which brings greater emotional balance (Siegel and Bryson 2012). However, sometimes talking isn't adequate . . . or even possible.

Talking can be too difficult, embarrassing, or scary at times. Sometimes children don't have the understanding or vocabulary to make meaning of their emotional experience. Brain imaging studies orchestrated by psychiatrist and trauma expert Bessel van der Kolk (2014) have shown that sometimes talking about feelings isn't even possible because stress responses have interfered not only with brain functions that enable speech but also with those that enable the body to sense what it is feeling. This makes sense as a survival response because if you are in the woods being chased by a bear, you don't want to stop to talk about it. Fortunately, during times of heightened stress, nonverbal channels remain open for communication through visual imagery, sound, and movement. This section explores how.

## Release

> My two-year-old daughter and I are waiting to pick up my son from school. A teacher, mistaking my daughter for a student, abruptly tells her that she's not where she is supposed to be and to join the other children. In that moment my little one has no words for her experience. Uncharacteristically, she begins to wail. Her body trembles. She can barely catch her breath. She needs to release these feelings, yet she is overwhelmed. I provide containment by holding her and singing softly, to the tune of "Twinkle, Twinkle, Little Star": "Mommy's here, my dearest one. You are safe. You are safe." Little by little, her breathing regulates. Her body relaxes. Only then can she share that the teacher's remark made her think, "Some people no like me."

In this example, music came to our aid when we were short of options. While labeling children's feelings can help temper a storm of emotions, I wasn't sure what her feeling was in the moment. I didn't even know what had ignited her wave of emotions until after the wave of emotion had passed. "You're really upset" felt inadequate to reflect the intensity with which she cried. I needed an alternative to talking, so I used a well-documented stress reducer: song (Allen et al. 2001).

Songs with familiar melodies can be particularly comforting. They are also effective at capturing the listener's attention while simultaneously allowing them to experience their emotions. Through song, I could reassure her without cutting short her expression of feeling. She could ride the wave of emotions knowing that she was sitting safely in a life raft. Holding her and singing to her also helped *me* feel contained as I witnessed her body release massive feelings through trembling, rapid breathing, and crying.

Neuroscience researchers and psychologists like renowned trauma specialist Peter Levine (1997; 2010) have discovered that letting go of feelings is necessary even if we don't understand them. For survival, animals facing a threat will fight, flee, or freeze. Some animals, Levine points out, literally shake to discharge unused fight-or-flight energy that remains after they play dead. Like animals, we too experience the fight, flight, or freeze response in the face of real or imagined threat. However, unlike animals, we do not typically give ourselves an opportunity to release the built-up stress. This energy needs to be discharged to prevent emotional, relational, behavioral, or health consequences. We need creative strategies to release the unused emotional energy.

> "You can pound on the drum. You may not pound on the door," I say as I redirect my son to a toy drum. Pound, pound, bang. BANG, BANG, BANG! . . . Bop. Bop. Tap. After a few brief minutes, his face relaxes and his arms drop to his sides. He lets out a deep exhalation.
>
> "Show me how angry you are," I say to a client, as I pass her paper and markers. She scribbles with fist clenched and arm flying back and forth in rapid, rhythmic movement until scarcely any white paper is visible. Her grip around the marker loosens. Her body relaxes. She slumps back in her chair.

The old convention was to punch a pillow to get anger out. Nowadays, violent video games are said to provide relief from anger, stress, and frustration. However, we now know that neither of these strategies is effective, and far from it. Rather than resolving intense feelings, punching something or playing violent video games has been shown to actually *increase* aggressive thoughts, feelings, and behavior (Anderson and Bushman 2001; Bushman, Baumeister, and Stack 1999). Punching pillows (or virtual bad guys) isn't the answer. However, moving your body is (Siegel and Bryson 2012).

Besides running, shooting hoops, or jumping on a trampoline, we can harness the physical effort of the arts to help children pass through storms of emotion. Creative arts options may be particularly useful for children who are not inclined toward athletic activities or have no access to them.

> **C/T** Shake your feelings out—Encourage your children to stretch, dance, leap, spin, or move in whatever way feels good to them. If they're reluctant, put on some music and jump and twirl around yourself; maybe they'll join in. Or simply say: "Sometimes dancing helps me feel better. Maybe you'd like to try it with me. Let's put on some music."

**C/T** Scribble, splatter, knead—Scribbling, splattering paint, or kneading clay works to discharge emotional energy like a stress ball. These artsy energy outlets can also evolve into creative and playful expression, helping children move beyond a feeling into a new emotional state.

**C/T** Badda boom—Whereas punching a pillow may increase aggressive feelings, banging on a drum can diffuse them or morph into a recreational activity in itself. Research shows that playing in sync with others activates a reward center of the brain and increases positive social behavior (Kokal et al. 2011; Valdesolo and DeSteno 2011; Valdesolo, Ouyand, and DeSteno 2010). Drumming with others decreases stress, improves immune function (Bittman et al. 2001; Fancourt et al. 2016), and contributes to overall improvement in the social-emotional behavior of children (Ho et al. 2011) and adolescents (Bittman, Dickson, and Coddington 2009). Direct your child to bang on a drum when upset. Sit alongside him and pick up your own drum. If you don't have a drum, play rhythms with "found sounds" like a plastic five-gallon water jug, bucket, or large food storage container.

**C/T** Rumble—To release emotional energy in a contained fashion, introduce a rumble of right and left hands in rapid alternation on a drum, table, or other object (a couch cushion or throw pillow will do). The rumble is also a fun and effective way to recharge and refocus—even if it is done silently in the air! While children rumble, you can conduct as you would an orchestra, raising your arms as a cue for louder sounds and lowering them for softer sounds. See how loud the rumble can become and how quickly your children can stop when you give the signal: 4-3-2-1-Stop! Take turns conducting.

## Contain

Twelve-year-old Ella is hesitant to discuss and make art about her feelings; however, when invited to create a container for them, she is gung ho. Using a shoe box and string, she designs a "locked door" behind which her feelings are held captive. Adding the finishing touches of paperclip padlocks and pipe-cleaner laser sensors (lest a feeling try to escape), she is freed up to begin expressing her feelings. With clay and paint, one feeling after another is brought to life, named, and given personalities, needs, and desires. Then in they go behind the shoebox door. It is she—and not those pesky feelings—who is in control. By making physical representations, she shifts unhealthy containment in the body to healthy containment in a box.

As important as it is to release feelings, it can also be frightening to do so. Children may believe that others cannot tolerate their feelings. They may feel wrong or ashamed for having them. Feelings typically build before peaking and falling like a wave, so it can be hard to trust that the wave will ever break. Most children are never taught how to ride this wave and, consequently, they fear losing control. By helping children release feelings in a contained way, however, they can begin to trust their ability to handle them.

In the example above, art helped metaphorically hold this child's feelings so she didn't have to do it alone. The box provided physical parameters for expression, while the added security features ensured that she would not be overwhelmed or overrun by the feelings to which she gave form. By making and playing with her creation, she also practiced managing when the feelings could come out and when they would go back in. Through this process, she worked toward mastering the real-life balancing act of releasing emotions and reining them in. In taking out and interacting with her feelings, she learned that she didn't have to ignore her feelings to be in control of them.

Containment can allow the controlled release of emotions, a little at a time, or safe boundaries for big bursts of emotional energy all at once. Here are some ways that art can help your children contain their feelings enough to feel safe letting them out:

**C/T** Bottle it up, literally (see fig. 5.5)—Bottles, boxes, bowls, treasure chests, and envelopes lend themselves well to containing experience. It's easier to write down a feeling, put it in a box, and close the lid than it is to express it out loud. I see this frequently in my work. A teen may not speak what's on her mind, but she will write it down and fold up the piece of paper into a compact square. A child may be afraid to share a feeling aloud but will draw it, put it in an envelope, and tape it up. "I don't need to know what it is," I say. "What's important is that you know what it is, and that you find a way to let it out." Children will feel as if their feelings are anonymous and safely stuffed away when, in actuality, the very process of transforming the feeling into a physical form begins to release them.

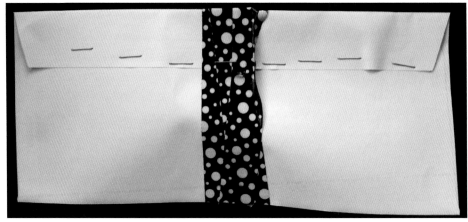

5.5 Bottle it up, literally

**C/T** The sky is blue, the grass is green—When a child is feeling untethered, you can provide containment by helping him connect with his body and surroundings. Labeling colors and shapes that you see around you is one way to feel more grounded. Start by saying: "I see a blue sky. Green grass. Purple shirt." See if he catches on. If not, ask: "What colors [or shapes] do you see?" Make it a game for younger children. For older children and teens, explain that this process can help calm the mind and body. You can move through the senses: "I hear birds singing. The washing machine chugging. What do you hear?"

**C/T** Go big with big feelings—The four edges of a piece of paper or the walls of a shoe box offer parameters for creative expression, yet sometimes that space isn't sufficient. When big feelings need big space, simply provide a larger container. Offer large sheets of paper outdoors at which to throw paint-dipped balls. Provide big rolls of duct tape and wads of newspaper to tape together. Roll out a long piece of butcher paper and give your children permission to dip their feet in washable paint before jumping on and running up and down the paper. Cover a bedroom wall with butcher paper and invite your teen to make a graffiti-inspired mural on it. These are some activities that permit big, physical expression within parameters.

### From zero to a hundred in one second

Twelve-year-old Liam is referred to therapy because, as his teachers and parents report, he goes from zero to a hundred in one second. He seems fine and then suddenly blows up for no apparent reason. "It's not like something happens that upsets him," his teachers say. "It just comes out of nowhere." It certainly looks like this, but explosive feelings don't come from nowhere. We are simply missing the early warning signs that something is amiss.

Zero to a hundred in one second, as you and I know it, is quick. In the world of art animation, however, a single second takes a whopping twenty-four frames to create. To understand what happens in the one second it takes any child to escalate from "everything's fine" to "everything's falling apart!" we need to look at that one second frame by frame. With art, we can literally do this.

Returning to the story above, I worked with Liam to illustrate the stages of escalation by creating a chart. He selected different colors to represent each stage of escalation, starting with "calm and relaxed" blue. Atop each color he added pictures of animals, representing what each stage felt like in his body. He started with the "please scratch my belly, I'm feeling relaxed" puppy and ended with the "bared teeth, tense body, I'm going to bite you" tiger. By referring back to this scale, over time he was able to more easily recognize the subtle shifts in his body as he moved between stages. When he noticed that his body was signaling he was no longer in the calm

**108**  stage, he learned to do something (like take a break, ask for help, or breathe deeply) to bring himself back to a relaxed state.

Along with increasing awareness of early signs of discontent, we can also use art to understand what ignites upset feelings in the first place. When the culprit is invisible, as in the case of Liam, it is often a thought. From a young age, children begin to make sense of their experiences by creating stories about themselves and the world around them. Even if a child is never called "bad," he may mistakenly interpret icky feelings as being bad inside. Children may believe that they are at fault for events that are not in their control. My own daughter, in an earlier example, had an enormous emotional reaction when she determined that "some people no like me" because a teacher sternly told her that she was in the wrong place. These are powerful thoughts that can stay with children and continue to affect them. Because of this, it's worth digging a little deeper to unearth the thoughts that are fueling the emotions in the first place.

> Using "Thought bubbles" (see fig. 5.6), Liam and I identify the beliefs that set off his rapid escalation of emotions. He writes: "I'm stupid. I'll never be able to do this." Then, we use "A buddy on my shoulder" (see figure 5.7) to create a friendlier, supportive voice. I draw a boy and, at my prompting, he draws a little "buddy" sitting on the boy's shoulder. I add an empty word bubble for a helpful thought. We make several photocopies of the resulting picture and keep them accessible for whenever he needs to check in with his thoughts and ask the little buddy on his shoulder for encouraging words. Using these creative strategies can stop the escalation of emotions before they get out of control. Months later, his outbursts at school have entirely disappeared.

The more in touch children are with early signals that something is amiss, the more they are able to cope with feelings and thoughts before they become overwhelming. This ability to notice and regulate feelings will follow them into their teens and adulthood. There are many simple ways you can teach this:

**C/T** Thought bubbles (see fig. 5.6)—When my children won't tell me what's on their mind (or when they're not sure themselves), thought bubbles often do the trick. Draw a figure (stick figures work) and an empty thought bubble on a piece of paper or sticky note pad. You may want to add a simple, distinguishing detail to suggest that the figure is your child, such as a hat, glasses, or skirt that she is wearing. Offer a pen and the drawing to her, saying: "I wonder what this person is thinking." Alternatively, draw a figure representing yourself with a thought bubble that says: "I wish I knew what happened to [child's name]." Then draw the child figure with an empty thought bubble. Offer the pen and paper to invite your child to complete her thought bubble.

5.6 Thought bubbles

**C/T** A buddy on my shoulder (see fig. 5.7)—Invite your child to describe or draw his own little buddy or imaginary creature that sits on his shoulder and whispers encouraging words. If you're feeling ambitious, bring out materials to make it into a three-dimensional figure. Brainstorm together with your child the encouraging words and phrases that the buddy likes to say. Does it have a catchphrase or a theme song? If not, make one up! For teens, ask what a friend or hero might say in a tough situation. Add an encouraging phrase to a picture of a loved musician or athlete. Or help your teen design a necklace, hat, decorative rock, or canvas with an encouraging reminder such as "breathe," "grateful," or "worth it."

5.7 A buddy on my shoulder ("It's OK.")

**110** **C/T** How do you know you feel that? (see fig. 5.8)—Help kids connect with emotional signals by asking them to describe what they feel in their body. Start with asking: "How do you know when you are hungry or when something hurts? What does that feel like in your body?" Once they get the idea, move onto feelings: "How do you know when you feel happy? Sad? How does your body feel?" Don't be surprised if younger children are literal, focusing on a stereotypical happy or sad face. Encourage them to describe their experience in terms of colors, size, textures, or movement. Provide an example of your own. You might like to offer an outline of a body within which the child can color in her feelings (search online for "body outline"). Consider doing this activity at a neutral time of day or when reflecting back on an upsetting moment earlier in the day. It may be easier for children to do this activity when they are not in the midst of big feelings.

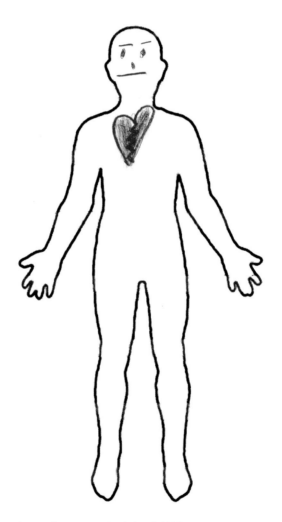

5.8 How do you know you feel that? ("When my body feels mad")

**C** The "uh-oh alarm" (see fig. 5.9)—Explain to your child that her body has a built-in alarm that sends messages to her brain when something doesn't feel quite right. For younger children, you can call it the "uh-oh alarm." Let your child know that the internal alarm is helpful, and it's important to listen to it. Invite your child to draw what her "uh-oh alarm" looks like (or make it out of boxes and paper, pipe cleaners, or other materials). If your child is stumped, offer a few suggestions of what it might look like, and then allow your child to take it from there.

5.9 The "uh-oh alarm" ("Thump! Thump!")

**C/T** Move with the feeling—When your child is experiencing feelings, ask what kind of movement it feels like. Give examples. If the child is angry, you might ask: "Does your angry feel kind of like *this?*" (e.g., squeeze your fists and scrunch your face tight), "or like *this?*" (e.g., run fast in place while shaking your arms and head quickly). If speaking to a teenager about his experience of anxiety, for example, you can ask him where he feels it and whether it feels more like a knot (e.g., clenched fists) or fluttery (e.g., shaking hands).

## A REFLECTION OF THE SELF

My son is about six years old, and I ask him who is his best friend at school. He names a couple of children and then stops and says, "Wait, no. My first best friend is me."

People often treat others more nicely than they treat themselves; we don't spend nearly as much time teaching children how to befriend themselves as we do teaching them how to befriend others. As pioneering self-compassion researcher Kristin Neff (2011) points out, self-criticism has become socially sanctioned—we believe it will motivate, but it really only holds us back from fulfilling our potential. It's necessary to remind kids to be their own best friend, particularly when they make mistakes or feel low.

Helping children become their own "first best friend" starts with modeling compassionate, rather than self-deprecating, talk when *we* make mistakes. We can also remind them to use encouraging self-talk instead of put-downs when *they* make mistakes (e.g., reminding them to say "It's okay, you can fix it" instead of "Stupid, now it's ruined"). Yet, practicing compassionate speech is only one, somewhat limited approach. In order to maximally nurture a kind-hearted relationship between your child and himself, it's worth turning to the arts to provide concrete, relatable experiences in self-love.

> "I'm just lazy," Camila says matter-of-factly. I'm not sure if she's come to this conclusion on her own or if she's been given the lazy label by some adult in her life. Either way, I'm not buying it. I want to understand better what's really beneath her lack of motivation in class. And more importantly, I want her to meet the less-than-desirable parts of herself that invite her to daydream. I want her to begin a friendship with them.
>
> I casually pass a box of markers across the table and ask, "Show me who comes along in class when you're supposed to be working? What voice inside you invites you not to work?" She draws two sharp-toothed characters that, as it turns out, are in cahoots with one another: "Distraction" and "Boredom." I add empty speech bubbles, inviting these characters to have a conversation. "You distract her, and then I'll make her bored," says Boredom. "Yeah, and you make her bored, and then I'll distract her," says Distraction.
>
> "So, are you just lazy?" I ask.
>
> She looks up at me and says, "I guess not."

By taking what's on the inside and transforming it into something on the outside, art makes a vague and abstract sense of self more tangible. Whether it's the part that doesn't want to get up in the morning, the part that loves to cuddle, or the part that gets overwhelmed easily, different parts of self can literally be seen (and changed) when they are painted, drawn, or sculpted. As in the 2015 Disney Pixar movie, *Inside Out*, in which a girl's emotions are given form through characters with their own personalities, needs, wants, and desires, children can use art to get to know, and befriend, the different parts that make up "me."

When we help children externalize parts of themselves, as in the example above, they have the opportunity to develop a more accurate and kinder self-understanding. This is even more important than we may realize. Children who grow up evaluating themselves based on their grades, appearance, and approval from others (all too common) tend to exhibit higher levels of stress, anger, and academic and relational problems (Crocker 2002). On the other hand, those who learn to value themselves as human beings, such as appreciating their own kindness, morals, or thoughtfulness, tend to do better academically in college *and* are less likely to use drugs and alcohol. It behooves us to invest time and interest in activities that help children connect with and value themselves as people. Here are some creative ideas to get started:

**C/T** What superhero are you?—Help your child design his own alter ego. Ask: "If you were a superhero, what would you look like? What powers would you have? Do you always have your powers, or are you just a normal guy sometimes? Are you ever one of the villains? What's he like?" You can also work with known characters from a favorite show. Ask: "Which of the characters from [name a favorite show] are you? Who are you when you're sad or mad?" Help your child get to know the characters by exploring their needs, hopes, and desires. Get to know them even better by encouraging your child to create stories or make up songs about them. With teens, seize a moment when they are watching a show, listening to music, or watching an influential online spokesperson. Ask: "Who's your favorite character?" or "Tell me about this person/song," and "What do you like most about this character/person/song?" Inquire if and how your child can relate or if she knows anyone like that.

**C/T** Mixed-up animals (see fig. 5.10)—Cut out different animal parts and piece them together to make a new animal. "If you were an animal, made up of all different animal parts, what would you look like?" Elaborate on the activity by asking creative questions such as: "What is this animal good at doing? How does this animal protect itself? Does it get along with other animals? Are there others like it or is it the only one of its kind?" For older children and teens, challenge them to create a hybrid creature most suited to dealing with challenges in their environment.

5.10 Mixed-up animal ("Me and my sister")

🅒🆃 "I am" image—Invite your child to choose any digital or magazine images he likes (a variety can be preselected and precut by an adult). Ask him to glue the images to a piece of cardboard or thick paper. Next, encourage him to choose an image that will "do the talking" through an "I am poem." Its structure enables children to express what matters to them in a complete-the-sentence format: I am, I wonder, I hear, I see, I want, I am . . . I pretend, I feel, I touch, I worry, I cry, I am . . . I understand, I say, I dream, I try, I hope, I am. Psychotherapist Nancy Weiss and veteran teacher Jane Raphael outline a similar process in their colorful book with helpful examples, *How to Make MeCards4Kids*™ (2013).

🅒🆃 The treasures inside (see fig. 5.11)—Invite your children to collect small objects that represent the special parts of them. You can provide materials such as small gems and buttons or natural objects, such as stones, shells, and flowers. Offer a choice of containers such as a small box, bottle, or jar. Explain: "The special things about you are like treasures. Let's find some things to put inside this treasure box that represent what you love about yourself or that are special about you."

5.11 The treasures inside

🅒🆃 Kind word rocks (see fig. 5.12)—Collect rocks with your child. Paint them different colors if you're so inclined, or leave them plain. Ask your child what she likes about herself. If it's difficult for your child to think of something, ask how a friend would describe her. Using a Sharpie marker, write

can add a thin layer of Mod Podge or other finish.

5.12 Word rock

**C/T** Self-hugs—Research finds that soothing, caring touch releases oxytocin, the neuropeptide that promotes feelings of calm, safety, and connection (Hertenstein and Weiss 2011). And this isn't just when we are hugged, held, or lovingly touched by someone else. The same happens when we caress ourselves (Neff 2011). Teach your children how to give themselves a hug by wrapping their arms around their chest and shoulders while standing or by hugging their knees into their chest while lying on their back. You can also show them how to place a hand over their heart or lovingly stroke the back of their hand. Make a daily habit of self-hugs before bedtime.

## Reinforcing values and beliefs

It's nighttime and my son is already in bed awaiting our much-too-drawn-out goodnight routine. I ask him to tell me one happy thing and one frustrating thing that happened at school today. He bargains for two of each. When he gets to his frustrating events, he begins recounting an incident with a difficult-to-get-along-with peer in class. Then he pauses. "Can we sing that song? You know, that something-something-something song where I think of someone?" I know precisely what he is talking about. "Okay," I say. "Think of someone who's hard to get along with." (But he doesn't need the instruction; he already has a classmate in mind.) "Picture that person. Ready?" Then, to the tune of "Twinkle, Twinkle, Little Star" we begin to sing: "May you be happy. May you be strong. May you be healthy. May you feel calm." My son smiles. "I think he especially needs the calm part," he says kindly. I smile back. "Yes, it sounds like it."

Children develop a positive sense of self not only by knowing their characteristics, preferences, and abilities but also through developing values and beliefs. In order to teach values such as kindness and compassion toward others, healthy choices, and hard work, we talk to our kids about right and wrong, give disapproving looks and smiles, and dole out consequences or praise. And when we're not there to give them "the look," we cross our fingers, hoping that they will still abide by these values.

**116**    However, for this hope to come to pass, we need to do much more than lecture children about what is "right" and give consequences when they do something "wrong."
Children need opportunities to embrace values and beliefs as their own and reap the
inherent rewards when they put those values into action.

The arts help children embody values through action. They provide fertile ground
for reflecting on and experiencing values directly, thus aiding in the integration of
those values into children's identities. Through the arts, children can celebrate, rehearse, or proclaim the values and ideals that we hope they will grow to exemplify. In
the above example, rather than telling my son to consider the struggles that might un-
derlie his classmate's behavior, he connected with our value of compassion through our
song, inspired by the practice of loving-kindness meditation. This not only reinforced
our value but also gave him a concrete (and catchy) tool with which to practice it.

Actively exploring, interpreting, and rehearsing values and beliefs helps children embrace internally what might otherwise remain someone else's rule. Through
the arts, children can begin to own a belief or value, closing the gap between "I
should" and "I am one who . . ." While creative self-expression doesn't guarantee
that kids won't make poor choices or experiment with unhealthy habits, it offers the
opportunity for children to embrace important values as part of who they are, making
them more likely to make healthy choices in the future.

**C/T** Hang it on your door (see fig. 5.13)—When I was a child, my friends and I
would draw "No Smoking" signs for our desks at school, modeled after ones we
had seen popping up in the community. We felt connected to the no-smoking
cause through our own art campaign. Invite your child to make a graphic sign
for her door that illustrates a value she holds important. Whether it's no smoking, no nose picking, or no fighting, making and displaying signs will reinforce
to your child the importance of those values to her, not just to you.

5.13 Hang it on your door

**C/T** Wear it on your sleeve—Values can literally be woven into the fabric of a child's identity by designing a T-shirt, stickers, buttons, or some other wearable item. For example, at a school where I worked, we used a T-shirt design competition to combat bullying on campus. The winning antibullying design was printed on shirts and worn by students and staff. You don't need a school-wide campaign to get going. Keep it simple. Give your children permission to write or draw value-laden messages, mottos, and pictures on their shoes, jeans, or bodies (if you're okay with that). Alternatively, invite your kids to draw on the bottoms of their shoes or buy an inexpensive pair of shoes or jeans specifically for drawing purposes. There are also plenty of professional-looking options online for uploading images and printing them onto shirts, mugs, tote bags, and more.

**C/T** Give to others—You don't have to wait for birthdays or holidays to give your children the opportunity to give to others. One day my kids set out small boxes in front of each bedroom, announcing that these were mailboxes. They started by sneaking scribbles and scraps of paper into each other's boxes. They thought it was hilarious. I capitalized on the opportunity to reinforce our family values of generosity, thoughtfulness, and gratitude. I joined in, sneaking in love notes, hand-drawn pictures, and thank-you notes. They caught on and continued enthusiastically "sending mail" (which expanded to gifting small treasures and beads) for many weeks to come. Older kids and teens may enjoy decorating a kindness jar, where family members can place notes of kindness or observations of kind deeds (see fig. 5.14). Alternatively, agree as a family to put loose change in the kindness jar and donate it to a local charity of your children's choice at the end of a designated period.

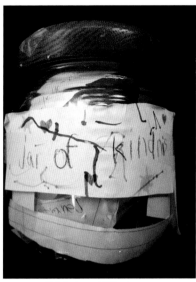

5.14 Jar of Kindness

**C** Sing well-wishes—As in the example above, create a song that sends wishes for happiness, health, and wellness to others. Before bedtime, invite your children to sing it while thinking of themselves, someone they love, someone they don't know well, someone they find challenging to be around, everyone as a whole, or all of the above!

**Taking safe risks, trying on roles, and imagining new ways of being**

It's seventh grade and a friend of mine comes to school each day embodying a different teen stereotype through her choice of clothing and jewelry: the rocker, the fierce academic, the nature advocate, the political activist. On one day, she dons a long, plaid skirt and button-down shirt. The next day, ripped jeans with peace signs and recycled can tops dangling on a string around her neck. She exemplifies the developmental stage of identity experimentation. Her choice of clothing and handmade jewelry is a tangible artistic expression of the different parts of herself, her roles, and who she hopes to become. Rather than experimenting through risky behavior as some teens do, she pushes the boundaries of her identity through safe risks of creative expression.

When children approach the teen years, they necessarily take more risks, try on new roles, and imagine new ways of being. As they shed their identity as a child, they begin figuring out who they are as individuals and in what groups they belong. While some risk taking is undesirable, or even dangerous, safe risks can be rewarding opportunities for growth. Wearing a funky ensemble to school or standing up to a friend who is cruel to another, for example, may be risks with social consequences but risks worth taking.

We don't need to wait until our children are teens to support the development of safe risk taking. The more opportunities we provide for them to safely experiment with their sense of self, the more tools they will have to avoid potentially harmful experimentation. Early practice with creative exploration of roles and identities can build a foundation of confidence for adolescence, when identity development demands are even greater. However, this isn't always easy. Providing these opportunities may require weighing the short-term cost of social risks against the long-term benefit of developing tools for self-assurance, as the following example illustrates.

I'm in the midst of an "Oh-my-goodness-my-child's-shoes-are-two-sizes-too-small-for-him-what-kind-of-mother-am-I?!" moment. I sweep my son off to the shoe store where, much to his delight, he spots neon pink shoes. He wants them. I hesitate. I generally avoid notions of gender-specific colors and themes, yet the reality is that my son's peers clearly distinguish between boy and girl items. I'm worried that if I buy him these "girl" shoes, he might get teased. I consider lying that they don't have his size. Then, I realize that the benefits of his self-expression far outweigh the social risk. I want to raise a confident child, not a child who is fearful of the reactions of others. I buy them. I tell him that I like his colorful choice, casually slipping in a comment that some kids think pink is just for girls (but that, clearly, it is not). At home, Daddy points out his own pink shirt for good measure. The very next day, a child teases him, "Why are you wearing girrrl shoes?" I feel heartbroken for him. I ready myself to intervene when my son laughs and confidently says, "They're not girl shoes." He skips away as the other child merely responds, "Oh."

Whether it's through their choice of shoe color, clothing, music preference, hair style, room decor, or nickname, children and teens are naturally inclined toward identity exploration through creative self-expression. As such, we may not need to do much more than recognize and capitalize on this propensity in order to satisfy their need for experimentation. At a minimum, we can tolerate their shoe selection and music choices (at least once in a while) and give them a fair amount of say in selecting their clothes (within the boundaries of safety and school expectations, of course). We can also check our impulse to hamper self-expression for fear of what others will think or say and, instead, coach them on how to handle difficult social situations, as in the example above. We can also champion their creative expression rather than teasing or belittling their sometimes awkward, trial-and-error process of identity exploration. If you'd like to give them an extra nudge, here are some additional ways to harness the arts to help them safely explore new ways of being:

**(C/T)** My body, my canvas—Create a body tracing for your child to fill in with symbols and colors that represent who they are or want to be. Either print out a small outline of a body or trace around your child's body on a large sheet of butcher paper for him to decorate. For teens, consider suggesting that they design a theoretical tattoo. While you can make it clear that your child won't be getting a real tattoo, this activity still allows your child to symbolically explore what's really important to him and what he wants to express to the world. You may turn this into an ongoing project, encouraging your child to add words or pictures weekly or monthly. Explore with your child how the images and words have changed over time or what themes have emerged.

**(C)** Paper dolls—One preteen with whom I worked made a paper doll with outfits using colored pencils and pictures cut out of fashion magazines. Similar to my school friend's experimentation with style, this art activity allowed my client to explore various roles and identities, including the safe expression of her developing sexuality, which she depicted by designing a low-cut top and a short, tight skirt for the doll. These were neither articles of clothing that she wanted to wear, nor ones that her parents would have allowed her to wear, but by designing these paper doll outfits she was able to safely explore feelings and ideas that the clothes *represented*. Help your child or preteen design outfits, hairstyles, and accessories. Draw, trace, or cut out pictures of clothing from magazines, rearranging them to make new ensembles. Doing this activity may even open up important conversations about social dynamics at school, such as different cliques and where your child fits in.

**(C/T)** My space—Like a giant art installation, your child's room can become a space for exploring and expressing identity through colors, textures, and images. It doesn't have to cost a lot of money—there are plenty of low-cost ideas online for upcycling items to redecorate a room. You don't even have to do a complete redecoration. Have your child pick one corner of her room to reinvent. Start by encouraging her to look online or at magazines for inspiration. Consider coming up with a theme such as "my space."

**(C/T)** Soundtrack to my life—Teens identify strongly with music genres, groups, and songs. Ask your child, "If your life was a movie, what would the theme song be?" You can print out the lyrics and encourage her to add decorative drawings around them. Provide a binder, where your child can keep decorated song lyrics and add to them over time. Suggest that your child pick a theme song for someone she respects, someone who makes her feel protected, and/or someone who makes her feel loved. She can decorate these lyrics, too. Alternatively, you can encourage her to make a playlist that represents the past year, the upcoming year, or a notable event.

## DE-STRESS

A father expresses concern over his son's homework avoidance . . . A mother comes to see me about her daughter's meltdowns during piano practice . . . A teen shares that she cheats to deal with the pressure she's under . . . A child's anxiety skyrockets when he considers the work he'll have to make up from having been out sick for a couple of days.

Headlines about kids and stress are not oversensationalized. Stress is affecting the current generation of kids like never before, and we need to heed the consequences.

The level of stress that children are under today is on par with that of adults (Bethune 2014), and the emotional health of college students is at a record low (Pryor et al. 2010). According to one California study, 70 percent of adolescents "often or always feel stressed by their schoolwork" (Conner, Pope, and Galloway 2010). In that study, 25 percent reported struggling with depression, 7 percent engaged in self-mutilation due to stress, and a whopping 44 percent cited three or more physical symptoms of stress within the past month, such as headaches or stomachaches. While there were other contributors to their stress including marital discord, both parents working outside the home, and social problems, the drive to succeed academically appeared to be the lead culprit.

Overscheduled calendars, hours of homework, and standardized exams conspire to produce harmful levels of stress in children and teens. If unmanaged, high levels of chronic stress can lead to unhappiness, insecurity, and trouble with learning, as well as more serious emotional, behavioral, and health problems. While we can actively work to reduce some stressors, such as ensuring enough down time for our children during the week and watching our own attitudes toward success, there are myriad stressors over which we have little or no control. Thus, aside from reducing stressors, we must teach our children how to de-stress.

When people consider the emotional benefits of art making, stress reduction often comes to mind. Children can experience art making as a place where they are free to make their own choices and truly be themselves. You may recall a time when you experienced a sense of pleasure, freedom, or relaxation while singing, playing an instrument, painting, doodling, or dancing. Perhaps your mind was freed from life's preoccupations. Perhaps you experienced a state of flow, a term coined by positive psychology expert Mihaly Csikszentmihalyi (1990) that describes the ecstasy of being in the "zone," or entirely engrossed in a creative task. Perhaps you benefited from the physical release of tension when drumming, dancing, or kneading clay. Perhaps your central nervous system was calmed by deeper breathing from activities like singing or playing a wind instrument. Perhaps you experienced a moment of awe in attending to the beautiful details of an environment for a still life that you were drawing. Perhaps you didn't notice these de-stressing functions at the time, but afterward you felt better. Indeed, the potential uses for art to help us de-stress are innumerable.

Set an intention to create space in your home (and in your family's schedule) to make art a regular strategy for de-stressing. This might involve setting up a semi-permanent "creative corner" in a room or doing a five-minute living room pickup to make space for dancing. Keep a stack of printer paper, box of markers, craft materials, or crocheting supplies in a convenient, accessible location. There are no rules about how and when to use art to help your children de-stress. Be proactive by integrating spontaneous "creative breaks" into your child's day or week, or use art breaks when your child is struggling during a task. By doing this, you are not only helping your children de-stress but also introducing tools that will serve them through turbulent teen years and into adulthood.

Creative breaks can be open-ended or you can approach stress reduction through art with more direction. Here are some ideas:

**C/T** Coloring in the now (see fig. 5.15)—Stress is decreased when we focus our attention on the present without judgment (Grossman et al. 2004). In order to effectively focus on what is here, now, we need to focus the mind on something other than racing thoughts, worries, plans, and preoccupations. Meditation practices that anchor one's attention on breath or a mantra can promote such focus on the present; however, even with age-appropriate adaptations, these can be difficult for children to practice—particularly after a traumatic experience and its associated intrusive imagery. Art activities like coloring in designs (including doodled ones) or drawing mandalas (circles containing concentric patterns) help make the present-oriented, meditative state of mind accessible. Encourage your children to focus on something pleasurable or enjoyable about drawing or coloring patterns, such as the movement of their hand, the colors that they choose, or how the picture changes as they add to it. Orienting them toward these experiences anchors their attention to the present moment.

5.15 Coloring in the now (Mandala)

**C/T** Show me that feeling—Earlier we referred to the "name it to tame it" principle of emotion regulation, coined by Daniel Siegel (Siegel and Bryson 2012). While adult assistance in naming feelings is a start, we can help children name their own feelings through visual expression. Whether through abstract lines, shapes, and colors or through selecting images from magazines, depicting feelings through art can make it easier for children to identify and understand them. Try: "Show me what it feels like when you get stressed" or "Show me what it feels like when you have a ton of homework and then I remind you to clean your room, on top of that," for example. The resulting

(C/T) Scribble your stress away—Scribbling can be a simple way to discharge stress held in the body. Not only is scribbling a way to express emotion, but the physical act of scribbling alone can loosen up stress-induced muscular tension. Once your child scribbles, you can invite him to do something with the scribble: rip it, bunch it up, throw it away, play ball with it. These are additional ways to get your child's body moving and loosened up. Alternatively, see if your child wants to transform the scribble into a picture by filling in the shapes with different colors or looking for images that emerge from the scribble. Sometimes the act of transforming an uncomfortable feeling like stress into something else, whether it's a flower, a monster, or an abstract drawing, can provide a sense of relief.

(C/T) Doodle dump—Whether your kids are having a hard time clearing their minds to settle down to sleep or you simply want to introduce a new way to unwind before bed, encourage them to dump whatever is weighing on their minds through a five-to-ten-minute doodle dump. Provide a small sketchpad or piece of paper for doodling any thoughts, feelings, concerns, or plans that are on their minds. Of course, you can suggest a doodle dump at any time of day. If your kids are struggling to get through homework, or coming home from school in a funk, declare a five-minute doodle dump break before getting on with other activities, chores, and tasks.

## CONFRONTING FEARS

A friend phones, concerned about her young daughter, Mia. Mia has recently become fearful of unfamiliar people. Nothing has prompted it, her mom says. It seems to have come out of nowhere. "Who is that? Why is he standing there?" Mia asks, as she keeps an eye on a man they are driving past. Her mom tries to reassure her, "He's probably waiting for someone." They arrive at a park. "I don't know that man," Mia says, pointing. Her mom encourages her to stay: "You're safe. I'm here with you." However, Mia's mind is made up as she pronounces, "I want to go home." At home, Mia can't stop talking about it.

My friend laments: "It doesn't matter what I say to her. She keeps going on about it." I suggest that she invite Mia to draw a picture of her worry. "It may help her see that she is not her worry. Worry is inviting her to believe that she is not safe. She can tell Worry to help her be cautious without getting in the way of having fun."

Later I receive a text: "Thanks! We did that drawing thing, and she was totally fine afterward."

124　　Fear can serve us well. It alerts us when it's time to pay attention to something important, whether it's a threat to our safety or a high-stakes situation. Anxiety gets our blood pumping and oxygen flowing, which can help us perform our best during sports, tests, and speeches. Fear primes our systems to fight or run if danger is near. But these feelings can also become overactive to the point of worrying about things that don't warrant so much energy and attention. At these times, we want to ease our children's worries.

My son wouldn't sleep because he was convinced that gophers lived in his closet. My daughter wept when saying goodbye during school drop-off. Children have fears of the dark, dogs, and imaginary monsters. These types of worries and preoccupations are a normal part of childhood. While most fears will eventually pass on their own, going through times of heightened anxiety can be stressful on both child and parent.

Art allows children to comfortably confront fears that they might otherwise try to avoid. Working with images, we can teach children how to turn the frightening into the humorous. We can equip them with imaginary shields against imaginary beasts or turn their fears into cuddly friends. Through pictures and songs, we can help our children not only get used to but also feel powerful over events of their lives that are unfamiliar and scary. This section explores how.

### Things that go bump in the night

> When I was young, I would sometimes get scary pictures stuck in my head at night (mostly monsters trying to grab me). My mother taught me to imagine a ginormous eraser, starting at one side of the image and working its way across to the other side, gradually erasing the picture. It worked . . . until I got to the other side. Once the picture was entirely erased, then "Pop!" the picture would come back. I'd start erasing all over again, just to have it reappear each time I finished. Even though it didn't quite work, my mother was on to something.

When you don't want to think about something, you can't just not think about it. If I said, "Don't think about a black cat," you would think of a black cat. Thinking of something else may work for a short while, but the troublesome image will more than likely return. Telling a child, "Don't worry, it's not real" doesn't do the trick, either. Irrational thoughts can't be appeased with rational talk. My son could not be soothed by repeated explanations of how gophers live underground and we lived on the second floor. He still insisted that gophers lived in his closet, which concerned him. Fears, worries, and anxieties come from a primitive part of the brain, tasked with emotions and keeping us safe from saber-toothed tigers. You can't convince a fear that it shouldn't be there. No. We need another strategy.

In order to get through to a fear you need to speak its language. My mother was right. You have to fight fire with fire (or, rather, image with image). The problem with the eraser trick, however, was that once I erased the scary monsters, I had nothing to imagine but a blank screen with eraser shavings. And pop! The monsters were back. Using mental imagery to *alter* the picture, instead of erase the picture, however, gives kids a fighting chance against those monsters (or, in my son's case, gophers).

To combat imaginary fears, encourage your child to work *with* the mind's imagery instead of trying to get rid of it. Here are some ways to work with frightening mental images:

**C** Fight it off—Because the eraser trick wasn't working for me as a child, I invented my own strategy using mental imagery. Snuggled under my blankets, I would imagine force fields forming around me like a protective bubble. There was a spikey force field, a rubber force field that would bounce monsters away, a super-thick metal force field that nothing could get through, and so forth. I'd invent countless force fields until, feeling safe and snug, I'd drift off to sleep. Whether it's imagining force fields or picturing superheroes blasting bad night invaders, explore with your children options for ways that they might visualize fighting off scary imaginary visitors. You might even suggest that they imagine teaming up with someone (a parent, sibling, friend, or stuffed animal) to defeat the scary characters.

**C/T** Make it funny (see fig. 5.16)—"Riddikulus!" chime the Hogwarts students in *Harry Potter and the Prisoner of Azkaban* (Rowling 1999) as they practice the charm that defends against the Boggart, a shape-shifting creature that assumes the form of your worst fear. But just saying the incantation isn't enough. To defeat the monster, students must make it assume a laughable form through the power of their wand and . . . their imagination. But the true power lies in the imagination. Even without the wand, you can teach your children to disarm a terrifying image by making it funny. When my daughter feared an underwater sea monster at night, I encouraged her to picture it with a funny little hat and outfit. She smiled at the thought of the sea monster wearing ridiculous shoes and a moustache. For good measure, she made its mouth disappear. Encourage your children to dress up the monsters or scary animals that they envision. They can also give these characters funny voices. If you want to take it a step further, help your child draw the image that scares him, adding giggle-worthy details or accessories. You can even turn it into a simple stuffed animal made out of felt, fabric glue, and pillow stuffing. Alternatively, stuff a tube sock and decorate it with button eyes and yarn hair to replicate the now silly monster. If you prefer to outsource a project like this, there are plenty of companies online that will turn your child's drawing into a plush animal toy. Search online for "plush from drawing" to find a selection of vendors.

5.16 Make it funny

**126**

- ⊙ Ward off evil (see fig. 5.17)—Making a magic wand out of a stick and ribbons, or an amulet out of clay, helps a child feel protected, brave, and in control. While "magical" objects like these might not protect a child from actual pain or harm, they may just be the perfect defense against imaginary threats.

5.17 Ward off evil ("Magic wand")

### School, shots, dogs, and other real-life scary stuff

My daughter has no problem going to preschool for the first time. She marches right in—not a worry, not a tear. She loves it. Until . . . week two. The gravity of the situation sinks in. She cries. She pleads. She clings to me. A week passes like this, and then another. I acknowledge her feelings. I remind her of the schedule and when I'll be back. I point out that she always has fun there. I try to phase out gradually. I think I have pulled out all the stops when I realize that I haven't done art with her yet. I stop talking and get creative.

At pickup and drop-off we snap pictures of her with teachers, friends, and favorite activities. At home we print them, cut them out, and paste them onto construction paper. I ask her what words she wants to add to describe the things she likes at school. The caption she instructs me to write under every picture is: "I love Mommy." We make brownies together, packaging them in goodie bags with hand-drawn notes that my daughter makes. Although we make these for her teachers, they are really more for her. By making something at home to take to school, she will experience a bridge between her two worlds. Finally, her big brother makes her a pipe-cleaner-and-bead bracelet (see fig. 5.18) "to help you when you miss Mommy." The next day she goes to school equipped with the handmade book of pictures, goodies for teachers, and magic bracelet. It is the first day in weeks that she doesn't struggle to say goodbye. After that, things quickly become easier for us both.

5.18 "Bracelet for when you miss Mommy"

Helping a child with anxiety about school is different from helping her with fear of monsters under the bed. Dealing with fear of dogs is different from dealing with fear of gophers in the closet. Although it is unlikely that anything bad will happen when going to school or crossing paths with a canine, anxieties about real life are grounded in actual, scary events such as being away from the primary caregiver or being confronted by an aggressive bark. While a child may respond positively to visual imagery strategies described in the previous section, imagining an invisible, protective bubble might not suffice when walking past a frightening dog. Such real-life events may require a different type of strategy.

Providing reassurance is a good first step to helping your child deal with real-life scary stuff, but you're not likely to be entirely convincing unless you get a little creative, too. It's difficult to talk people out of their worries. Even if they *know* there's nothing to worry about, the *feeling* of worry remains. Anxiety is the body's way of saying: "Something is amiss. Pay attention." There's a good reason we can't easily disable that alarm signal with a mere pep talk. On the other hand, creative strategies speak the emotional, visual, and visceral language of fears that inhibit rational thought. Art may therefore stand a better chance. The following are easily adaptable creative approaches to help your children cope with real-life fears:

**C/T** Develop self-talk through song—We all talk to ourselves so much throughout the day that we hardly notice when we are doing it. Constructive self-talk (as opposed to negative self-talk) can help us through anxiety-provoking situations by reminding us of what's going on and how to get through it. However, it can be difficult to counteract overpowering, worrying thoughts with reassuring ones. Songs are ideal for teaching children positive self-talk for tough situations because they are easy to remember, catchy, and playful. For example, if a child is anxious about dogs, in addition to talking to children about general safety guidelines, you might also sing (to the tune of "The Farmer in the Dell"): "The dog is barking 'hi.' The dog is barking 'hi.' Heigh ho the derry-o, but I just walk on by!" If your teen is anxiously waiting to hear the outcome of an application or job interview, you might sing: "Will I hear today? Will I hear today? I don't know, but I don't care, 'cause either way I'm okay!" Alternatively, find a line from the chorus of a popular song that seems fitting. Taylor Swift's "Shake It Off" was popular among my teen clients to help them shake off their social and test anxiety.

**C/T** Transitional objects—These are objects of affection, typically thought of as a "lovey" or "blankie," that help a child self-soothe when a parent is gone; however, a transitional object can actually be any object that helps a child or teen deal with any change, move, or separation. The object can serve as a reminder of the child's connection with someone special or offer an internal sense of safety and security, even away from home. For my daughter in the example above, making brownies to give to her teachers served as a transitional object. It connected an experience at home with me to an experience of her teachers at school. The bracelet that my son made for her was also a type of transitional object—something that she continued to carry in her lunch box, months later, as a reminder of her connection to home. Teens and adults benefit from transitional objects, too: a painted stone or shell, a special charm hung on a necklace, a picture of the family. Work with your child or teen to come up with something that you can make together to ease the difficulty of separation or change.

**C/T** Flesh out the picture—The brain's default mode is to focus on the negative (Carretie et al. 2001) because remembering dangerous details in our environment has historically been necessary to our survival as a species. Today, however, this natural propensity can get in our way. Pleasant or reassuring details that could otherwise help alleviate anxiety over an upsetting event may be omitted from memory. If your child experiences something scary, invite her to imagine the scene as you help her recall positive or reassuring details. If it's too difficult for her to picture it, help her draw it. Include helpers that were on the scene as well as the resolution to the situation ("and then the firefighters came and put out the fire" or "and then the tow truck came and helped" or "Grandpa was holding me and everyone was okay").

Consider making a book about the event. Add text to reinforce positive beliefs about the outcome, such as "and then we were all safe and happy." If your child avoids thinking about the memory, try creating a metaphorical story that contains similar themes instead. After a trip to the emergency room with my son, we drew a story about a train that got derailed and had to go to the train doctor to get fixed. The doctor helped the train, and it was back chugging up and down the branch line again in no time at all. We read the story several times, at my son's insistence, until it seemed that he had resolved the incident in his mind.

If your child becomes overwhelmed or withdrawn in response to any of these activities, do not force him to continue. If you are concerned about the impact of an event on your child, and he is unresponsive to your attempts to help, you may wish to consult a trained professional.

# 6

## Raise Successful Kids

> To raise new questions, new problems, to regard old prob-
> lems from a new angle, requires creative imagination and
> marks real advance in science.
>
> —Einstein and Infeld (1938)

> Creativity now is as important in education as literacy and
> we should treat it with the same status.
>
> —Sir Ken Robinson (2006)

Research trends demonstrate that active engagement in the creative arts positively affects the cognitive and academic performance of children (Asbury and Rich 2008) and increases student engagement, effort, and grit in completing schoolwork (Chand O'Neal 2014). Top executives insist that the arts are key to developing the types of creative problem solvers they are seeking to manage their companies (Alfono 2013). And government officials point to the arts as necessary to education, human understanding, and accomplishment (National Performing Arts Convention 2012). When it comes to raising successful kids, even an occasional serving of art will do your child good.

### MAXIMIZE THE NUTRITIONAL CONTENT OF ART

I'm driving my son to a weekend activity. He is captive for the next fifteen minutes, so I seize the opportunity to quiz him about his upcoming class presentation on Galileo.

"So what made Galileo a hero?" I ask him, recalling his teacher's prompt.

"Uh. I know, but I don't know how to explain it."

I try to guide him. He's getting frustrated. He clearly doesn't want to be thinking about this right now (if ever).

Inspired by Lin-Manuel Miranda's 2015 musical *Hamilton*, a rapped musical about early American history, I try a different approach:

"Yo. Yo. Galile-o," I begin (I am clearly no rapper). "Yo. Yo. Yo," I continue, not sure what to say next. "Galile-o. The church says Earth's in the center, yo! But Galileo, he said no, no!"

"That's terrible, Mom!" my son exclaims, laughing. Oh good, I have his attention now.

I continue: "Galile-o. He said no, no. It's the sun, yo! You're wrong, POPE. And if you don't believe me, come and check out my super cool . . ." I pause to see if he will fill in the rest.

"TeleSCOPE!" he finishes off. "You know why I like Galileo, Mom? Because you make up silly raps."

The freshness of vegetables, and how they are cooked, significantly affects their actual nutritional benefits. Just like veggies, how we serve up the arts matters. The Baby Einstein DVD series (which includes *Baby Mozart* and *Baby DaVinci*) is a clear example of this. The first of these popular videos for youngsters was developed on the heels of a 1993 study by Rauscher, Shaw, and Ky which reported that adults listening to ten minutes of Mozart temporarily raised their scores on an IQ subtest. The problem with marketing products based on the study was fourfold: gains lasted for a mere fifteen minutes at most, improvements were in a narrowly defined area of intelligence, the study was not generalizable to children, and there was no support for enhancement of general intelligence. Nevertheless, the "Mozart Effect" hit prime time. Some governments began requiring a daily dose of Mozart in classrooms and new moms were given Mozart CDs after delivery. Capitalizing on this trend, the Baby Einstein brand was launched, and by 2009 it was estimated to be worth around $400 million—despite serious scholarly doubt that Mozart would make children smarter. Then, in 2007, a University of Washington research team showed that viewing DVDs like *Baby Mozart* was actually associated with decreased vocabulary word development (Zimmerman, Christakis, and Meltzoff 2007). Lawsuits were launched, and refunds were given. The touted benefits of those DVDs were tantamount to feeding kids wilted, overcooked veggies with no nutritional value.

Intelligence and academic success will not increase by watching puppets dance to classical music. Nor by passively listening to music that is not enjoyed or looking at flashcards of Renaissance paintings. As in the above story about my son's Galileo presentation (and my breathtaking rapping skills), in order to maximize the nutritional content of art, we need to cook it up with children's preferences and interests, mixed with active engagement (rather than passive consumption). Add a helping of discussion. Voilà! This is a recipe for success. Here are some examples:

- A British study found that when ten- and eleven-year-old children listened to preferred music, they performed better on visual-spatial tasks (Schellenberg and Hallam 2005). Listening to popular music that they enjoyed, and not Mozart, improved their scores.

- Several studies produced by the Dana Arts and Cognition Consortium (conducted over four years, across seven universities) revealed positive and lasting results from active participation in musical training (that is, learning how to read music and play an instrument). Outcomes included better scores on geometry and map reading tasks, improvement in reading accuracy and speed, and increased phonological awareness (an important skill for reading and spelling) (Asbury and Rich 2008).

- Low-income preschool students in a one-year arts enrichment program involving active participation and discussion showed greater language comprehension than those in a non-arts program. Those in the arts program for two years made even greater gains in literacy, math, and science skills than those enrolled for only one year (Brown and Sax 2013).

- Kids who were taught how to listen during classical concerts, with discussion afterward about what they heard, showed improvement in listening to and following instructions in the classroom (Hallman 2014).

When we serve up the arts in ways that maximize their nutritional value, we not only see measurable improvements in academic and cognitive arenas, but we also see growth in related areas that support learning. The arts can hone attention skills, alleviate distracting feelings about personal problems, increase motivation, promote critical thinking and observation skills, facilitate retention and retrieval of information, develop out-of-the-box thinking, and much more. The rest of this chapter will examine how these skills can be cultivated for success through the arts.

## WHY CREATIVE THINKERS MATTER . . . A LOT

"Our daughter isn't very creative. Maybe you can help her with that," a friend of mine remarks as I sit down with her daughter and my son to do sticker books (with scene pages, stickers, and corresponding numbers for sticker placement). "Where does this sticker go?" the girl asks me. "Well," I begin, "the book suggests that you put it on this page, but that's only a suggestion. You can come up with your own idea and put it anywhere you want." I give her examples. It doesn't take long before she is placing stickers that "belong" on page 5 onto page 8 instead, and those that "belong" on page 3 onto page

1 instead, thus creating her own, unique scenes. Contrary to the impression of her parents, she is creative. She only needs permission to be so. When her parents return, they are in awe of how differently we approached the task: "It never would have occurred to us to do it that way." It never would have occurred to me *not* to do it that way.

Creativity is a process that involves skills, such as innovation (thinking outside the box to approach a task or subject in a new way) and risk taking (a willingness to make mistakes or be wrong). It also promotes critical thinking (making well-thought-out judgments through observation and analysis) and problem solving (which may require recognizing patterns and abstract thinking). While the arts are not the only way to exercise one's creativity, they play a key role in developing skills necessary for creativity. And, advantageously, these creativity-boosting skills can be applied to anything: science, math, writing, engineering, parenting, cooking, teaching. Thus, the arts are a prime arena for preparing children for success in whatever career, hobby, or interest they may pursue.

Education and business innovation expert Sir Ken Robinson asserts that creativity is essential for both personal success and the future of society (Azzam 2009). Gone are the days when working hard and getting a college degree guaranteed career and financial stability, if not satisfaction. Bachelor's degrees are now so common that they don't count for as much as they once did. Even young adults with master's degrees may struggle to find meaningful employment. To be competitive, job candidates need more than good grades and degrees from top universities. They need to be creative thinkers to have that necessary edge. Sir Ken Robinson warns that businesses and society at large need creative thinkers to solve the mounting economic, technological, and environmental problems that will determine the future of our world. Not only do young people need to be creative in order to be successful, but also society will need them for survival. Creative thinking matters . . . a lot.

Everybody has the capacity for creativity, but not everyone knows how to cultivate it. The above story, of my friend and her daughter with the sticker book, is a good example. Many of us have been taught to be rule followers by our parents, schools, jobs, or society. When it comes to making art, many of us have been taught to copy examples, follow instructions, or try to make it look like it's "supposed to look." When we've been taught this way, we tend to pass down the same approach to our own children and others as well.

Ping is at her three-year-old granddaughter's preschool for its annual children's art show. Besides displaying and selling art made by the children and staff, it also offers art tables for the children and their siblings. Ping silently observes her granddaughter at a table with another little girl. They are each given an upside-down section of an egg carton, googly eyes, and pipe cleaners. The other girl goes to town gluing eyeballs—maybe a dozen of them—all over her three egg-carton humps. Meanwhile, Ping's granddaughter weighs the options and glues a single eyeball to the top of each of her three humps. Moments later, a well-meaning classroom aide confiscates the other girl's twelve-eyeball creation, says "No," and plops down a two-eyeball prototype of a caterpillar (previously unseen by the girls). "Oh, *that's* what it's supposed to look like!" shrieks Ping's granddaughter, as Ping silently laments the missed opportunity to reinforce creative thinking and risk taking, independent decision making, and the formation of creative identity.

Certainly, it's important for children to learn how to follow directions. I may intentionally choose an art project that requires careful attention to step-by-step instructions for children with difficulty following multistep directions or breaking down large tasks into small parts, so they can practice these very skills. However, for most children, a much more relevant and wide-reaching skill that will serve them throughout their lives is creative thinking. Most children will learn how to follow directions without us insisting that the stickers go in a predetermined place. And most children will learn the colors of animals, without us insisting that they be colored accurately. The arts are one of the few arenas in life where children can bend the rules and exercise their creative muscles. Sometimes this simply means staying out of their way. At other times, it may be beneficial to intentionally guide them in this direction.

Depending on how structured or open-ended an activity is, different types of guidance may be warranted for developing creativity. Too much structure or too much freedom can be equally detrimental. While a lot of structure can get a child stuck in the habit of following prefabricated instructions, too much freedom can feel overwhelming and make it difficult to begin. Our task is to help our children find that sweet spot in between, where creativity can flourish. Here are some tips to keep in mind, based on the degree of structure or open-endedness in a given activity:

### Highly structured activities

Highly structured activities include projects that come with step-by-step instructions, color-coding, or pictures of the final product. They are useful in promoting creative thinking because they provide opportunities to break the rules. When you keep the following tips in mind, structured activities can teach children and teens that you can simultaneously build on the ideas of others while deviating from them. Structured activities can also teach that there are many ways of approaching the same task:

- Point out that instructions are just suggestions (see fig. 6.1)—Reflect out loud: "That's their suggestion, but you can come up with your own idea. Do you want to use the color that they suggest, or do you want to use a different color? If you want to, you could make that gold or green or just leave that part blank. It's up to you. What do you think?" If your child wants to follow the instructions or sample, don't fight it. Simply say, "It sounds like you like their idea."

6.1 Instructions are suggestions ("Ice-skating girls with tree-eating dinosaurs")

- Model "breaking the rules"—If you are doing the same or a similar activity alongside your child, show how you deviate from the suggested method, colors, or procedure. Narrate what you are doing: "I think I'd prefer to put this sticker over here instead of where they have suggested that we put it. There. I think that looks good . . . where are you going to put yours?"

- If an example is necessary, give several—Children are often provided with a sample of the final product, especially in school or formal art classes. Many craft kits also come with a picture of what the child will make. If an example is necessary (or has already been provided), give several other examples either verbally or visually. This teaches that there are many ways to approach the project.

- Include additional art materials—Explore with your children other art materials that can enhance the original materials for the project. For example, if using a sticker book, play around with adding stickers from other sheets or books. If they are painting a wooden car, look for ribbons, pipe cleaners, hardware, or other items that can be glued onto it.

- Avoid "shoulds"—If you hear yourself starting to say "should," "shouldn't," or "supposed to," STOP! These are all surefire ways to stop creativity and exploration in their tracks: "That sticker's supposed to go there" . . . "You shouldn't cut clay with scissors" . . . "You should use a color other than black because it'll make your picture all muddy." If you'd like to provide some gentle artistic guidance, use nonjudgmental phrases like "I see" or "I notice" and "I wonder," emphasizing the child's ability to make his own choices: "I see that your colors are blending together to make a brownish color. I wonder if that's working for you, or would you like some suggestions on keeping your colors separate? It's up to you." (For more discussion and examples of nonjudgmental language, see appendix 1: "Guidelines for Talking about Art and Life.")

### Open-ended activities

New or unusual materials alone can spark imaginative thinking; for example, you might offer materials like Model Magic (a lightweight, non-messy, air-dry clay), finger paints, found objects, or recyclables (like old keys, paper towel tubes, or leaves). Sometimes the material itself provides enough structure to get creative juices flowing, but other times your child might need a little nudge. Even with familiar materials like pencils and markers, your child or teen may need more structure to get started. A blank piece of paper can be intimidating.

- Wonder aloud about the art materials—"I found this and thought it was cool. I wonder what we can make out of it." Explore the material together. What does it make you and your child think of? Together, you can come up with a unique project.

- Model risk taking—Teach your children that it's okay to experiment without any particular plan in mind. Talk out loud about your process of experimentation as you play around with a material. For example, you might start rolling a ball of clay and say, "I'm not sure what I'm going to make here, but I'm just going to dive in and see what happens."

- Look online—If you and your child are stumped for ideas, look online together for craft suggestions using the materials that you have. A simple search for "crafts with toilet paper rolls" or "crafts with leaves" will get you started.

- Set a challenge—To provide more direction with open-ended materials, create a challenge. You might suggest, "Let's see if we can build the tallest tower ever with these materials." Alternatively, come up with a theme, such as "Fall" or "Winter," to get started.

- Stop fixing (see fig. 6.2)—It's tempting to offer our children solutions to life's **137** problems. Art problems are no different: "Tape won't work; we'll need to use a stapler" . . . "Here, I can fix that" . . . "In order to make this we're going to need . . ." As well intentioned as we may be, giving our children the answer cuts short their opportunity to explore, experiment, and learn from mistakes. Sometimes it's helpful to offer assistance or suggestions, but first invite them to work through the problem with you: "Hmmm, I notice that it's not sticking. I wonder what you think we should try instead?" In this way, you are helping them exercise creative problem solving, a skill applicable to life.

6.2 Stop fixing

- Make it a game—The idea of a game invites playfulness and removes pressure. Framing an art activity as a game can encourage a rule follower to loosen up, and an art-phobic kid to give it a try.

  ○ Scribble drawing (see fig. 6.3)—"I learned a new drawing game. Start by making a scribble all over the paper. Then, look at the shapes and lines that you made. Look for pictures or objects in those lines and shapes. Add color and details to make a picture!" Older children and teens may enjoy trading their papers and seeing what they can make of one another's scribbles.

6.3 Scribble drawing ("Sea horse")

○ Turn-taking drawing—"Here's how we play. Without talking, we're going to make a picture together by taking turns drawing shapes or lines on a piece of paper." As neither of you knows what the other is thinking, the drawing will evolve over time. This exercises not only creative thinking but also creative collaboration, too!

## FROM PRESCHOOL TO GRADUATE SCHOOL

Any good preschool teacher can tell you that when children make art, they are developing preacademic skills. Coloring, beading, or using scissors hones prewriting skills of fine motor and eye-hand coordination. Drawing lines and shapes to represent people or trees, as early forms of symbolic representation, prepares for another form of symbolic communication: reading. The ability to tap to the beat of a metronome predicts the brain's ability to track syllables; therefore, engaging in rhythmic activities may also facilitate language learning and reading (Carr et al. 2014). Through art, kids learn about shapes related to math, and when they dance they gain spatial awareness. When they mix paint, they learn the science of color and experimentation. Kids learn how to make choices and solve problems through art making.

It makes sense to have preschoolers make art. But what about high school students, or even graduate students? We don't hear much about them making art to enhance cognitive and academic skills. Yet more and more top graduate programs are beginning to appreciate the role of the arts in developing crucial skills overlooked by traditional teaching approaches. It turns out that from preschool to graduate school, the arts offer unique opportunities to develop cognitive skills for future success.

A striking example of the capacity of the arts to enhance cognitive and professional skills is the inclusion of art classes in medical school programs. Historically, medical students may have taken drawing classes to learn about human anatomy; however, today they are taking art classes to hone a range of sophisticated cognitive skills that will make them better doctors. More than twenty medical schools in the United States, including Yale, Harvard, Cornell, and Brown, have incorporated thoughtfully designed art classes into their curriculum. Here's why.

### Observation skills

Art hones observation skills. Whether sketching something in front of you or viewing a painting, you are developing an ability to see more accurately. This is a skill that is fundamental to many adult professions and roles. Whether it's making an accurate diagnosis, a viable hypothesis, or an appropriate assessment of needs, observation skills are crucial. And our propensity to stare at handheld devices is hampering our ability to observe the world around us.

Observation skills involve gathering information about an object, person, or event through the senses. While this sounds straightforward enough, being a keen observer is actually harder than it may seem because the brain works by constantly editing, anticipating, and abstracting what is seen. The brain also tends to interpret what is seen by drawing from the past, making it more likely to miss obvious details. This is why two people can have entirely different accounts of the same event. Medical doctors can't afford this common type of observational inaccuracy when making a diagnosis. That's one reason why medical schools have introduced classes in the fine arts—to help bring back the art of firsthand observation (e.g., Genovese 2015; Jones and Peart 2009).

Studies demonstrate that artists see with keen observation (Dingfelder 2010). Eye scans reveal that when looking at the same image, artists tend to spend more time taking in entire scenes, including seemingly empty space, whereas people untrained in the arts spend more time looking at objects, especially people (Vogt and Magnussen 2007). This suggests that artists spend more time seeing all that is in front of them, while others try to categorize and make meaning out of what they see, without as much attention to detail and context. Not surprisingly, trained artists are also better able to recall details later. Quick translation of visual information into familiar categories, while important to daily functioning, may lead us to miss critical information staring us in the face.

There are several ways to cultivate an artist's brain:

**C/T** Invite your child to take a photo of something that she has never noticed before, each day for one month (see fig. 6.4). Make a printed or digital collage out of the photographs at the end of the month.

6.4 Something I've never noticed before

**C** Play "I spy" describing objects not only in terms of color but also in terms of texture, shapes, lines, patterns, light, and shadow.

**C** Look for images in the clouds together.

**C/T** Challenge your child to replicate an image that is turned upside down. Or, invite your child to shade in the space around an object (the negative space), instead of drawing the object itself.

**C/T** Ask your child to study an image carefully, then put the image away while she draws or recalls as many details as she can.

**C/T** Enroll your child in a formal drawing class.

💡 **C/T** TRY THIS:

Invite your child to select an object to draw. It can be anything: a person, tree, favorite stuffed animal, apple, or anything else. You can even have your child sit in front of a mirror to draw his own face. Provide a piece of paper and a pencil or pen. Your child's task will be to draw the object without taking his eyes off of it and without lifting the pencil from the paper. This is called a blind contour line drawing (see fig. 6.5). Instruct your child to let his eyes slowly move along the object and, as he does, slowly move his pencil along the paper to draw what he sees. Resist the urge to look down at the paper. Resist the urge to lift the pencil. When he is finished, he can take a look! Remind your child that the point isn't to make it look like the object he is drawing. It's more like a game with often funny and surprising outcomes. Try doing the activity alongside your child for the added benefit of bonding time.

6.5 Blind contour (self-portrait of a teenager)

Imagine this: more than two hundred fifth-graders, each with a bag of miscellaneous items and fifteen minutes to create their own chair. Their only requirement: use at least three different materials provided. Go! This is exactly what the United States Department of Education and the Guggenheim Museum in New York initiated, over the course of four years, in order to measure the impact of art training on problem-solving skills (Korn 2010). The results were promising. Those students who participated in the Guggenheim Learning through Art program, described above, demonstrated an increased tendency to make deliberate choices, plan ahead, use multiple approaches to a problem, identify resources other than those readily available to them, and work through challenges with focus and an attitude of exploration. In short, they became more sophisticated problem solvers.

We all encounter daily problems that need solving, whether in school, relationships, home, or work. Some problems are relatively mundane ("How will I get all three kids to their respective activities *and* get ready for work?" or "What will we eat for dinner with so little in the house?"). Other problems have broader significance ("What can we do to clean our air?"). Yet we rarely think about tools for effective problem solving and how to acquire them.

Contrary to what most people think, problem solving isn't about getting to the right solution as quickly as possible. When we rush to identify one right answer, we may miss other possibilities. We may lose the ability to think flexibly and become frustrated or perpetually stuck. This is why some medical schools train their students to ponder problems together, encouraging the expression of differing—even conflicting—opinions (Naghshineh et al. 2008). They appreciate that working with others is a more efficient and effective route to diagnosis and treatment than striving to get the right answer alone. How do top medical schools prepare future doctors to work in this manner? They discuss paintings.

"Discussions of art may be one of the most fertile grounds for teaching critical thinking skills precisely because there is no one right answer," says Visual Thinking Strategies cofounder Abigail Housen (2001–2), whose decades of method development and research outcomes support her assertion. Visual Thinking Strategies, a carefully designed process for facilitating group discussions about art, helps kids use existing skills and knowledge to make meaning from what they see. Students learn to identify clues in the painting that support their ideas, listen to each other, and seek additional details to develop or change their ideas. This process fosters respect for perspectives of others, increases confidence, and enhances public speaking skills. It also improves critical thinking skills (Housen 2001–2)) and promotes academic achievement in math, science, and language arts (Curva et al. 2005).

While Visual Thinking Strategies is commonly implemented by trained facilitators in museums and schools, there's no reason why you can't use a similar strategy with your own children to give them a boost in critical thinking. The next time you are looking at art together, whether you are at a museum, near a billboard, or looking at a movie poster, simply ask these three questions from the Visual Thinking Strategies curriculum:

1. What's going on in this picture?
2. What do you see that makes you say that?
3. What more can you find?

Listen intently. Repeat back what you hear your child saying to you. You can play, too, or get siblings or friends involved. Allow for not knowing and for many answers to emerge. Even if you know what the artist intended to communicate, resist correcting your child or steering him toward a "right answer." Alternatively, adapt the Visual Thinking Strategies process to music. The next time you are listening to music in the car or at home, play a game in which you ask your child these three questions: 1) What's going on in this song? 2) What do you hear that makes you say that? 3) What more is going on in this song?

## Mindfulness

Originally associated with Buddhism, and traditionally cultivated through meditation practice, mindfulness has made it into the mainstream and is now taught to students and professors, employees and executives, and high-level athletes. Mindfulness, the practice of nonjudgmental acceptance for whatever is present, isn't just about personal fulfillment and peace of mind. It enhances focus, concentration, and calm, even in the midst of distraction, chaos, and intensity (Kabat-Zinn 2013). It heightens our awareness of internal chatter (the ever-present voices in our head of which we are typically unaware) that influences our thinking and choices. Mindfulness also helps us be more open to details in the present that we might otherwise miss. It's no wonder that one of the reasons cited by medical schools for incorporating art classes into their curriculum is the intention to cultivate mindfulness (Pevtzow 2013).

Just like focusing on breath or a mantra during meditation, creative expression is also a path to mindfulness, whether we are rendering an image in someone's likeness, expressing an emotion in the abstract, or translating music into movement. Creative expression invites noticing a variety of details, such as lines, shadows, colors, and shapes or subtle movements of arm, wrist, hand, and fingers. By attending to these experiences, we stay present with what is actually occurring rather than thinking about past or future. For medical students, these skills translate into an increased ability to listen and observe when meeting with a patient, rather than half-listening while ruminating about the prior patient or anticipating the next.

There are many formats for teaching mindfulness, including breathwork, walk-ing meditation, and body scans, during which attention is brought to various parts of the body. For some, however, these more traditional entry points into mindfulness are difficult. Perhaps especially for children:

I'm lying on the floor, doing my "meditation homework" for a course I'm tak-ing. A recording of a voice prompts me to focus attention on my breath. My son decides to join in. He lies down on his back, too (literally on top of me), and begins to suck air audibly in and out of his mouth. The soft voice on the recording continues: "Now, shift your attention to your toes. What do you notice there? You do not need to wiggle your toes to feel them."

My son interrupts. "Mom, she said to wiggle your toes. You're not wiggling your toes."

"Shhh . . . " I quietly try to guide him back into silence (or, rather, toward an approximation of silence). The recording continues: "Maybe you feel the cool air on your toes. Or a tingling sensation. You don't need to feel your toes to feel what is there. Feel into your toes." My son reaches down and grasps his toes. "She said feel your toes, Mom! Feel your toes!" I burst out laughing. "Yes, sweetheart."

My attempt at meditation fell flat, but this situation offered a mindful parenting opportunity to practice nonjudgmental acceptance for what was present: my very wiggly, unfocused son grappling with meditation. He would clearly need a different approach.

It's not surprising that when children are taught meditation, they are often guided with visual and imagination-based cues. For children, imagining that they are blowing up a balloon, or paying attention to the rise and fall of a small stuffed animal on their belly, is more relatable and accessible than being directed to pay attention to their breath per se. Likewise, the physical, sensory, and imaginative world of art can help children anchor their attention more readily in the present than harder-to-grasp experiences like feeling sensations in the toes, as in the example above. It just takes a little intention on our part to help children maximally benefit from the mindfulness-boosting qualities of art. Here's how.

One of the hallmarks of mindfulness practices is the ability to refocus the mind when it wanders. The mind drifts during art making, just as it does during breathwork or body scans. Thus, art making in and of itself does not automatically engender nonjudgmental attention to the present. On the contrary, art has a ten-dency to evoke self-judgment. It can stir up feelings of inadequacy, frustration, and impatience. Without a specific anchor for one's attention, these judgments can quickly dominate. When capitalizing on art to promote mindfulness, keep these two strategies in mind:

- Redirect the mind during art making toward visual, tactile, or motor elements: the brilliance of a color, the relaxing repetitive motion of a pencil going back and forth, or the squishy sensation of clay, for example.

- Engage in art, dance, or music activities without a preconceived plan. Take each moment as a happy surprise that invites another creative moment, and another, and another. This is improvisation: creative decision making from one moment to the next. Improvisation increases activity in areas of the brain that enable self-expression and reduces activity in areas involved in self-monitoring (or "fear of making mistakes") (Limb and Braun 2008). Research discussed earlier in this book has shown that reducing the fear of making mistakes builds a growth mindset (Gunderson et al. 2013), which is associated with increased academic achievement (Gunderson et al. 2018).

Here's one activity you can try with your child that uses these strategies.

TRY THIS:

For this activity, your child will need a large piece of paper, paints, and a paintbrush. If you do not have paint, you can use a marker, crayon, or pencil instead. Explain to your child that the game is to focus attention on the movement of the brush (or drawing implement) rather than on thinking about what she will paint. After loading the brush with paint, give the prompt: "Let's start by just moving our fingers. Notice how they move and how the brushstrokes are created from that movement." Encourage your child to take her time. Next: "Experiment with focusing your attention on how your hand moves. How is it the same or different from moving your fingers? What do you notice about the brushstrokes now?" Progressively invite focus on movement of the wrist, elbow, shoulder, and eventually the whole arm: "Notice what it's like to use your whole arm. How does that feel? What do the strokes look like now?" Reload the brush with paint as needed. Encourage your child to experiment and play: "What happens if you go through the same process while holding the brush in your other hand?" Ask your child to notice any thoughts that arise while she is painting, and then return her attention to the motion of the body and the difference it makes.

## Comprehension, retention, and recall

"Six farm eggs, a cake for tea, a pound of pears, and don't forget the bacon. . . . Six fat legs, a cape for me, a flight of stairs, and don't forget the bacon. . . . Six clothes pegs, a rake for leaves, a pile of chairs, and don't forget the bacon." So goes the classic children's story of a little boy attempting to remember a shopping list in *Don't Forget the Bacon!* by Pat Hutchins. Of course, in the end, he forgets the bacon.

Many of us have strategies for learning and recalling information, such as repeating information over and over again in our head or saying it aloud. Rote memorization strategies like these, however, are some of the least effective because they neglect important components of memory making—namely associations with previously stored information and emotional significance (Klemm 2007). The key to long-term storage lies in understanding how the brain recalls memories and makes meaning—through stories, images, emotional connections, and sensory experiences (Petty and Cacioppo 1986). These are all avenues tapped into by the arts.

Images, movement, and music are particularly suited to helping the brain make sense of, retain, and access information. Case studies reveal that patients with Alzheimer's disease and other forms of dementia may spontaneously recall memories while viewing images during collage making (Stallings 2010) or painting (Huebner and Rossi 2009) and may recall past personal experiences up to six months after hearing familiar music from an earlier time in their lives (Lord and Garner 1993; Sacks 2008). Memory-impaired individuals can also retain new information more easily when it is sung rather than spoken (Simmons-Stern, Budson, and Ally 2010) and demonstrate better information recall following training in imagery-based memory techniques (Kaschel et al. 2010).

Magicians and World Memory Championship winners use vivid mental images and stories to remember information quickly, allowing them to perform tricks that require memorizing the order of a deck of cards or lists of thousands of numbers, for example. Far from magical, these cognitive tools for enhancing information retention are accessible to most any layperson. According to research by Dresler et al. (2017), training in the use of memory-enhancing visualization tools actually reshapes connectivity within and between brain regions, changing brain patterning to resemble that of memory champions. In this study, subjects remembered more than twice as many words after training in the memory palace visualization strategy (described below). Had our young man in the story *Don't Forget the Bacon* visualized baking a greasy bacon-and-pear cake with six fried eggs on top, perhaps he would have remembered everything on the list.

There are numerous image-, movement-, and music-based strategies for learning, retaining, and recalling information that you can introduce to your children. Here are several worth exploring:

**C/T** Make a metaphor—Some graduate programs challenge students to create images in order to demonstrate comprehension of new material, rather than writing papers alone. By using images to represent abstract concepts, students move beyond regurgitating ideas in words to building a firmer understanding of material through metaphoric associations. In addition to improving comprehension, pictures are simply easier to remember than words (Grady et al. 1998). You can help children learn new information, especially abstract concepts, by helping them come up with a metaphor. Ask: "What does this new thing that you're learning remind you of? What is it like?" Once your child finds a metaphor, encourage him to draw it to anchor the new concept in his mind. A study by psychologists Wammes, Meade, and Fernandes (2016) found that drawing pictures of words leads to more effective recall than writing them!

**C/T** Paint a mental image—Research suggests that the stranger the picture and the more vividly you imagine it, the stronger your recall of it will be (Toyota 2002). Challenge your children to imagine or draw a bizarre scene including the information that they want to retain and recall. For example, if your child needs to remember to put her report about elephants in her backpack before leaving for school, she might picture an elephant crashing through the front door while swinging the backpack around with its trunk, or she might imagine an elephant walking out the front door, wearing a giant backpack. When your child goes to the front door in the morning or sees her backpack, her brain will likely associate this item with the outrageous image of the elephant, thus triggering her brain to remember what she needs to do.

**C/T** Tell a story (see fig. 6.6)—It is easier to recall information that is linked together through some form of interaction or cause-and-effect than to remember information in fragments (e.g., Bower 1970). If your child needs to memorize information, help him come up with a story (even a nonsensical one) that connects the pieces of information together. Drawing, visualizing, or enacting the story may further support the retention and recall of the information (Wammes, Meade, and Fernandes 2016; Toyota 2002; Macedonia and Kriegstein 2012).

6.6 Recall information with stories and images

**C/T** Build a memory palace—In ancient Roman times, the memory palace, or method of loci, was used to memorize and pass on large amounts of information. In more recent times, it has been shown to more than double retention and recall of information (Dresler et al. 2017). One reason is that when we recall a place, even a virtual space (spatial memory), the associated memories from that place surface as well (episodic memory) (Miller et al. 2013). It's long been established that these two forms of memory exist within the same hippocampal region of the brain, and researcher Jonathan Miller and colleagues have also shown that they are closely intertwined. Here's how to build a memory palace:

Encourage your child to imagine a space to which she can travel and in which she can store information. It can be a castle, house, school, or other space. Help your child draw a floor plan. Invite her to imagine walking into rooms where she can see representations of the information she wants to store there. They can be literal representations, metaphors, or visual stories associated with the information to be learned. Different rooms can house specific categories or types of information. Later, when she needs to recall the information, she can mentally walk back through the imaginary space. As she enters each room in her imagination, she will associate it with the visual representations that inhabit the room and, thus, recall the information.

**C/T** Use rhythm and rhyme—The ancient tradition of oral storytelling relied on rhythm and rhyme, and so did I when I learned that "In 1400 and 92, Columbus sailed the ocean blue" or that the word "Mississippi" is more easily spelled to the rhythm "M-I-s-s-I-s-s-I-p-p-I." Chants, raps, rhythm, and rhyme are all well-documented strategies for learning and retaining information, making the top ten of most mnemonics lists. Help your children invent their own rhymes for information or routines that they need to remember. To spice things up, invite your children to clap, snap, tap, or drum along.

**C/T** Let your body do the talking—Research has shown that kids who gesture with their hands when they talk can learn and recall information better than those who don't (Cook, Yip, and Goldin-Meadow 2010). What's more, observing gestures from a teacher or parent when being taught also improves learning and recall (Cook, Duffy, and Fenn 2013). Model and encourage talking with your hands when telling stories, teaching concepts, or tackling homework. You can also teach your child to pair information or concepts with a physical action. When learning a foreign language, for example, pair an unfamiliar word with a related action rather than simply drilling the word with its meaning. Enacting new words has been shown to improve recall and usage (Macedonia and Kriegstein 2012).

Ⓒ/Ⓣ Write a song—Children learn their ABCs through song, so why not other information? Change the words to a familiar tune, like "Row, Row, Row Your Boat" or a popular new release, to capture the information to be remembered.

Ⓒ/Ⓣ Put on an act—Actors embody other personas to evoke emotions and convey stories, but what many don't realize is that taking on the persona actually helps them memorize and recall their lines (Noice and Noice 2016)! Multilinguists (people who speak three or more languages) use a similar approach in learning new languages (Keeley 2014). By embodying a persona that they associate with a specific language, they are able to retain and recall more vocabulary. Keeley reveals that the secret may lie in engaging emotionally with the material being learned. Once engagement is achieved, memorization of material follows automatically. Whether acting out literature, historical events, math equations, or science concepts, encourage your child to act it out with personality and emotional qualities to help commit the material to memory.

Just as individuals have preferred learning styles, they also have preferred memory cues. Ask your children which strategies work best for them. Learning strategies are more effective when enjoyable. If a strategy doesn't work the first time, remind your child that new learning strategies, like sports or other hobbies, require practice for mastery.

## BUT I AM PAYING ATTENTION

I cross the auditorium of the school where I am working, approaching a high school student who busies himself by drawing on the sole of his shoe during an assembly. The kids around him sit attentively, watching the speaker on stage. He looks anything but attentive. I crouch down and quietly inquire:

"Is that helping you pay attention?"

"What?" He is noticeably confused by my question.

"Is that helping you listen? If it is, great! If it's not, I'll hold your pen for you until the speaker is done so it doesn't distract you." He looks stunned.

"Yeah. It is helping me. Thanks."

Looking attentive isn't a sign that someone is paying attention. In actuality, sometimes it's when people look the most engaged that their minds are miles away. Meanwhile, those who seem distracted may be much more tuned in to what is going on than it appears. I regularly invite attendees at my lectures to draw, doodle, or crochet while I speak. Some are surprised by my invitation. Many are relieved. Here's why:

Doodlers rejoice! Despite what teachers or bosses have likely stated, research supports doodling as having attention-focusing benefits that help more with retention and recall of information than sitting and listening alone (Andrade 2009). Doodling engages the brain just enough to prevent it from drifting off into daydreams, while not interfering with our ability to pay attention. It doesn't matter what a doodler doodles. Even shading in simple shapes, such as squares and circles, has been shown to help people remember more information than their non-doodling counterparts.

Microsoft founder Steve Jobs was a doodler. Albert Einstein is said to have been a doodler. John F. Kennedy doodled words, tracing them over and over again. Doodling can help keep the brain online, so it doesn't drift too far afield during a boring lecture. Purposeful doodling, involving the capturing of key ideas through simple symbols and words, has even more advantages. This kind of doodling helps us think through and process material being presented. Graduate school students benefit from this type of doodling to synthesize newly learned material. Top companies incorporate group doodling into meetings and brainstorming sessions to promote effective collaboration and creative thinking among employees. Professional doodlers (called graphic facilitators in the industry) are even hired to visually capture important ideas at meetings and negotiations. If your child doesn't retain information while arbitrarily doodling, he may benefit from this more structured doodling approach of translating key information into graphics.

Despite the known benefits of doodling, encouraging your child to doodle during class is complicated by the fact that most teachers frown upon it. It's one thing if your child is a college student sitting in a large lecture hall. It's quite another if she's one of thirty in a small classroom. Even if your child clearly benefits from doodling to process and retain auditory information, her teacher may still not buy into the idea. Nevertheless, you can help your child reap lifelong benefits of doodling in a way that doesn't get her in trouble at school.

**C/T** Work with the teacher—If your child benefits from doodling, find out how your child's teacher feels about doodling in class or during assemblies. Ask if there's a way to make it work so that it meets the needs of your child and the teacher. Would the teacher be open to it if the student doodled on a separate piece of paper (rather than on a worksheet)? Would she be open to it if the student doodled symbols and words directly related to the class material, instead of doodling hearts and stars? Are there certain classroom periods during which doodling might be permitted?

**C/T** Educate your child—Teach your child what you know about the benefits of doodling. Ask your child if it is easier or harder to pay attention when he doodles. Your child may already be using this as a learning strategy but not realizing it, especially if he's being told not to doodle by teachers and getting the wrong impression that he is a "daydreamer" or "not good" at paying attention in class. It's these types of negative beliefs about oneself that can lead to poor academic performance, and not the doodling itself. Explain that while there's nothing wrong with doodling, if it doesn't work for the teacher, he may have to come up with other strategies for learning or focusing.

**C/T** Doodle at home—If doodling isn't allowed at school, you can still encourage the development of this skill at home. Doodling can help with homework, creative problem solving and, ultimately, college and career.

○ Mix it up with homework—Instead of leaving your child to plow through yet another boring textbook chapter, mix things up during homework time by reading aloud a section to your child while she doodles the main concepts. The creative change in routine alone may promote interest and motivation, thus enhancing learning.

○ Secret Messages—Help your child develop doodling skills by leaving symbolic notes for each other. Make it a game to decode what the other person said. For example, you might leave an "I Love You" note by drawing an eye, a heart, and the letter "U."

○ Family meetings (see fig. 6.7)—Whether you are debating family plans for the weekend, negotiating a new bedtime, or solving a sibling squabble, introduce doodling to capture the main points of the discussion and promote creative problem solving. Grab a large sheet of paper that everyone can see. Either assume the role of "master doodler" or take turns as the doodler. While the family talks, jot down symbols and words that stand out. Use the doodle to review points of the conversation and create solutions.

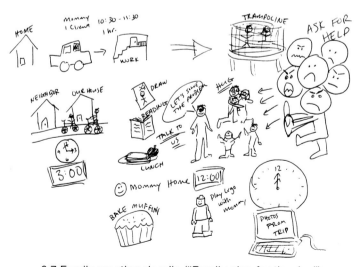

6.7 Family meeting doodle ("Family plan for the day")

Training in the arts requires a great deal of attention. Performing a series of correct musical notes or dance steps, for example, requires simultaneous interaction with the environment, emotional control, and aesthetic expression. Just as taxicab drivers (before the age of satellite navigation) developed more robust memory centers through repeated use of those brain regions (Maguire et al. 2000), those who repeatedly and rigorously engage in arts activities are likely to develop stronger and more efficient attention networks. These attention networks, scholars believe, can also positively affect other cognitive skills (Posner and Patoine 2009).

Practicing an art form doesn't just improve artistic performance. It makes stronger neural connections for enhanced learning in other domains as well. But practice doesn't always come easy, and children are unlikely to be motivated by the long-term and crossover benefits of dedicated practice in the arts. "It's time to practice" is often met with "Do I have to?" For starters, it's important for children to find the art form enjoyable. In order to incentivize practice, help them discover an art form about which they feel passionate or excited. Children not inclined toward singing may love drumming. Children who don't enjoy drawing may easily immerse themselves in clay work. Children may dislike tap but light up with hip-hop. The options are many; you can help them discover an artistic outlet that they would like to pursue through workshops, online channels, how-to books, or regular exposure at home.

The inherent motivation from an arts activity that your child truly enjoys may be enough to yield attention-focusing benefits. You may find, however, that interest and motivation wax and wane. Here are some tips for handling times of low motivation:

- Appeal to your child's goals—Children and teens may be more willing to invest effort in an activity if reminded of the benefits they'll reap (that is, benefits about which they care). "I know how important it is to you to have healthy teeth" is more likely to result in my children reaching for their toothbrushes than "I need you to go brush your teeth now," which typically results in "Ahhh, Mom, just a minute" delays and reminders. The same principle applies to helping your child practice an instrument, review a dance routine, memorize lines, or work on an art piece for a special occasion, contest, or school project. Here are a few examples of ways to appeal to your child's needs, interests, and goals:

  ○ "I notice that you don't always like to practice, but boy do you like it once you've nailed a song."

  ○ "I've heard you say you really want to do well at your dance performance next week."

  ○ "I notice that you want to play after school, *and* I know that you also really want to enter the art contest next week."

- Set an expectation and routine—Ask your child to make a plan for practicing her instrument, dance, or other art form. When is the best time for her to practice? How often and for how long? Come up with specific expectations together. Will your child have a twenty-minute break after school and then practice for thirty minutes before doing anything else? Will your child have one snack after school and then go through her dance routine three times? Invite her to draw the plan and post it somewhere visible. She may also want to add a picture that illustrates a long-term achievement goal. Help your child stick to the agreed-upon plan: "You wanted to do your practicing after watching one show. You've watched one show. Now we're going to turn off the television so you can stick to your practice plan. Once you've practiced you can watch another show if you'd like." Or: "You planned to finish your art project when you got home from school. I notice you haven't done that yet. I know the neighbors are going to want to play soon. Let's set up your art project to work on now, so you're ready to play later."

- Provide an audience—Children and teens may be more invested in practice when someone is on the receiving end of their creative efforts. My children are more likely to practice their instruments, and practice longer, when I sit down to listen than when I set a timer and send them off to practice alone. The same goes for any performance art or even visual arts. Making art with or alongside children provides a secondary gain: special bonding time.

- Address underlying factors—There are many invisible barriers to motivation for lessons and practice: frustration, fatigue, boredom, an upsetting event with a peer or teacher, an impending cold, separation anxiety, shifting interests, and more.

My daughter loves to attend dance class, asking daily when she gets to go back. One week, out of the blue, she says she doesn't want to go. I insist that we go. And I end up allowing her to watch with me through the observation window instead of participating. The following week she doesn't want to attend either.

I ask: "What happened?"

"I just don't want to go."

"Are you tired of it?"

"I don't know. I just don't want to go."

Sometimes children can't articulate why they want to stop an activity. They need help finding the words. Being careful not to belabor it, I offer several possibilities until I finally hit upon something:

"I wonder if something happened in your class that upset you? . . . Did something happen with another kid?"

"Yes! They don't listen to the teacher, and they hang on the barre, and then we don't get our stickers at the end of class."

Bingo. We make a plan to talk with the teacher about my daughter's concerns. She agrees.

When your child resists practicing or attending lessons, approach him about his experience with compassion and curiosity. Offer suggestions as to why "some kids" occasionally don't want to practice or attend lessons. If you're still stumped, try playing a game whereby you name the best and the worst thing about something in your day and then ask your child about the best and worst thing about practicing, going to a lesson, or attending class. Alternatively, play a round of two truths and a lie, whereby your child names two true reasons and one fake reason for not wanting to practice. You guess which one is the lie.

- Respect shifting interests—Different parents place different value on sticking with an instrument or art activity after a child has lost interest. Some children will naturally dedicate themselves to an interest or activity, whereas others will dabble. My son maintains sharp focus on and dedication to his activities of choice. My daughter is a dabbler. Both styles have merit. Regardless of your child's age, how you address shifting interests will depend on personality and timing of the request to shift gears. If your child is part of an ensemble that requires participation for a final performance, it is reasonable to expect her to finish the session before taking a break. Make a plan together: Does your child need a short break before resuming an activity? Does she want to explore a new dance style or instrument? Or is she interested in shifting gears altogether?

When my son requests a break, it is usually just for that week because he is tired, wants to play, or wants to test who's in control. Sometimes we allow him to make that call. Often, we encourage him to go to his lesson, appealing to what motivates him by pointing out that he always has fun when he attends. When my daughter requests to shift gears, it's usually because she has lost interest in the activity or is now excited about something else. We let her know how many more weeks she will continue with the current activity, with our commitment to shift lessons to her new area of interest upon completion.

- Avoid overscheduling—Children and teens need ample free time to play and be creative without formal instruction from grown-ups. However, precisely where the line is between enriched and overscheduled may be different for each child. Consider: Is there enough time for sleep, homework, and hanging out with friends or family? Is your child complaining that he doesn't have enough down time, or is he clamoring for more activities in the week? When motivation to invest in a creative endeavor is low, examine the whole picture of your child's schedule.

- Avoid power struggles—Power struggles breed disconnection and resentment. If you find yourself in a power struggle over practicing or getting your children out the door to their lessons, hit the reset button. Bring it up with your child at a neutral time by saying, "I notice it's been really hard to get out the door for lessons lately. I wonder if you could help me understand this better." If he must continue with the activity, despite his wish to discontinue, explain your long-term goals for him and why you believe it is important to persist. Ask for his input on how to make getting to lessons or practicing easier for you both. Address underlying factors that contribute to the struggle. If you can uncover and address these, he may be reinvigorated to keep at it. (For more on avoiding power struggles, turn to appendix 1: "Guidelines for Talking about Art and Life").

## HIDDEN BARRIERS TO ACADEMIC SUCCESS

A teacher approaches me in the hall with a hurried, "Good morning," and continues on. "My students aren't motivated. They won't do their work. They don't pay attention. Some of the kids are bullying other kids. Help." I agree to help. I team up with an art therapist colleague to intervene. One day a week, over the course of a year, we work with these students to paint a mural in the school courtyard.

The project is collaborative, teaching social skills and encouraging a sense of camaraderie. It is long-term, teaching them to persist through difficult tasks by breaking down a large project into smaller parts. Beautifying the courtyard promotes investment in the school community. Their participation draws positive feedback from staff and students alike. For these students, who are labeled as either apathetic or troublemakers, this is a positive change. Now, they feel proud and useful. Their overall investment in school improves. They are more inclined to participate in class and are friendlier to one another on campus.

Aside from attention and learning difficulties, two significant barriers to academic success are low motivation and emotional distress. Persistent feelings of frustration with school or homework, being pigeonholed as a certain type of student (such as disruptive or lazy), or a poor fit between teaching styles and learning styles can negatively affect a child's emotional world and motivation level. Common life circumstances can also disrupt a child's ability to concentrate or care about what is going on in the classroom. This applies not only to negative events (such as loss, death, family conflict, divorce, peer issues, or illness) but also to destabilizing positive events (such as a move, a new baby in the family, or an upcoming graduation). At these times, it's not memory tricks or attention building that we're after. Rather, it's addressing the underlying problem of motivation or emotional distress.

In some instances, as in the example above, there are opportunities for arts integration in the classroom that can address hidden barriers to academic success.

Educators may be open to learning about studies of arts-based school interventions, such as the work of Rosal, McCulloch-Vislisel, and Neece (1997), who integrated visual art and creative writing into a ninth-grade English curriculum with impressive results. By integrating literary characters and themes with an arts-based exploration of self-image, personal strengths, and family history, students showed improved grades and attitudes about school, their families, and themselves. Or educators may be curious to learn about programs like the John F. Kennedy Center's Changing Education through the Arts (CETA) program. CETA examined thirty-two schools across Washington, D.C., revealing that students who received arts-integrated curricula were more engaged in schoolwork than their peers who did not receive arts-integrated education (Chand O'Neal 2014).

Of course, despite these striking results, the logistics of introducing arts integration into a school can be complicated. It may be difficult for parents and educators to find the time, leverage, or resources to incorporate the arts into school curricula. Fortunately, the power of art can be harnessed at home to accomplish similar goals:

- Identify the root of the issue—Don't settle for the mindset of "she just needs to try harder." If there is academic difficulty, it is nearly always because something is going on beneath the surface related to emotional or social distress, attention or learning difficulties, boredom, or some other disruption. If your child won't talk about it or can't identify it, sometimes answers will surface through the arts. These activities may offer some clues:

  - Invite her to share a favorite song to which she most relates or most often listens at the moment.

  - Ask him to use pictures or metaphors to describe what it's like for him at school or home. If he is willing, you can work together to make a collage from magazine pictures about "the biggest problem in my life right now."

  - Invite her to take a picture of something that represents her most dreaded school subject (such as the textbook). Alter the image with a photo filter app.

  - Show him a few poems written by youth with themes such as friendship, confidence, or stress, to which he may be able to relate. Ask him to circle any words or phrases that stand out to him. Teens may want to use some of these words or phrases that may have meaning to them as prompts for writing more.

- De-stress—Some kids can hunker down and tackle all of their work at once. Others find school and homework to be unbearably overwhelming. It is well documented that breaking up long stretches of work can actually boost focus and productivity (Ariga and Lleras 2011). Invite your child to take art breaks (even short ones) during homework by knitting, beading, drumming, or participating in another creative outlet (maybe even practice time!). Unlike social media breaks that can harm emotional health (Steers, Wickham, and Acitelli 2014), art breaks can reenergize and de-stress (Kaimal, Ray, and Muiz 2016). Alternatively, invite your child to surround his work environment with art and plants. This, too, can enhance productivity (Knight and Haslam 2010).

- Music to motivate—For some students, listening to music is a distraction while doing schoolwork. For others, it's a big help. Research suggests that music can energize as well as motivate through tedious or challenging tasks by shifting focus away from negative aspects of the task (Fenske 2012). Although music during homework may not be the answer for every child, you may want to experiment with this before insisting that homework be done in silence.

- Make time to make art about feelings and life challenges—If you believe that your child's academic difficulties stem from a recent or upcoming emotionally disruptive event, turn to chapter 5, "Raise Happy Kids," which offers ideas for using the arts to address underlying emotions.

Supporting your child's emotional health at home through the arts, in order to maximize academic motivation and success, is not a substitute for assessment and treatment of significant or prolonged emotional or academic disruption. Seek support from a qualified professional if you observe noteworthy or persistent changes in behavior including, but not limited to, changes in academic performance, socialization, interaction with family members, sleep patterns, eating habits, or mood. Bear in mind also that some children cope with difficulties by "keeping it together" or academic overperformance. Just because a child seems fine or is getting good grades doesn't necessarily mean she is okay on the inside. If your family has experienced a recent stressor, positive or negative, check in with all of your children.

# 7

## Tap Into Your Own Inner Artist

Whether you fancy yourself an artist or run in the opposite direction when you hear the word "scrapbooking" (or both!), we can all invite a little more creativity into our lives. Just as we can strategically apply art to help children grow socially, emotionally, and intellectually, we too can tap into art for our own benefit.

Small shifts in the ways we think about moments in life can lead to big changes in how we feel about and respond to them. Developing a more creative mindset in life can be enough to change our experience of parenting (and cultivating it doesn't require any setup or cleanup!). Once developed, an artist-like perspective is always accessible, allowing us to be curious about experiences, see new possibilities, gain perspective on challenging situations, and maintain centeredness. Let's take a closer look at how.

### DEVELOP A CREATIVE MINDSET

It is an hour after I tucked in my daughter for bed. She is still squirming and occasionally glancing in my direction to make sure I'm still here. She whines, "But I don't know how to close my eyes." She's already been potty twice. She's been too hot, too cold, thirsty, and unable to find a certain stuffed animal that's gone missing. Indeed, she is the queen of nighttime shenanigans. Leaving her in her room never works—she won't stay in. We've tried bedtime routines, clear limits and consequences, and relaxing visualizations. Nothing works for long. So, I bitterly resign myself to lying down in the room with her each evening, sometimes for an hour or more, until she falls asleep. I feel frustrated waiting here, thinking of all the things I still need to do before retiring to

**157**

bed myself. Then I notice the glow from her nightlight as it backlights her face. A line of golden light runs along her forehead, like the silver lining of a storm cloud. I look at her as a portrait artist would, focusing on the details of her face and resting body. As my mind shifts, I feel in love all over again. Frustration and resentment vanish. I feel fortunate to be with her. I realize that part of me will miss these moments when she's older.

Creativity in the everyday sense has less to do with producing a song, painting, or dance—and more to do with how we look at the world. Generally speaking, artists and other creative people share similar approaches to life that can be equally useful to our experience of parenting. According to researcher-authors Scott Barry Kaufman and Carolyn Gregoire in *Wired to Create* (2015), creatives tend to surround themselves with beauty, seek out new experiences, and maintain curiosity about life. Creative people observe . . . everything. They are interested in what others think or feel and approach struggles as an opportunity for growth and creative expression. Imagine approaching parenting with this orientation in mind.

Interestingly, many of the qualities of creatives mentioned above have also been identified as habits worth nurturing for happier and healthier lives and relationships. Research from the field of positive psychology has linked the feeling of awe at experiencing beauty (in nature or art, for example) with healthier immune systems (Stellar et al. 2015). Meanwhile, scholars note that curiosity is a key habit for general satisfaction, a meaningful life, and growth-oriented behavior (Kashdan and Steger 2007). Indeed, friendly curiosity toward any experience (that is, approaching our internal and external worlds with nonjudgmental interest) is a key principle of Mindfulness-Based Stress Reduction, a cutting-edge practice shown to have numerous physical, mental, and emotional health benefits (Grossman et al. 2004). In short, the artist's way of looking at and experiencing the world is valuable for life.

When we look at our children through the lens of an artist, we may be able to approach parenting with more awe and less judgment. A more creative outlook on life in general, and on parenting in particular, can be nurtured through simple mental exercises that do not require art making at all.

**P** See your child for the first time—Have you ever tried to look at someone very familiar to you as if seeing them for the first time? Artists do this. They look for novelty and not the norm. They focus on the detailed interplay of light, shadow, shapes, and lines that make up the object or person in front of them. Mundane objects and familiar people take on new, rich meaning through the eyes of an artist. We can do the same when we look at our children. Take a moment to look intently at the details that make up your child. Observe the lines, shapes, colors, and texture of her skin, hair, and clothes. Take in the landscape of her face. Notice her rumpled clothes, her tousled hair, or the smudged dirt on her cheek. Do this any time: while sitting at the dinner table, watching her play, or giving her a bath. You may just find that you see her with a refreshed sense of love and awe.

**P** Remember a time of awe—When we're not feeling so in love with our children or parenting, we can purposefully evoke the feeling of love, amazement, or awe by recalling a time when we *did* experience these feelings. Maybe you had these feelings when your child was first born or when you visited a beautiful or awe-inspiring place. Remember this place and time, and the accompanying feelings of love, amazement, or awe. Close your eyes if it helps. Place a hand over your heart. This gesture can serve as a signal to connect with soothing, loving feelings. What do you notice? Now that you know you can bring up these feelings at will, try to evoke them with the same hand-to-heart gesture, while you pause to watch your child play, eat, lounge, or sleep. Practice this exercise when you feel happy and connected with your child. It'll be easier. Next, try this exercise during times when you feel neutral. This will prepare you for when your children are tired, angry, frustrated, or defiant. It's more challenging to look at them with a sense of love and awe at these times. But with practice it *is* possible to feel a sense of wonder and amazement at those little (and big) beings, even in their most difficult moments.

**P** Get curious—Whether mundane or extraordinary, artists have the same task: to ponder, explore, and notice what is before them. We can cultivate a similar sense of curiosity about our children (and their behavior) rather than succumb to expectations and frustration over what is unfolding before us.

It is the morning of my daughter's first birthday. She throws herself on the kitchen floor, legs kicking and fists pounding. "Hey, Honey," I call to my husband, with an equal amount of surprise and interest. "Come here. I think . . . she's having a tantrum." I have dealt with plenty of tantrums far worse than this in my years of working with children and families. However, this is my daughter's first, and I am seeing it with fresh eyes. I am intrigued.

Years, and many tantrums later, I lose my sense of curiosity about her occasional outbursts. I am stuck in "Here we go again!" My experience of the present is tainted by the history of accumulated tantrums. More often than not, I am no longer curious about them. I am tired of them. I hear the frustration in my voice. I decide to make a change and ask myself, "What's going on here, now?" I try to look at this tantrum as if it's the first. As curiosity returns, frustration fades.

Curiosity is important because it shifts us into a present state of mind. It draws us to our children, even in their most difficult moments, because of a genuine desire to know more about them and their behavior. This puts us in the right frame of mind to choose how we respond to what is happening, rather than yield to knee-jerk reactions rooted in assumptions, expectations, or familiar

*Tap Into Your Own Inner Artist*

patterns. Fortunately, curiosity is a conscious process that can be cultivated. When you feel fed up with a particular behavior or habit, as we all do from time to time, cultivate curiosity by asking yourself questions like: What's going on here? How is my child feeling right now? What do I see that tells me that? What is her body doing in response to these feelings? How might this be for her? These questions are similar to those used in Visual Thinking Strategies, from chapter 6, which are used to explore the meaning of art.

## FIND INSPIRATION IN THE MUNDANE

There are days when I feel as if I am watching paint dry. My firstborn is an infant, and I am adjusting from a fifty-hour-a-week job to full-time mom. It is glorious, stressful, and mundane all at once. I feel unproductive and uncreative. One evening, I report to my husband that the most noteworthy thing I have done all day is trim my nails. I know right then: something has to change.

Something indeed changes one night in the wee hours, as I gaze at my sleepless baby. I imagine the superhighways of his brain lighting up with blue and white lights. I picture them speeding to and fro, making connections, and growing new pathways in a beautiful intricate web. "Look at what I did today," I think to myself. I know that infant brains make more than 1 million new neural connections every second (Center on the Developing Child 2009), but it isn't until this mental image appears that I understand the statistic on a personal and emotional level. It dawns on me right then: "I am having the most productive day of my life."

Parenting is challenging. It is both rewarding and, at times, boring. Feed, burp, change, repeat. Wipe, bathe, brush, repeat. Nag, drop off, pick up, repeat. From infancy to teen years, many parents feel stuck at least occasionally in the rut of routines and needs. In this crazy job, seeing through a lens of creativity can help us not only cope with the mundane but also discover inspiration, renewed love, and happiness.

Stephanie longs to bring more inspiration and creativity into her life. She is a busy mother and wife, whose career is on hold. "Cooking," she announces to me one day. "That's something I want to be creative with. But it stresses me out. It never turns out how I imagine it will, and I end up frustrated with nothing to show for it." I give her a creative challenge: "Imagine you're on one of those cooking shows where you have to make something out of a few ingredients in a sealed box. Don't look up a recipe. Don't go to the grocery store. Tonight, just look in your kitchen and see what you have to work with. Then pull something together. Being creative isn't about fancy ingredients and complicated recipes. It's about being innovative. It's about making something special from

Cooking, decorating, dressing, rearranging furniture, wrapping gifts, gardening, and uploading pictures to social media sites can all be acts of creativity. However, we forget their creative potential, as they have become habitual. We may even resent them because, while performing them, we're worrying about what else needs to be done or what we'd rather be doing.

Creativity is about expressing something personal, combining materials or knowledge in a new way, or turning something ordinary into something special. When we consciously apply these creative principles to ordinary tasks, we can change our approach and attitude toward them. The next time you find yourself stuck in a rut or resenting a routine, challenge yourself to apply one of these creative principles to your daily life. Even if the ordinary doesn't become extraordinary, at least you can make the task more palatable. Here are some sample activities to inspire you:

**P** Express something about yourself, your family, or your life—When I was first planning my wedding, I felt overwhelmed by the many tasks involved. Then it occurred to me: "But I do know how to make art." The overwhelming task suddenly became a multisensory expression of love. "Planning a wedding" was stressful. "Expressing our love" was fun and creative. By seeing tasks as an opportunity to express something about yourself, your family, or your life, you can change the way you think and feel about it. Sure, it's difficult to figure out how to make driving to school or brushing teeth an expression of love. But if you're up for a challenge, you probably can! Perhaps you pretend the drive to school is like looking at a photo album together. Whenever you see something that reminds you of a time together, point it out. "Look at that. Remember when we rode our bikes up here? And look! Remember when we went to dinner at that restaurant after your field trip? Here's your school. Remember your first day of kindergarten?" Or try packing school lunches with an element of self-expression in mind. It doesn't matter if anybody recognizes what you're conveying with the PB & J, cheese stick, or carrots that they won't eat. It's your own experience of the process that matters. What else can you transform into an act of self-expression?

**P** Combine knowledge or materials in novel ways to create something new— Necessity is the mother of invention. From using a sun visor to prevent soap in the eyes during hair-washing, to labeling left and right shoes by cutting a sticker in two and placing each half on the inside of each shoe, tackling common parenting problems in creative ways will make life easier and more interesting. The story of Stephanie, above, is another example of combining materials in a novel way. By working with simple ingredients found in her

*Tap Into Your Own Inner Artist*

kitchen, she not only saved time but also was challenged to think creatively. Consider some of your daily challenges and how you might approach them in novel ways. Your ideas don't have to be complicated or ingenious. Simple is creative, too.

**(P)** Take an ordinary behavior, object, or gesture, and make it special (see fig. 7.1)—Taking something ordinary and making it special is a basic human act. Since prehistoric times, people have embellished, adorned, and otherwise transformed objects, places, and times of significance through the arts. This process of "making special" is believed to have sustained us by bringing us together, commemorating events, and helping us deal with changes that come with the passing of time (Dissanayake 1992). Birthdays, deaths, weddings, and holidays are most easily recognized as times when the arts are used to connect, commemorate, or reflect. But what about "making special" in day-to-day life? Arranging lunch foods to look like a funny face, making up a silly dance before bath time (my kids invented the "shake your booty" dance to commemorate bath time), or even making up a story at bedtime instead of reading a book—these are all ways to make simple moments a little more special.

7.1 Making applesauce special

Life is relatively pleasant after my second child is born. My eldest behaves lovingly, or at least neutrally, toward his baby sister . . . until she becomes mobile. She starts crawling and Big Brother's toys are under continual attack by her cavernous, drooling mouth. Everything changes. He yells at her, pushes her down, snatches. We try moving things out of her reach, but that doesn't work for long. It seems as if overnight she figures out how to stand . . . and then climb. Into her mouth things go. Big Brother cries, shoves, and shouts. Baby Sister bites back. He is furious. She is persistent. I am exasperated. Day after day it is the same. I am stuck.

I like to tell my kids, "If it doesn't work, try something different." After all, insanity has been defined by an unknown author as "doing the same thing over and over again and expecting different results." Yet, here I am, doing the same thing over and over again without resolution: "No, that doesn't go in your mouth. We don't push. STOP. We don't push!" Baby screams. Son cries. ARGH! Is nothing working?

Just because a behavior repeats doesn't necessarily mean that nothing is working. Children need repetition in order to learn. They will play out the same scenarios to master a new skill (clothes are on the floor again), understand a new concept (it's still not safe to throw sand), or process an emotional experience. They may simply need more practice. Years later, my children are still practicing the fine art of conflict management with each other daily (and will surely continue to do so). Yet, while children need repetition, there are also plenty of times when a different approach will actually yield a preferred outcome. The above example was one of those times. We'll return to it in a moment.

All parents get stuck. We may get stuck because we've encountered a new situation. We're not always prepared to deal with the first tantrum, the first "I hate you," or the first fender bender. At other times, we may have the know-how but are *reacting* from our feelings about the situation rather than *acting* from our understanding of it. We have the tools but simply cannot access them. At times like these, we may become inflexible and expect our kids to just do as we say. Or we may become unhinged out of frustration, fear, or anger. Operating at either end of the spectrum (rigid thinking or chaotic emotion) interferes with problem solving (Siegel and Bryson 2012). However, an image-based strategy can help bring balance, thoughtfulness, and preparedness in approaching challenging situations. Let's take a look at how:

Working with mental imagery is a well-documented strategy for changing one's behavior or performance. Olympic athletes use it to achieve peak performance (Jones and Stuth 1997; Ungerleider and Golding 1991). Musicians use it to enhance their concert performances (Keller 2012). Mental imagery is so powerful that research even supports its use to heal our bodies (e.g., Lengacher et al. 2008; Maddison et al. 2011).

**164**　Moreover, visualization supports optimal *actions* and *reactions* in unexpected or undesirable situations (Orlick 2016). Intentional use of mental imagery can help us prepare for those times when we can't access our parenting tools, and we feel particularly stuck.

Because the brain experiences imagined events as if they are real (Ji et al. 2016), mental imagery may be more effective than simply planning how we'd like to respond to our children. By imagining how we'd ideally like to interact with our children, playing it out like a movie in our mind, we can rehearse optimal parenting performance and prepare to approach undesirable scenarios calmly.

In particularly difficult situations, finding metaphors through mental imagery can also help us uncover new solutions and shift how we feel in the moment to enable a more effective response. Let's take a look at this more closely by returning to the previous story:

> My son's toys are once again under threat of Baby Sister slobber, and I brace myself for the next firestorm. I stop and ask myself, "If I could draw a metaphor for the problem, what would it look like?" As the conflict escalates, it is neither feasible nor of interest to me to actually draw. So, I make mental art. The image of a brick wall springs to mind. Indeed, I am feeling walled off, tense, and disconnected. Then I ask myself, "If I could alter that image, how would I change it?" This time, the wall image vanishes and the image of open arms appears in my mind. With this image, the feeling in my body shifts. I relax and realize that the problem isn't my son's reaction to his sister. Nor is it the drool. The problem is my frustration toward my son for not being more patient with his baby sister. I am trying to protect her and, in so doing, walling him off. This, in turn, fuels his anger and impatience toward her. The wall shows me how disconnected I have become from my son. The image of the open arms is my solution, both metaphorically and literally.
>
> This time, instead of reminding him (ad nauseam) to stop pushing his sister and that it is his responsibility to put things away if he doesn't want them in her mouth, I go to him with compassion, love, and understanding. I approach the situation with "open arms." I empathize with his plight and give him a hug. With that, my son also relaxes. He becomes more open to my suggestions and more tolerant of his sister.

Empathizing and connecting before instructing is not a new approach to parenting. It is up there with the best practices in parenting. I know this tool well, but because I was stuck, frustrated, and not thinking flexibly, I simply could not access it in this situation. Working with metaphor and mental imagery allowed me to tap into that wisdom. (The next section, "Access your inner resources," explores this further.)

I encourage parents to come up with their own images to break through "stuckness": a skillful tap dancer; hands cupping a precious stone; tending to a flower; riding an ocean wave. In my own role as a parent, I continue to hold onto the image of open arms. I call upon this image at times when I'm feeling particularly pushed, tired, or irritated. With this image, I am better able to respond from a place of caring and connection than from a place of control. With this image, I can more easily remember that when children are least lovable, they need love from us most.

**TRY THIS:**

(see fig. 7.2):

1. Find a neutral moment to think of a parenting situation where you feel stuck. Picture it. How does it feel in your body? What emotion does it bring up in you?

2. Come up with a metaphor that fits your experience. What is it like? A brick wall, a jigsaw puzzle, a wave crashing over you?

3. Notice the image that comes to you. Try not to overthink it. What pops into your mind? If you struggle to come up with an image, start by thinking about what feeling you are experiencing at the moment. What color might it be? Can you give it a texture or a form? If you need additional help, try looking at images online or in a magazine to find an image with which you connect.

4. Once you have your image, ask yourself what you would like to add to or change about it. What does it need? How can you transform it? With what would you like to replace it? For example, would it be easier to ride the wave instead of standing beneath it?

5. Once you have a new image, notice how it feels in your body when you visualize it. Has anything changed? Does it give you any clues as to what made you feel stuck? Does this new image give you any ideas as to how you might approach the situation differently? How might your metaphorical strategy translate into an alternative strategy with your child?

7.2 Overcome parenting "stuckness" with metaphor

*Tap Into Your Own Inner Artist*

When you're hungry, you go to the fridge. When you're upset, you call a friend. Friends, family, community groups, teachers, books, money, food, stuff you own . . . these are all resources. Although we may take them for granted, they are generally available to you when you need them. You know where they are. You know how to get to them. Inner resources are different. They are harder to see and can be more difficult to access, especially when we are angry, tired, or overwhelmed. Inner resources are strengths inside us like creativity, problem-solving ability, insight, physical and emotional self-awareness, communication skills, and parenting know-how. We are all filled with internal resources, ready and waiting for our use. The issue is accessing them when you need them most.

**Step 1: Identify your resources**

We need to know what inner resources we have at our disposal before we can access them. Just as you might buy a box of Band-Aids, with the foresight that someday they will come in handy, it is wise to prepare your internal first aid kit for difficult moments of parenting. Of course, we cannot locate self-compassion on the shelf above the heart or relaxation in the cabinet under the lungs. Internal resources are invisible and often intangible. This is where art comes in handy.

   TRY THIS:

To familiarize yourself with your internal resources, start by making a collage from images and phrases that you cut out of magazines. As you flip through pictures, contemplate the question: "What skills or qualities do I have that help me as a parent when I'm at my best?" Work spontaneously. Images may stand out to you. Make a small pile of cutouts to consider and sort through them later to make your final selection. When you've settled on a stack of pictures and words, arrange them on a piece of paper and glue them down. Look at the images you have selected. What do they say about you? Does anything surprise you?

Alternatively, you can forgo physical art making in favor of mental art making. Have paper and pen handy, find a quiet place, and then close your eyes. If you are uncomfortable closing your eyes, a soft gaze on the floor works, too. Now think of a time when you were at your best as a parent (perhaps it wasn't even with your own kids!). If you struggle to think of a specific memory, try creating an ideal scenario. Visualize the scene (whether from an actual memory or imagined scenario). Where are you? What are you doing? How is the child responding? Next, become aware of how you feel. What emotions do you discern? How does your body feel? Are you able to be relaxed, present, loving, confident, knowledgeable, playful, and/or a good listener? If so, you've just tapped into your internal resources. If not, you can also try imagining how someone you admire might interact with a child. Once you have completed the visualization, jot down (or doodle) the resources you discovered within.

When you're stressed, tired, overworked, or upset, that's when you need your inner resources most . . . yet, this is also the most difficult time to engage with them. Other than taking a deep breath or giving ourselves a time out, many of us do not know how to connect with our internal resources in parenting. The creative arts help us not only to identify our resources but also to tap into them when we need them most. When our rational self has left the building, the arts offer an alternative route to finding it again.

TRY THIS:

Just as actors use mental imagery to create authenticity in their portrayal of characters, we can do the same. Now that you have identified some internal resources, you can regain perspective at a challenging time by visualizing yourself or your child in your best moments.

I'm attending a fundraiser for my son's school. As we watch a slideshow of our little ones, with sentimental songs about growing up playing in the background, many of us get a little choked up. One of the moms, a professional comedian, jokes, "Why is it that I don't care much for my kid until I see pictures of him set to a soundtrack?" We erupt in laughter. Not only is her remark funny, but also it resonates.

Of course she cared for her child, as we all do, but she was speaking to the familiar experience of losing touch with feelings of love and connection. She also unknowingly identified a powerful tool to access the best in us in the hardest of parenting times: music. Indeed, a simple song can bring tears of affection.

Music reduces stress, anxiety, and pain in children and adults (Hartling et al. 2013; Klassen et al. 2008; Martin et al. 2018; Nilsson 2008; Suresh, De Oliveira, and Suresh 2015; van der Wal-Huisman et al. 2018). Moreover, it provides a gateway to positive feelings. Research suggests that even sad music induces positive responses in the listener, including nostalgia, wonder, and peace (Taruffi and Koelsch 2014). Listening to music (or poetry) that elicits "chills" is associated with blood flow patterns in the brain similar to those elicited by euphoria-inducing stimulants like drugs, sex, and chocolate (Blood and Zatorre 2001; Zeman et al. 2013). Furthermore, music or songs can remind us of a particular time in life and evoke associated feelings from that time. This is because the amygdala in the brain, which processes emotional experiences (including emotional responses to music), interacts with the neighboring hippocampus, which encodes and stores memories (Gosselin et al. 2007; Phelps 2004; Richardson, Strange, and Dolan 2004). Knowing this, we can capitalize on music to help us remain more connected and in love with our children, even when they are least lovable. Experiment with the following music-based activities:

(P) They're playing our song!—Identify a special song or piece of music that you associate with your child, as one often does with a romantic partner or friend. It doesn't matter if it's a top 10 hit, a lullaby, or a symphonic work. If you're struggling to identify one, start listening until you find something that moves you or brings up warm feelings in you. Or search online for "parenting songs that make you cry." Once you've identified a song or piece of music, listen to it with your full attention. Sing it. If your kids complain about it, hear it silently in your head. Imagining music produces effects in the brain similar to those produced by actually listening to it (Kraemer et al. 2005; Zatorre and Halpern 2005). If you're feeling really inspired, make an entire playlist that evokes feelings of nostalgia and love for your children. As you listen, watch them as if you're watching a clip from a movie of their lives. Notice what it touches inside you. Notice the impact of those feelings on your approach with your children in that moment.

(P) Match music to your mood—Make music playlists that soothe, energize, or inspire you. Although it may sound counterintuitive, it is also useful to make a playlist that reflects how you feel when you are upset. This is because listening to music that matches how you feel validates and helps you release those feelings in order to shift out of them. For example, if you feel angry and you want to feel calm, first listen to music that matches your anger, then listen to a series of songs or pieces that feel progressively less angry to you, and then finally listen to music that you find calming. This technique, used in music therapy, was first noted by pioneering psychiatrist Ira Altshuler (Davis 2003; Michel and Pinson 2005).

And just because you feel angry doesn't mean that you have to listen to a song about anger. We all have different preferences for music because of different associations that we make with what we hear; so, what is relaxing for one person may be annoying to another. There are no absolutely right or wrong choices. What is right for you is what works for you (Nilsson 2008).

(P) Belt it out—Try singing along, playing along, drumming along, conducting along, or even dancing along to the music. Active music making engages even more of the brain, which literally crowds out stressful thinking (Tramo 2001).

(P) Mix up the mundane with music—Use music to transform your experience of any mundane activity: paying bills, doing laundry, cooking, washing dishes, cleaning the bathroom, sorting mail, answering email. For added benefits, you may spontaneously find yourself singing or moving along to it.

Like music, movement also offers a passageway to our most difficult-to-access **169**
parenting resources. Scores of compelling studies teach that how we move and hold
ourselves physically affects how we experience ourselves (e.g., Carney, Cuddy, and
Yap 2010, 2015; Cuddy, Wilmuth, and Carney 2012; Huang et al. 2011). While
ongoing research investigates whether or not our body posture affects our hormones (Carney, Cuddy, and Yap 2015; Fosse 2016; Ranehill et al. 2015), research
consistently demonstrates that it impacts our behavior and can leave us feeling
empowered . . . or anxious.

Likewise, our body language influences how others perceive and respond to us
(e.g., Cuddy, Wilmuth, and Carney 2012). We form impressions of others in less
than 100 milliseconds—based on body language alone (Gruenfeld 2013). And when
verbal and nonverbal messages are in conflict with each other, it's what the body
tells us that we will remember. Actual words account for only 7 percent of social cues
(Mehrabian 1981). Given this, just imagine the impact of body-based messages such
as a clenched jaw, furrowed brows, or raised shoulders when parenting. I've never
seen a parent limber up before tackling a parenting moment. But maybe we should.

**TRY THIS:**

Check in with your body *before* responding to a challenging parenting moment.
Notice what is present in your body when your buttons are pushed. For me, my brow
furrows, I purse my lips, and I tend to hold my breath. With practice, I've come to
quickly recognize these signals of tension, and I use them as a cue to "STOP!" before
responding. I know that I am not ready to engage yet. It's time to prepare my body first.

After taking stock of your body, try one of the following movement-based strategies to shift your physical state toward a relaxed, open, energized, or confident one:

P Tense and relax—It is common to hold tension in our bodies without noticing it. To relax tight muscles (even ones you're not aware of as being tense),
tense and release different muscle groups from head to toe. For example, try
clenching your hands into fists and letting them go. Then try lifting your
shoulders up to your ears and letting them drop. Using this progressive relaxation technique, see if you can purposefully relax your forehead, eyes, mouth,
neck, shoulders, arms, hands, back, chest, belly, buttocks, legs, and feet.
Now take stock again. What do you notice? Bring awareness to your body
throughout the day. Use red traffic lights, or some other visual reminder, as
a cue to check for signs of tension and then consciously release them. Once
accustomed to relaxing your body in neutral times, you can more easily in-
voke this skill in challenging moments with your child.

P Take a power pose—People who assume "power poses," or expansive stances associated with powerful roles, report feeling more confident (Carney, Cuddy,

and Yap 2010, 2015; Cuddy, Schultz, and Fosse 2018; Cuddy, Wilmuth, and Carney 2012; Huang et al. 2011). If you ever feel emotionally closed off, tentative, or disempowered when parenting, this technique might be helpful for you. When you have a quiet moment away from your children, stand with your legs apart and hands on your hips (like Wonder Woman or Superman), outstretch your arms in the air (like an Olympic gold medalist), or assume another "expansive" pose of choice, with arms extended away from the body and chest open. Maintain this pose for two minutes, holding it with as much energy as possible even if your arms get tired. Notice how you feel afterward.

If you are unable to take a power pose in private, you may wish to adopt a subtler version of an expansive pose because hands on hips and a wide stance may appear defensive or aggressive rather than open and welcoming. Try doing a strong upward stretch with arms reaching toward the sky or take a deep breath to expand the chest. A confident, open posture can be helpful whether crouching down at eye level with a four-year-old or looking up at a teen. How do you feel?

Ⓟ Conjure up a soothing image—Think of something that evokes a feeling of relaxation: a calm body of water, warm sun on your back, a cat purring on your belly. Experiment with pairing a movement with the image, however subtle. It may be a gentle swaying of your body, placing your hand on your heart, or stroking the back of one hand with the other. Soothing touch taps into what self-compassion guru Kristin Neff calls the mammalian caregiving system, evoking within us feelings of safety and calm (Neff 2011). Notice how your body feels when visualizing with movement. Breathe.

Ⓟ Synchronize movement to breath—Try raising your arms in sync with a slow inhalation and lowering them in sync with an elongated exhalation. Deep breathing, particularly with extended exhalation, signals calm and resets the nervous system, thus lowering heart rate and blood pressure (Radaelli et al. 2004). As you slowly lower your arms, try bringing them down across your chest to give yourself a hug.

Ⓟ Shake out your tension—Literally shake out residual stress with the assistance of upbeat music. Holding onto an object can facilitate movement. Look for "found objects" that swing around (like tissues or streamer wands) or "found sounds" that make noise (like homemade shakers made from plastic Easter eggs or containers filled with rice). Move and shake them up and down, side to side, forward and back, and all around. Try this by yourself or with your children. You may succeed not only in calming yourself but also in breaking them out of their funk, too.

Ⓟ Walk around—Walking facilitates creative thinking, too (Opezzo and Schwartz 2014).

**THE INNOVATIVE PARENT**

It's dark outside, and Ping is behind schedule for bedtime with her two young granddaughters. After a long day that began with sleep deprivation, her patience is being tested by repeated requests for replacement food at dinnertime: "Can I have blueberries instead?". . . ("After dinner.") . . . "And yogurt!". . . ("For dessert.") . . . "And applesauce!". . . ("If you'd rather have that for dessert, that's fine.") . . . "Can I just eat the chicken without the sauce?". . . ("Fine.") . . ."I don't want the snap peas". . . ("You always liked snap peas; just eat two.") . . . "Can I have a carrot instead?" . . . ("Fine.") . . . "Is it time for dessert yet?". . . ("Not until you finish your dinner.") . . . "I want a cheese stick". . . ("Fine.") . . . "Can I have milk?". . . ("Fine.") . . . "Can you make it warm?". . . ("Argh!")

Sensing Ping's frustration, her older granddaughter tenderly asks, "Do you not love us anymore?"

Ping stops in her tracks and runs over to give both girls a kiss and a hug. "Of course I love you. I will always love you."

That was a wake-up call. Children may blame themselves for our lack of self-care. Self-care for the caregiver is equally important for the caregiver and the child.

Typical advice for self-care includes going out for a walk, calling a friend, reading a book, or getting a massage. These may be possible on your birthday but unrealistic on a daily basis. We don't have the time. We feel too guilty. So, instead, we put our needs aside. Multitasking and endless repetitive demands of parenting sap our energy in addition to our ability to concentrate, remain calm, problem-solve, and be creative. We keep going when we are depleted, even at the expense of functioning effectively or feeling good. But self-care doesn't always have to look as we might imagine it.

"I should do more self-care," I hear myself say. Exercise more. Sleep more. Dance. Make art. Why don't I do those things anymore? My excuse: I have children. Translation: no time. One day I decide to do something radical. I turn on music that I like. Not the tolerable modern-folky kids' music that has become my standard daily fare. No. Honest-to-goodness-I-like-this-music type of music. It is a moment of relief. And insight. I realize I need to think more flexibly about self-care. I swap excuses for better-than-nothing-twenty-minute home workouts. I stop fretting about not painting at an easel and begin looking at my world through a creative mindset again, pointing out the dancing colors, light, and shadows I see to my children. I feel more inspired and rejuvenated.

The mindset for innovative parenting applies to self-care. If you try no other activities in this book, give yourself the gift of five to ten minutes to replenish your internal resources with these next activities:

*Tap Into Your Own Inner Artist*

💡 **P** TRY THIS:

Based on an ancient yoga exercise, the Light Stream technique has been used as a tool for relaxation, sleep, and relief from pain (Shapiro 2012). It requires no materials, just a moment of your time to make some "mental art." Find a relaxed position and, if you feel comfortable doing so, close your eyes. Alternatively, you can gaze softly at the floor in front of you. Next, notice how your body currently feels (physically, emotionally, or both). Now, give that feeling a form: What shape would it be? What size? What color and texture? Does it have movement or direction? Visualize this form inside your body. Next, picture a light coming down through the top of your head. Give this light a comforting or soothing color. Watch the light as it comes down through the top of your head, entering your body, and targeting the form. See it go into and around the form. Watch as the light changes the form. Keep watching. Next, visualize the comforting light filling each part of your body: your limbs, your torso, your shoulders, your head. Once you can imagine your body entirely filled with this soothing light, rest there a moment. Open your eyes. How do you feel?

💡 **P** AND TRY THIS:

Do this next activity either by yourself in a quiet place or alongside your children (see fig. 7.3). They can do this, too. Grab a piece of paper and any colorful implements for drawing, such as pencils, crayons, or markers. Roughly draw the outline of a body (or you can print one from online). If this already feels too complicated, trace your hand instead. Next, think of people, pets, things, and activities that rejuvenate you. Choose as many or as few as you'd like. Assign each a color (make a key code on the side to remember which color goes with which person, animal, thing, or activity). Now fill or surround the body or hand shape with the colors you selected, showing how these relationships and experiences affect you. You may draw pictures, use simple lines and shapes, or shade in parts. Consider: How do they fill me? How are they a part of me? Where do I feel them most? How do they change my internal landscape? Once you are done, reflect on your drawing. How did you feel while you worked on it? How do you feel looking at it now? What does this drawing tell you about yourself and what you need?

 family

 friends

deep breath / meditation

exercise

sleep

7.3 Replenish your resources

The creative arts have much to offer in the realm of self-nourishment; yet, for many, the idea of making art evokes feelings of pressure or anxiety. As much as the arts can help fill us up, they can also awaken the inner critic. For this reason, it's worth looking more closely at how to harness the creative arts to relax and recharge.

## RELAX AND RECHARGE

The adult coloring phenomenon is going strong, and I have a standing-room-only crowd at a university-based workshop on the stress-reducing benefits of coloring. I instruct the participants to color for five minutes, using colored pencils on coloring book pages that they select from a large array. After the five minutes are up, I invite them to share their experiences: "Relaxing" . . . "Fun" . . . "Took my mind off of other things." I pause, look around the room, and announce: "Raise your hand if this activity stressed you out." Up goes a sea of hands, to which I respond: "Ahh, good. Let's address that."

Art is commonly thought of as a leisure activity—something done for enjoyment, relaxation, or perhaps distraction. However, benefits of the creative arts have been shown to include improved quality of life, mood, motivation, confidence, coping, sense of well-being, sense of meaning, self-esteem, and ability to focus on positive life experiences. Moreover, engagement in the arts can reduce stress, anxiety, depression, fatigue, and pain (Martin et al. 2018; Puetz, Morley, and Herring 2013; Stuckey and Nobel 2010). The creative arts can facilitate improvement in vital signs and immune function; positive changes in parts of the brain associated with stress, reward, and emotions; earlier discharge among medical patients; and the use of less medication for inducing sleep (Stuckey and Nobel 2010). However, for many, making art may feel anything but beneficial. A lot of people have had negative experiences growing up when they were made to feel ashamed of their art. Directly or indirectly, they got the message that they were not artists and simply stopped making art. Even those who continue to make art, as a hobby or career, may find it difficult to silence the voice of the self-critic. So, while art can bring enjoyment and relaxation, it can also feel like a chore. This is true for all forms of creative expression. It is challenging enough to find time to relax and recharge as a parent, without also having to deal with our inner critic. So, how can we maximize the benefits of the arts when self-judgment is lurking?

Let's return to the scene at the coloring workshop from above.

"What stressed you out about this coloring activity?" I inquire. Hands shoot up: "I didn't know what colors to choose" . . . "I wanted it to be perfect" . . . "I was worried about making a mistake" . . . "It bothers me that it's not finished." I suggest that the participants consider how these thoughts may come up in other areas of life. Art, after all, has a tendency to reveal thought patterns that influence us not only during art making but also in other realms of life. Indeed, their answers confirm this: "Yes, I struggle with making choices" . . . "I tend to be perfectionistic" . . . "I always want things to be done. I'm not very good at being in the process."

"Try this," I say. "We're going to color for another five minutes, but this time let's focus our attention on something pleasurable while coloring. It can be the back and forth movement of your hand. It can be the colors as they brighten up your page. It doesn't matter what it is. Discover one pleasurable part of this experience and focus your attention on that." At the end of the five minutes, I again invite reflection on the experience. The consensus: "Much better!"

When it comes to maximizing the relaxation-inducing potential of the arts, process almost always trumps product. In other words, it's the process of creative expression, rather than how the product looks or sounds, that matters. Research has shown that forty-five minutes of free-choice art making reduces cortisol levels, a marker of stress in the body, regardless of experience or talent (Kaimal, Ray, and Muiz 2016). Thirty to ninety minutes of process-oriented art therapy in hospital settings reduces pain and anxiety, and improves mood, regardless of age, gender, or diagnosis (Shella 2018). How "good" an artist you are, or believe yourself to be, is irrelevant. When you focus on the experience of the process, concerns about making "good art" (or making it "look like something") diminish. The outcome is no longer important. This is a novel experience that is in itself freeing. After all, how often do we get to *not* care about outcomes, results, and products in life?! Moreover, as witnessed in the example above, a focus on the process of creative expression gives us an opportunity to reflect upon thoughts and struggles that occur during art making, so we can gain insight into current life challenges. In groups, this can facilitate meaningful dialogue, empathy, and social connection.

Process-based arts offer a unique opportunity for stress-reduction through mindfulness, fun, and self-expression. Let's look at each of these in turn.

### Mindfulness for self-care

Mindfulness, or the process of focusing awareness on the present moment without judgment, has been widely documented for its emotional, physical, and cognitive health benefits (Grossman et al. 2004). It is commonly nurtured through meditation practice; however, the arts have been increasingly recognized as mindfulness cultivating in their own right. In meditation, the mind may be anchored in the present by focusing on breath or a mantra. In the example above, when my workshop attendees focused on a pleasurable experience while coloring, they were orienting their minds toward the present, rather than engaging in judgmental thinking about the art and future thinking about what it should look like. This was a mindfulness activity disguised as coloring.

Some find art making, movement, music making (like drumming), or music listening to be a more comfortable entry point to mindfulness than formal meditation. You may find that doing something (in a non-doing kind of way) can help quiet the mind and keep it in the present more readily than seated, silent meditative practice can. The combination of focus, relaxation, and skill can open a passageway to being "in a state of flow" or "in the zone," a pleasant experience of full absorption and energy (Csikszentmihalyi 2013). One trick is to find a process-based arts activity that allows you to focus your attention on a specific experience in the present moment, whether it be movement, color, sound, sensation, or another element. Try some of these:

- Experiment with watercolors with no goal in mind—Focus your attention on the colors as they spread or on the movement of your hand and arm. Alternatively, find something that is uniquely pleasurable to you during the experience and focus on that.

- Doodle patterns—Draw a shape. Then break up the shape with straight or curvy lines, creating smaller shapes inside your larger shape. Finally, fill in each smaller shape with a different pattern: dots, scallops, crisscrosses, diamonds, or whatever you'd like. Work spontaneously, focusing on the process rather than the outcome. Avoid erasing. Instead, use every unwanted mark as an inspiration for a new pattern to emerge.

- Rediscover the magic of art—Scribble on a paper towel with different water-based colored markers. Next, drip water on top of the colors for a surprising effect! Focus on the sensations as you dip your fingers into water and allow droplets to fall from your fingertips. Watch intently as the colors spread and transform.

- Color detailed pictures or mandalas—Research supports the premise that coloring mandalas (circles containing geometric patterns) provides an optimal amount of focus for decreasing anxious or other negative thoughts (van der Vennet and Serice 2012). You can draw your own, print them from online, or buy an adult coloring book containing mandalas or other themes, such as oceans, animals, or cities. Some find mandalas more relaxing, due to their abstract nature. Others find pictures more gratifying. Experiment to see what you prefer.

- Meditative drumming—If you don't have a drum, find something in your house that can serve as a drum (e.g., a large plastic container, water jug, or bucket; even a thick pillow will do). Find a quiet place to sit and start a simple rhythm. It's easiest to play if you don't think about what you are doing; just feel it in your body. You may find yourself moving to the beat. Play for five minutes with your eyes closed or while gazing softly at the floor in front of you. Focus on the rhythm, the sensation in your hands, or the movement in your body. Notice also how your rhythm, bodily sensations, breath, or mental state change over time. Are you able to get into a rhythmic "groove"? Do you experience a sense of timelessness? Do you feel more relaxed?

🅿 Listen intently to music without lyrics—Choose a piece of music that you find soothing or relaxing. It can be one with a slow and repetitive rhythm, an orchestral piece, or a nonrhythmic one that creates an atmosphere conducive to meditation and deep relaxation (i.e., ambient music you might hear in a yoga class). Whatever works for you. Get in a comfortable position and listen intently to the sounds and/or rhythms. What instruments do you hear? What do you notice during the silence? How does the music swell and subside in volume? Has your breath changed in any way?

🅿 Move what needs to be moved—Without any planning, move slowly as you discover tight spots that need to be released or stretched. Breathe into those spots and experiment with tiny adjustments of your body to see if you can release the tension. Continue to breathe if you pause to stretch, as holding your breath increases tension. If you prefer, allow the movement to flow slowly and continuously without pausing. Move your body into different positions and in different directions, being sure to explore opposite sides. Experiment with moving as slowly as you can. Use soothing or ambient music if it will support your experience. Do not do anything that feels uncomfortable or that you have been advised to avoid. There is no right or wrong way to do this activity. What do you notice in your body or breath as you do this activity? How do you feel afterward in body, mind, and spirit?

As you paint, doodle, drip, drum, listen, move, or color, your mind will wander. That's just what minds do. When you notice that you're judging, planning, worrying, or entertaining some other thought while engaged in an art activity, try labeling it as "judging," "planning," or "worrying." Then, shift your attention to something about your art (e.g., "red" or "shimmery"). Alternatively, reconnect with the motion that you are making (e.g., "round and round" or "flick, splatter"). This will reconnect your mind to the present moment. Ultimately, the more you train your mind to focus on the present and notice when it's not present, the more you will experience a state of relaxation that will permeate the day.

## Have fun, experiment, and be a kid again

I am leading an art experience for adults on a one-day retreat. "Trace one of your hands. Take a moment to consider what you want to welcome more of into your life. Using magazine images, words, or pictures that you draw, fill in your hand." When the group is finished, I invite them to share their creations. One gentleman holds up his piece, a hand filled with ocean waves and a sun. "Tell us about it," I say. Based on the beach image, I imagine that he will talk about self-care or inviting more calm and relaxation into life. But he doesn't. "Look at the sun!" he says excitedly. "That's how I used to draw suns when I was a kid!" He continues in joyful disbelief, "I can't believe it. This totally took me back! This was really fun."

One way that the arts help us recharge is by allowing us to let go and have fun. With the arts, we can make messes, experiment, and play (things we don't often do as adults, despite their documented emotional and mental benefits). It's an opportunity to be spontaneous when nothing, really, is on the line. This kind of playfulness is serious business for adults because fun activities that focus on experiencing the process rather than achieving a goal help adults deepen connections, strengthen problem-solving skills, and increase creative thinking (Brown and Vaughan 2009). As such, process-based arts are productively unproductive!

Unless an art form is already part of your downtime repertoire, you may find it difficult to choose it over playing with that new app on your phone. Here are some ideas to get started:

**P** Sign up—Register for a dance, poetry, music, improv, or art class. Look into one-time workshops, local clubs, or meet-ups. Consider art forms that have piqued your interest at some point in life (perhaps photography, woodworking, pottery, jewelry making, or flower arranging). Many people benefit from the structure, community support, and time away from home that classes offer.

**P** Daily art challenge—Challenge yourself to make one drawing a day or take one picture a day for thirty days. There are plenty of online "daily art challenge" sites to inspire.

**P** Go back in time—Think back to the types of arts or crafts that you enjoyed doing as a child or teenager. Try something similar. Or draw a picture in the way that you might have drawn in early elementary school years. Recall what and how you used to draw. Perhaps take a moment to recreate that now.

**P** Get down and dirty with your kids—Many of us use those precious moments when the kids are occupied to tidy up the house or check email. Or we may sit back to supervise, taking pleasure in watching our kids enjoy themselves. Many parents rarely jump in. The next time your kids are making art, dancing around to their current favorite song, or drumming on pots and pans, see what it's like to join in the fun.

Back pain, headaches, anxiety, bickering with your partner, snapping at your kids . . . repressed feelings will sooner or later be expressed, often in undesirable ways. Vegging out in front of the TV or computer may relax and distract momentarily, but it won't help get to the core of the issue. Conversely, the arts provide essential opportunities for getting in touch with feelings or needs and expressing them.

Besides warding off unwelcome side effects of accumulated stress, research indicates that expressing yourself is important for cultivating a meaningful life (Baumeister et al. 2013). If you express yourself through art, it doesn't matter whether or not you share it with others. In fact, it need not communicate anything specific at all. Art making can be about authentic self-expression that reflects what is meaningful to you. This, in itself, can be rejuvenating. If this isn't reason enough to take a few moments to try some of the following activities, invite your children to do them with you. Then you can use the excuse that your kids will benefit from them, too.

- **P** Clarify feelings—Use lines, shapes, and color to express how you are feeling right now (or steal some of your kid's Play-Doh and sculpt it). Alternatively, take a photo. Then let the image inspire a poem. Poems need not rhyme. They can be thought of simply as a song without melody or as prose broken up into lines for effect. If you want to write sparingly, try a haiku-like poem. If you prefer more structure, create a poem by cutting out phrases or words that stand out to you from poetry, song lyrics, or text (from magazines, newspapers, or the internet). Assemble and affix them using glue or tape in a meaningful sequence or random pattern. Decorate the page if you wish. Use this process daily to serve as a creative journal of feelings.

- **P** Discharge stress—Think of something that causes you stress. Use pencil and paper to express how it feels through drawing, scribbling, scrunching, or ripping. Think about how your expression of stress reflects how you actually respond to stress.

- **P** What I give. What I receive.—Trace your hand, embellishing it with doodles or cutout images representing all that you give in a day. Next, fill the outside of the hand—the negative space—with things that you receive, want to receive, or want to allow yourself to receive.

- **P** Celebrate life—Research has shown that habitual appreciation for positive aspects of life can facilitate psychological well-being (Davis et al. 2016). Make a flower arrangement with varied colors and textures. Or cut out pictures and words from a magazine to make a collage that represents things in life for which you are grateful.

*Tap Into Your Own Inner Artist*

ⓟ Celebrate yourself—Snap pictures of things that make you feel good and that you wouldn't normally document. Challenge yourself to photograph one thing each day for a week that represents an accomplishment or something that fills you with a sense of pride: your kids, a pile of dishes that you let sit in favor of self-care, your "to do" list with everything crossed off, or a thriving plant on the windowsill. Or the next time you are on the phone or waiting for an appointment, simply doodle your name and decorate it, or take a selfie and have fun embellishing it with a photo-altering app. We are not often, if ever, thanked for our efforts as parents. It's worth taking a moment to acknowledge YOU.

Remember that even brief creative moments to clear the mind, have fun, or self-express can make a profound difference in our efforts to raise connected, happy, and successful children.

You've finally finished this book, after several interruptions calling you to parent duty. You close it and look up. You see clutter on the floor and briefly reimagine the items as time capsule artifacts from this moment in your life. Maybe you smile. Then you hear yelling in the other room. A door slams. Slightly tense, you approach to figure out what the heck is going on and who slammed that door. Maybe you start to hum an upbeat or calming tune, or imagine one that reminds you of the love you have for your children. Or you shake out your arms and stretch to the sky. Change of plan. You detour to get a piece of paper and pen instead.

You don't really know what to draw, as responding to children with art is new to you. You don't have a plan, so maybe you draw a large question mark and slip it under your child's door. Nothing. You tap gently and say, "I notice it's quiet in there. I wonder if you saw what I delivered under the door." Maybe your child opens the door. Maybe your child shoves little torn pieces of what used to be your question mark back under the door to you. You resist feeling rejected, understanding this gesture is communicating a need—even if you're unsure *what* the need is. You respond with a gesture of connection. You take one of those little torn pieces and draw a heart, and pass it back under . . .

Welcome to the creative world of innovative parenting. Thank you for being here.

# Epilogue

Unlike any other mind/body practice:
… the arts enable us to express what is within, even when words are not possible.
… the arts connect us to others in a way that feels organic and safe.
… the arts enhance positive emotions as well as reducing negative ones.
… the arts are accessible to all.

Can we get these benefits from just singing, dancing, acting, drawing, and writing? Yes *and* No.

This book contains strategies that integrate the arts with mental health practices, such as the language of nonjudgment to facilitate connection, self-expression, reflection, and insight. This approach enhances the social, emotional, and cognitive benefits of the arts, while preventing unintended consequences, such as anxiety, self-judgment, and excessive vulnerability.

Why is this important?

This approach to the arts can sustainably address issues that affect the public broadly, such as those related to trauma, end-of-life, chronic pain, loneliness, and intolerance.

Let's take trauma, for example.

An estimated 15 to 27 percent of the public has experienced some form of emotional, physical, or sexual abuse (Chiu et al. 2013). And nearly two-thirds of our population reports a childhood experience of at least one adverse event (abuse, neglect, or household dysfunction/violence), which can negatively affect health, mental health, and achievement across the lifespan (Anda et al. 2006; Felitti et al. 1998).

According to trauma expert Bessel van der Kolk (2014): "Trauma almost invariably involves not being seen, nor being mirrored, and not being taken into account. Children will go to almost any length to feel seen and connected."

The arts enable us to be seen and connected.

Every national tragedy involving violence underscores the need for innovative programs that build social, emotional, and cognitive skills, for prevention and healing. The arts allow individual expression within the context of community. Their nonverbal element makes them accessible to persons of diverse backgrounds and abilities. The process of creative expression reveals unconscious information that,

**181**

when reflected upon, can facilitate meaningful dialogue, empathy, social connection, and emotional well-being.

A study that followed 753 kindergartners into early adulthood found that greater social-emotional competence (such as the ability to consider the needs of others, manage feelings, solve problems with peers, cope with disappointment, and focus) predicted greater educational attainment, employment, and mental health, and less substance abuse, involvement in crime, and use of public assistance—regardless of gender, race, number of parents in the home, socioeconomic status, early childhood aggression, early academic ability, and other factors (Jones, Greenberg, and Crowley 2015).

*The Innovative Parent* aims to empower the public with tools, rooted in the field of creative arts therapies, for addressing myriad challenges faced by children and teens.

Moreover, this book offers creative approaches to self-care for adults. Thus, it is intended as a gift for all.

# Appendix 1

*Guidelines for Talking about Art and Life*

The following guidelines have been modeled throughout this book and have been consolidated here, with additional examples, for convenient reference. Art is a metaphor for life, so as you practice effective language in the process of art making to encourage self-expression, exploration, reflection, creative thinking, and even setting limits, you are honing communication skills for other areas of life—with children *and* adults. And guess what? Your children will learn these skills from you, too.

## MAKE NONJUDGMENTAL OBSERVATIONS

Nonjudgmental observations open communication, foster connection, encourage creativity, and prevent resistance. A nonjudgmental observation remarks on something that is observable, without interpretations, assumptions, or value judgments—whether positive or negative. A judgment-free observation often begins with "I see" or "I notice," followed by a specific, observable action. For example:

| Recommended | Not Recommended |
|---|---|
| *Nonjudgmental or neutral statements about that which is literally observable, beginning with "I see" or "I notice."* | *Judgmental statements involving interpretation, assumptions, or value judgments—either positive or negative.* |
| "I notice you're not touching the clay." | "You don't want to do this activity?" <br><br> *This discourages participation and problem-solving.* |
| "I see you're drawing lots of circles." | "What's *that* supposed to be?" <br><br> "Is it a _____?" <br><br> *This communicates that art has to look like something and that self-expression itself is not enough. It discourages creativity.* |
| "I notice a lot of colors in this corner." | "I like it. That's beautiful." <br><br> *This inhibits further dialogue. It can set up performance expectations and anxiety, or disconnection if the artist does not agree. It can also be construed as meaningless if overused.* |

| Recommended *(cont.)* | Not Recommended *(cont.)* |
|---|---|
| "I see you ripping up your paper." | "You're ruining your beautiful art!" <br><br> *This is a judgment about the art (it's beautiful) and what is happening to it (it's getting ruined). Thus, it may stifle creativity, self-expression, and communication, while provoking resistance.* |

## EXPRESS CURIOSITY

Sometimes a nonjudgmental observation is enough to spark a reply. At other times, you may want to follow up with a statement of curiosity beginning with "I wonder . . ." This is a nonthreatening way to make an inquiry because it does not suggest any conclusions have been reached. For example:

| Recommended |
|---|
| "I wonder what you're going to do next?" <br> *This encourages independent decision-making and engagement.* |
| "I wonder what your plan was when you started?" <br> *This strengthens problem solving and planning.* |
| "I wonder if you would like to try that?" <br> *This invites participation, engagement, and creative risk taking.* |
| "I wonder if you can tell me more about this?" <br> *This encourages reflection and dialogue.* |
| "I wonder what happened?" <br> *This teaches that events precede feelings which, in turn, encourages problem solving and development of coping skills. Unlike statements like "I wonder why you're angry?" or "I wonder what's wrong?" it does not interpret how a child may be feeling or assume that anything is wrong.* |
| "I wonder what made you decide to do that?" <br> *This encourages reasoning skills.* |

## ENCOURAGE PREFERRED QUALITIES

Nonjudgmental observations can also be used to encourage preferred qualities. This kind of "praise" reinforces useful skills that will carry over to other activities. Children benefit from praise that is accurate, is specific, and addresses behavior over which they have control (e.g., effort) rather than traits (e.g., intelligence). For example:

| Recommended | Not Recommended |
| --- | --- |
| "I notice you are focused. I see you have finished most of your music practice." <br><br> *This observation reinforces the effort (to focus) and links that behavior to the completion of a task.* | "Good job getting your music practice done." <br><br> *This statement emphasizes only the outcome of the effort and not the behavior required to achieve it.* |
| "I noticed your sister had a big smile when you said you would share your paints." <br><br> *This observation teaches how the action (of sharing) makes someone else feel and specific enough for the child to feel truly seen and heard.* | "I'm proud of you for sharing." <br><br> *This statement does not connect the action (of sharing) with how it makes someone else feel; therefore, it may not reinforce subsequent sharing as effectively. Also, it reinforces the need for approval rather than intrinsic rewards from sharing.* |

Of course, we may occasionally notice ourselves saying, "Good job," "I'm proud of you," or "I like it." When that happens, just add a specific observation to reinforce effort and/or behavior afterward. For example: "Good job . . . You solved the problem, and you did it all by yourself!"

## PREVENT POWER STRUGGLES

Simple shifts in our choice of words can help our children be more receptive to our communication. The use of "Let's," "AND," and "What's your plan?" removes the power differential in our language and encourages cooperation. For example:

| Recommended | Not Recommended |
| --- | --- |
| "Let's clean up now." <br><br> *"Let's" is inclusive and nonthreatening.* | "I want you to clean up now." <br><br> "I need you to clean up now." <br><br> *"I want you to" and "I need you to" suggest a power differential that may invite resistance.* |
| *Context: Child has stated that an activity is boring.* <br><br> "I hear that you find this activity boring AND how might you make it more meaningful to you?" <br><br> *"And" validates the perspective of the other person. This response encourages engagement, creative thinking, problem solving, and connection.* | *Context: Child has stated that an activity is boring.* <br><br> "I hear that you find this activity boring, BUT you have to do it." <br><br> *"But" negates the perspective of the other person and has authoritarian overtones that may trigger resistance. Moreover, it discourages ownership of the decision to participate meaningfully.* |

*Guidelines for Talking about Art and Life*

| Recommended *(cont.)* | Not Recommended *(cont.)* |
|---|---|
| "What was your plan?" | "Why did you do that?!" |
| *"What" (and "How") elicit more information because questions starting with these words usually cannot be answered with a simple "Yes" or "No."* | *"Why" implies disapproval, which might inhibit creative expression and may provoke anxiety, self-judgment, resentment, or resistance. Moreover, children (or adults) often don't know why they have done something. The question may be difficult to answer or lead to falsehoods.* |
| *"What was your plan?" encourages engagement, critical thinking, problem solving, and connection.* | |

## REMEMBER BEHAVIOR IS COMMUNICATION

The vast majority—93 percent—of communication is nonverbal: tone of voice and body language, including facial expressions, gestures, posture, and eye contact (Mehrabian 1981). When we seek to understand and address the underlying needs expressed by undesirable behavior, rather than focusing on limits and consequences alone, we can promote connection, teach self-regulation, and change behavior more effectively in the future.

The following guidelines for identifying underlying needs are based on a hypothetical scenario in which a child has been found drawing on the underside of a table. A typical adult response might be a rant like: "Why did you do that? You know you're not supposed to write on the table! Now I have to clean it up. You're going to lose a privilege."

Instead, try these steps:

| Steps to Identifying and Addressing Underlying Needs | Examples |
|---|---|
| 1. State what you see (start with "I see" or "I notice"): | "I see you drawing on the table." <br><br> *This nonjudgmental observation, when spoken neutrally or with curiosity, minimizes defensiveness and keeps lines of communication open.* |
| 2. Inquire about underlying needs (start with "I wonder"): | "I wonder what made you decide to draw on the table?" <br><br> *"I wonder" orients the child toward curiosity about her own behavior. It promotes self-reflection.* |
| 3. Suggest possible underlying needs: | Curiosity: "Did you wonder what it would look like?" <br><br> Attention: "Did you need my attention?" <br><br> Upset: "Did something happen?" <br><br> *Younger children may need help identifying underlying needs. While older children and teens may find it easier to identify what they need, they may still benefit from assistance.* |

| Steps to Identifying and Addressing Underlying Needs *(cont.)* | Examples *(cont.)* |
|---|---|
| 4. Find alternatives that respect limits (start with "What" or "How"): | Curiosity: "How can we experiment without drawing on furniture?" |
| | Attention: "How can you get my attention without drawing on furniture?" |
| | Upset: "What are some ways to express your feelings or feel better without drawing on furniture?" |
| | *If ideas are not forthcoming, then offer alternatives:* |
| | Curiosity: "What about gathering different materials to experiment with?" |
| | Attention: "How about asking me to stop what I'm doing so we can spend time together?" |
| | Upset: "What if we tape a large piece of paper to the door for expressing your feelings?" |
| | *Help your child put the alternative into action to meet his need.* |
| 5. Teach responsibility taking and natural consequences (start with "Let's"): | "Let's use this sponge to clean off the marker. *Then* we can experiment with drawing on other materials." |
| | "Let's clean this up. *Then* you can do something else." |
| | *If there is resistance or refusal to help:* |
| | "I see you're not ready to clean it yet. Let me know when you're ready. When the table is clean, you can play." |
| | *So as not to initiate a power struggle, remember the formula for staying positive: When X, then Y. ("When the table is clean, you can play.")* |

For repeat offenses by children or teens, address the underlying needs and provide more structure, limits, or consequences. Consider making the items in question (markers or scissors or whatnot) available only under supervision (e.g., "Let's put the markers in another place. When you want to use them, I can get them for you."). Work together to create a plan to prevent repeat occurrences.

## SET LIMITS FOR SELF-CARE

Limits are important for safety, practical reasons, and also for our own self-care. They teach skills such as consideration of others, awareness of time constraints, and ability to handle setbacks and disappointments. It's okay to let children know when something isn't working for you and why. For example:

**188**     Scenario 1: Your child is pulling out the paints, and you both need to leave soon.

| Steps to Setting Limits | Examples |
|---|---|
| 1. Affirm the activity: | "I see you have a creative idea." |
| 2. Take responsibility: | "Unfortunately, painting doesn't work for me right now." |
| 3. Give your reason: | "It takes a lot of cleanup, and we need to be out the door in ten minutes." |
| 4. Explore alternatives: | • Encourage problem solving: "What can we do to solve this?"<br>• Offer an alternative time or place: "You can paint as soon as we get home. Let's leave this all set up so it's ready for you when we get back."<br>• Offer a different activity: "You can draw until we leave, instead."<br>• Adapt the activity: "You have five minutes to paint before we need to clean up, so let's start with one color and one brush right now." |

Scenario 2: Your child is singing loudly in the car.

| Steps to Setting Limits | Examples |
|---|---|
| 1. Affirm the activity: | "It sounds like you've learned a new song." |
| 2. Take responsibility: | "Unfortunately, singing loudly in the car doesn't work for me right now." |
| 3. Give your reason: | "I'm tired and need to concentrate on my driving." |
| 4. Explore alternatives: | • Encourage problem solving: "What can we do to solve this?"<br>• Offer an alternative time or place: "You can sing as loudly as you want as soon as we get home."<br>• Offer a different activity: "How about finding shapes in the clouds instead?"<br>• Adapt the activity: "Maybe you can sing more quietly or sing it in your head." |

No matter how much of this language we master, what counts most is our body language and tone of voice (Mehrabian 1981). Children may feel unsettled or provoked by a discrepancy between our words, tone of voice, and body language. And all of these may be difficult to control when we are tired or overwhelmed. Therefore, self-care is essential. (Refer to self-care strategies offered in chapter 7: "Tap Into Your Own Inner Artist.")

*Appendix 1*

# Appendix 2

*Supplies to Get Started*

The activities in this book are designed to require few or no special materials. Most drawing activities can be done with a piece of paper and pen or pencil. However, you may choose to acquire a wider variety of materials to use. This list can get you started:

## BASIC SUPPLIES

Drawing utensils: pencils, pens, markers, colored pencils, crayons

Paper

## ADDITIONAL SUPPLIES

Drums (or plastic buckets, or five-gallon water jugs, or plastic containers with lids on which to drum)

Fabric, pipe cleaners, yarn, puff balls

Found objects, rocks, boxes, cardboard tubes from paper towel rolls

Magazines, glue or glue dots, scissors

Masking and cellophane tape

Paper in a variety of colors and sizes

Scarves and costumes to enhance movement-based activities

Shakers (or plastic Easter eggs or small storage containers, filled with rice)

Smart phone or camera to take pictures

Water-based paint and paintbrushes

Modeling clay or other sculpting material

Boxes, bins, or tubs for quick cleanup and supply storage

Hand wipes and paper towels

Larger sheets of paper to place under smaller pieces of paper

Paper plates or cardboard to place under projects

Sheets, newspaper, or paper bags to cover surfaces

# Appendix 3

*Where to Put All That Art*

Keeping art is a valuable way to communicate how special your child is to you, yet you can't possibly keep it all. What to do?

## WEAR YOUR FEELINGS ON YOUR SLEEVE

Let your child know that you wish you could save everything he does, but sadly you can't. Saying this with feeling can take the sting out of it for your child. Also, your child can be the problem solver. Ask: "Since we want to save this, and we don't have room, what can we do to remember it?"

## LET YOUR CHILD CHOOSE

Help build decision-making skills by having your child choose pieces that are particularly meaningful to her to be saved. Make or purchase a portfolio or plastic container in which you will store them, and into which you can add things each month. Date the art pieces on their backs. With more time comes greater objectivity in the selection process.

## PHOTOGRAPH IT

Consider memorializing through digital photographs. Invite your child to do the documenting. If you are so inclined, you can design and print a book of your child's art from the photos taken.

## REPURPOSE IT

Use art destined for the recycle bin to inspire a new project. Cut out drawings and glue them onto blank cards, ornaments, or packages. Use large sheets of artwork to wrap a gift. Cut strips to create a paper chain. Cut out geometric or other shapes from paintings and glue them onto a canvas to create an entirely new piece of art. Transfer old drawings onto a T-shirt or pillowcase, using fabric markers or iron-on transfer sheets. Or use disposable art to decorate the inside of a cardboard box house.

## MAKE DESTRUCTION FUN

Smashing a sandcastle when it's time to leave can be even more exciting than building it in the first place. Brainstorm options for how to dismantle large sculptures: "It's time to take this down. How do you want to do it? Do you want to take a flying ninja leap at it? Or try to knock it down by rolling a ball at it?"

## BE PROACTIVE

Let your child know up front that he can work as large as he'd like but that, depending on how big it gets, you may not be able to save it. Remind him that you can photograph it before dismantling it or keep it up until the end of the day (or week) before taking it down. Offer more than one acceptable option so that your child has a sense of control over the situation: "Do you want to leave it up until tonight or do you want to leave it up until tomorrow after school?"

# Appendix 4

*A Word on the Creative Arts Therapies*

The information contained in this book draws from the professional domain of the creative arts therapies.

The creative arts therapies emerged as academic disciplines and professional practices in the mid-twentieth century.

Art Therapy, Music Therapy, and Psychodrama (1940s)

Dance Movement Therapy (1960s)

Drama Therapy (1970s)

Poetry Therapy (1981)

All of these fields are represented by national organizations, which are, in turn, represented by the National Coalition of Creative Arts Therapies Associations.

The creative arts therapies expand possibilities for health care because they can be delivered in a variety of settings and in groups.

## WHAT DO CREATIVE ARTS THERAPISTS DO?

Creative arts therapists are mental health professionals dually trained in the arts. They use creative processes to assess needs and develop individualized treatment plans for disability and illness, health and wellness. Their work often emphasizes reflection on the process of creative expression to facilitate the emergence of personally derived meaning. These are the major distinctions between creative arts therapists and others who may use the arts for therapeutic benefits.

## HOW DOES ONE BECOME A CREATIVE ARTS THERAPIST?

Becoming a creative arts therapist typically involves master's level accredited training (although there are some BA and PhD pathways). The curriculum involves mental health, arts, and professional practice theory and competencies. Training also involves supervised clinical internships and adherence to a strict code of ethics and standards. Creative arts therapists can also be registered, board certified, and/or licensed through supervised experience, examinations, and continuing education.

## WHAT IS UNIQUE ABOUT CREATIVE ARTS THERAPISTS?

Creative arts therapists are well suited to addressing a broad array of problems that are difficult to identify and/or treat. Below is a sample list:

Abuse and domestic violence

Acute and chronic pain

Alzheimer's disease and dementia

Anxiety, depression, and mood disorders

Autism

Community building

Developmental and learning disabilities

Eating disorders and body image

Elderly-related concerns and conditions

Family and relationship issues

Grief and loss

Hearing, visual, and speech impairment

Infant-parent bonding

Medical conditions—such as cancer, AIDS, Parkinson's, neonatal intensive care

Mental illness

Personal development, wellness and prevention

Prevention of behavior problems in at-risk youth

Stress management

Substance abuse and addictions

Terminal illness

Trauma and post-traumatic stress disorder

Traumatic brain injury and stroke

You can check the websites for or contact any of the following national organizations:

American Art Therapy Association

American Dance Therapy Association

American Music Therapy Association

American Society of Group Psychotherapy and Psychodrama

International Expressive Arts Therapy Association

National Association for Poetry Therapy

National Coalition of Creative Arts Therapies Associations

North American Drama Therapy Association

UCLArts & Healing

# References

Adams, M., S. Foutz, J. Luke, and J. Stein. 2006. "Thinking through Art." *Isabella Stewart Gardner Museum School Partnership Program, Year Three Preliminary Research Results*.

Adler, J., and H. Hershfield. 2012. "Mixed Emotional Experience Is Associated with and Precedes Improvements in Psychological Well-Being." *PLoS ONE* 7 (4): e35633.

Alfono, E. 2013. "Does Business Need the Arts to Be Innovative? Five Executives Weigh In." *Huffington Post*. Updated December 6, 2017.

Allen K., L. Gloden, J. L. Izzo Jr., M. Ching, A. Forrest, C. Niles, P. Niswander, and J. Barlow. 2001. "Normalization of Hypertensive Responses During Ambulatory Surgical Stress by Perioperative Music." *Psychosomatic Medicine* 63:487–92.

American Psychological Association Task Force on Violent Media. 2017. "The American Psychological Association Task Force Assessment of Violent Video Games: Science in the Service of Public Interest." *American Psychologist* 72 (2): 126–43.

American Psychological Association Zero Tolerance Task Force. 2008. "Are Zero Tolerance Policies Effective in the Schools?" *American Psychologist* 63 (9): 852–62.

Ames, L. B., and F. Ilg. 1989. *Your Four-Year-Old*. New York: Dell Publishing.

Anda, R. F., V. J. Felitti, J. D. Bremner, J. D. Walker, C. Whitfield, B. Perry, S. R. Dube, and W. H. Giles. 2006. "The Enduring Effects of Abuse and Related Adverse Experiences in Childhood: A Convergence of Evidence from Neurobiology and Epidemiology." *European Archives of Psychiatry and Clinical Neuroscience* 256 (3): 174–86.

Anderson, C., and B. Bushman. 2001. "Effects of Violent Video Games on Aggressive Behavior, Aggressive Cognition, Aggressive Affect, Physiological Arousal, and Prosocial Behavior: A Meta-analytic Review of the Scientific Literature." *Psychological Science* 12 (5): 353–59.

Andrade, J. 2010. "What Does Doodling Do?" *Applied Cognitive Psychology* 24 (1): 100–06.

Anshel, A., and D. Kipper. 1988. "The Influence of Group Singing on Trust and Cooperation." *Journal of Music Therapy* 25 (3):145–55.

Anxiety UK. 2012. *Anxiety UK Study Finds Technology Can Increase Anxiety*. https://www.anxietyuk.org.uk/for-some-with-anxiety-technology-can-increase-anxiety/.

Ariga, A., and A. Lleras. 2011. "Brief and Rare Mental 'Breaks' Keep You Focused: Deactivation and Reactivation of Task Goals Preempt Vigilance Decrements." *Cognition* 118 (3): 439–43.

**198** Asbury, C., and B. Rich, eds. 2008. *Learning, Arts, and the Brain: The Dana Consortium Report on Arts and Cognition*. New York/Washington: Dana Press.

Azzam, A. 2009. "Why Creativity Now? A Conversation with Sir Ken Robinson." *Teaching for the 21st Century* 67 (1): 22–26.

Baumeister, R. F., K. D. Vohs, J. L. Aaker, and E. N. Garbinsky. 2013. "Some Key Differences between a Happy Life and a Meaningful Life." *Journal of Positive Psychology* 8 (6): 505–16.

Baumrind, D. 1966. "Effects of Authoritative Parental Control on Child Behavior." *Child Development* 37 (4): 887–907.

Bennett, M. P., J. M. Zeller, L. Rosenberg, and J. McCann. 2003. "The Effect of Mirthful Laughter on Stress and Natural Killer Cell Activity." *Alternative Therapies in Health and Medicine* 9 (2): 38–45.

Benson, H. 2009. *The Relaxation Response*. New York: HarperCollins.

Beres, A., Z. Lelovics, P. Antal, G. Hajos, A. Gezsi, A. Czeh, E. Lantos, and T. Major. 2011. "Does Happiness Help Healing? Immune Response of Hospitalized Children May Change during Visits of the Smiling Hospital Foundation's Artists." *Orvosi Hetilap* 152 (43): 1739–44.

Berman, R. 2014. *Permission to Parent*. New York: HarperCollins.

Bethune, S. 2014. "Teen Stress Rivals That of Adults." *American Psychological Association* 45 (4): 20.

Bittman, B. B., L. S. Berk, D. L. Felten, J. Westengard, O. C. Simonton, J. Pappas, and M. Ninehouser. 2001. "Composite Effects of Group Drumming Music Therapy on Modulation of Neuroendocrine-Immune Parameters in Normal Subjects." *Alternative Therapies in Health and Medicine* 7 (1): 38–47.

Bittman, B. B., L. Dickson, and K. Coddington. 2009. "Creative Musical Expression as a Catalyst for Quality-of-Life Improvement in Inner-City Adolescents Placed in a Court-Referred Residential Treatment Program." *Advances in Mind-Body Medicine* 24 (1): 8–19.

Blair, C., and C. C. Raver. 2014. "Closing the Achievement Gap through Modification of Neurocognitive and Neuroendocrine Function: Results from a Cluster Randomized Controlled Trial of an Innovative Approach to the Education of Children in Kindergarten." *PLoS ONE* 9 (11): e112393.

Blood, A., and R. Zatorre. 2001. "Intensely Pleasurable Responses to Music Correlate with Activity in Brain Regions Implicated in Reward and Emotion." *Proceedings of the National Academy of Sciences of the United States of America* 98 (20): 11818–23.

Bodrova, E., and D. Leong. 2006. *Tools of the Mind: The Vygotskian Approach to Early Childhood Education*. 2nd ed. New York: Pearson.

Bornstein, R. 1997. *That's How It Is When We Draw*. New York: Clarion Books.

Bower, G. 1970. "Imagery as Relational Organizer in Associative Learning." *Journal of Verbal Learning and Verbal Behavior* 9:529–33.

Bradberry, T., and J. Greaves. 2009. *Emotional Intelligence 2.0*. San Diego, CA: TalentSmart.

Bransford, J., A. Brown, and R. Cocking, eds. 2000. *How People Learn: Brain, Mind, Experience, and School*. Washington, DC: National Academies Press.

Bronson, P., and A. Merryman. 2009. *Nurture Shock: New Thinking about Children.*
New York: Hachette.

Brouillette, L., and W. Fitzgerald. 2009. "Arts-Based Experiences as Preparation for Future Learning." *Arts & Learning Research Journal* 25 (1): 68–86.

Brown, E., and K. Sax. 2013. "Arts Enrichment and Preschool Emotions for Low-Income Children at Risk." *Early Childhood Research Quarterly* 28 (2): 337–46.

Brown, S., R. Nesse, A. Vinokur, and D. Smith. 2003. "Providing Social Support May Be More Beneficial Than Receiving It." *Psychological Science* 14 (4): 320–27.

Brown, S., and C. Vaughan. 2009. *Play: How It Shapes the Brain, Opens Imagination, and Invigorates the Soul.* New York: Penguin.

Burkland, L., J. D. Creswell, M. Irwin, and M. Lieberman. 2014. "The Common and Distinct Neural Bases of Affect Labeling and Reappraisal in Healthy Adults." *Frontiers in Psychology* 5:221.

Burton, J. M., R. Horowitz, and H. Abeles. 2000. "Learning in and through the Arts: The Question of Transfer." *Studies in Art Education* 41 (3): 228–57.

Bushman, B., R. Baumeister, and A. Stack. 1999. "Catharsis, Aggression, and Persuasive Influence: Self-Fulfilling or Self-Defeating Prophecies?" *Journal of Personality and Social Psychology* 76 (3): 367–76.

Capaldi, C., R. Dopko, and J. Zelenski. 2014. "The Relationship between Nature Connectedness and Happiness: A Meta-Analysis." *Frontiers in Psychology* 5:976.

Carney, D., A. Cuddy, and A. Yap. 2010. "Power Posing: Brief Nonverbal Displays Affect Neuroendocrine Levels and Risk Tolerance." *Psychological Science* 21 (10): 1362–68.

———. 2015. "Review and Summary of Research on the Embodied Effects of Expansive (vs. Contractive) Nonverbal Displays." *Psychological Science* 26 (5): 657–63.

Carr, K. W., T. White-Schwoch, A. T. Tierney, D. L. Strait, and N. Kraus. 2014. "Beat Synchronization Predicts Neural Speech Encoding and Reading Readiness in Preschoolers." *Proceedings of the National Academy of Sciences* 111 (40): 14559–64.

Carretie, L., F. Mercado, M. Tapia, and J. Hinojosa. 2001. "Emotion, Attention, and the 'Negativity Bias,' Studied through Event-Related Potentials." *International Journal of Psychophysiology* 41 (1): 75–85.

Carter, C. 2008. "Happiness Is Being Socially Connected." *Greater Good Magazine: Science-Based Insights for a Meaningful Life*, October 31, 2008.

Catterall, J. 2005. "Conversation and Silence: Transfer of Learning through the Arts." *Learning through the Arts: A Research Journal on Arts Integration in School and Communities* 1 (1): 1–12.

Center on the Developing Child, Harvard University. 2009. *Five Numbers to Remember about Early Childhood Development* (Brief).

Chand O'Neal, I. 2014. *Selected Findings from the John F. Kennedy Center's Arts in Education Research Study: An Impact Evaluation of Arts-Integrated Instruction through the Changing Education Through the Arts (CETA) Program.* Washington, DC: The John F. Kennedy Center for the Performing Arts.

Chartrand, T. L., and J. Bargh. 1999. "The Chameleon Effect: The Perception-Behavior Link and Social Interaction." *Journal of Personality and Social Psychology* 76 (6): 893–910.

200  Chiu, G. R., K. E. Lutfey, H. J. Litman, C. L. Link, S. A. Hall, and J. B. McKinlay. 2013. "Prevalence and Overlap of Childhood and Adult Physical, Sexual, and Emotional Abuse: A Descriptive Analysis of Results from the Boston Area Community Health (BACH) Survey." *Violence and Victims* 28 (3): 381–402.

Chopra, D. 2005. *Magical Beginnings, Enchanted Lives: A Holistic Guide to Pregnancy and Childbirth.* New York: Random House.

Christie, W., and C. Moore. 2005. "The Impact of Humor on Patients with Cancer." *Clinical Journal of Oncology Nursing* 9 (2): 211–18.

Cigna. 2018. *Cigna U.S. Loneliness Index: Survey of 20,000 Americans Examining Behaviors Driving Loneliness in the United States.* https://www.cigna.com/assets/docs/newsroom/loneliness-survey-2018-full-report.pdf.

Cohen, L. 2002. *Playful Parenting.* New York: Random House.

Cole, S., J. Capitanio, K. Chun, J. Arevalo, J. Ma, and J. Cacioppo. 2015. "Myeloid Differentiation Architecture of Leukocyte Transcriptome Dynamics in Perceived Social Isolation." *Proceedings of the National Academy of Sciences* 112 (49): 15142–47.

Colt, G. H. 2012. "Sibling Rivalry: One Long Food Fight." *New York Times*, November 24, 2012.

Conner, J., D. Pope, and M. Galloway. 2010. "Success with Less Stress." *Health and Learning* 67 (4): 54–58.

Cook, S., R. Duffy, and K. Fenn. 2013. "Consolidation and Transfer of Learning after Observing Hand Gesture." *Child Development* 84 (6): 1863–71.

Cook, S., T. Yip, and S. Goldin-Meadow. 2010. "Gesturing Makes Memories That Last." *Journal of Memory and Language* 63 (4): 465–75.

Crocker, J. 2002. "The Cost of Seeking Self-Esteem." *Journal of Social Issues* 58 (3): 597–615.

Cruwys, T., S. A. Haslam, G. A. Dingle, J. Jetten, M. J. Hornsey, E. M. Desdemona Chong, and T. P. S. Oei. 2014. "Feeling Connected Again: Interventions That Increase Social Identification Reduce Depression Symptoms in Community and Clinical Settings." *Journal of Affective Disorders* 159:139–46.

Csikszentmihalyi, M. 1990. *Flow: The Psychology of Optimal Experience.* New York: HarperCollins.

———. 2013. *Flow: The Psychology of Happiness.* London: Ebury.

Cuddy, A. 2012. "Your Body Language Shapes Who You Are." *TEDGlobal*, June 2012. https://www.ted.com/talks/amy_cuddy_your_body_language_shapes_who_you_are.

Cuddy, A., S. J. Schultz, and N. Fosse. 2018. "P-Curving a More Comprehensive Body of Research on Postural Feedback Reveals Clear Evidential Value for Power-Posing Effects: Reply to Simmons and Simonsohn (2017)." *Sage Journals* 29 (4): 656–66.

Cuddy, A. J. C., C. A. Wilmuth, and D. R. Carney. 2012. "The Benefit of Power Posing before a High-Stakes Social Evaluation." *Harvard Business School Working Paper* 13-027.

Curva, F., S. Milton, S. Wood, D. Palmer, C. Nahmias, B. Radcliffe, E. Fogartie, and T. Youngblood. 2005. *Artful Citizenship Project: Three-Year Project Report.* Tallahassee, FL: The Wolfsonian.

Davis, D. E., E. Choe, J. Meyers, N. Wade, K. Varjas, A. Gifford, A. Quinn, J. N. **201** Hook, D. R. Van Tongeren, B. J. Griffin, and E. L. Worthington Jr. 2016. "Thankful for the Little Things: A Meta-analysis of Gratitude Interventions." *Journal of Counseling Psychology* 63 (1): 20–31.

Davis, W. B. 2003. "Ira Maximilian Altshuler: Psychiatrist and Pioneer Music Therapist." *Journal of Music Therapy* 40 (3): 247–63.

Dingfelder, S. 2010. "How Artists See." *American Psychological Association* 41 (2): 40.

Dissanayake, E. 1992. *Homo Aestheticus: Where Art Comes from and Why.* New York: Free Press.

Docter, R., and R. del Carmen (directors). 2015. *Inside Out.* Pixar, Walt Disney Productions.

Dresler, M., W. Shirer, B. Konrad, N. Muller, I. Wagner, G. Fernandez, M. Czisch, and M. Greicius. 2017. "Mnemonic Training Reshapes Brain Networks to Support Superior Memory." *Neuron* 93 (5): 1227–35.

Dunn, E., L. Aknin, and M. Norton. 2008. "Spending Money on Others Promotes Happiness." *Science* 319 (5870): 1687–88.

Dunn, R., A. Honigsfeld, L. Shea Doolan, L. Bostrom, K. Russo, M. Schiering, B. Suh, and H. Tenedero. 2009. "Impact of Learning-Style Instructional Strategies on Students' Achievement and Attitudes: Perceptions of Educators in Diverse Institutions." *The Clearing House: A Journal of Educational Strategies, Issues and Ideas* 82 (3): 135–40.

Dunning, D., K. Johnson, J. Ehrlinger, and J. Kruger. 2003. "Why People Fail to Recognize Their Own Incompetence." *Current Directions in Psychological Science* 12 (3): 83–87.

Dweck, C. 2006. *Mindset: The New Psychology of Success.* New York: Ballantine Books.
———. 2012. *Mindset: How You Can Fulfill Your Potential.* London: Constable and Robinson.

Einstein, A., and L. Infeld. 1938. *The Evolution of Physics: The Growth of Ideas from Early Concepts to Relativity and Quanta.* New York: Simon and Schuster.

Fancourt, D., R. Perkins, S. Ascenso, L. Carvalho, A. Steptoe, and A. Williamon. 2016. "Effects of Group Drumming Interventions on Anxiety, Depression, Social Resilience and Inflammatory Immune Response Among Mental Health Users." *PLoS ONE* 11 (3): e0151136.

Feeney, J. A. 2000. "Implications of Attachment Style for Patterns of Health and Illness." *Child: Care, Health, and Development* 26 (4): 277–88.

Felitti, V. J., R. F. Anda, D. Nordenberg, D. F. Williamson, A. M. Spitz, V. Edwards, M. P. Koss, and J. S. Marks. 1998. "Relationship of Childhood Abuse and Household Dysfunction to Many of the Leading Causes of Death in Adults: The Adverse Childhood Experiences (ACE) Study." *American Journal of Preventive Medicine* 14 (4): 245–58.

Fenske, M. 2012. "Why Does Music Motivate Us?" *Globe and Mail*, February 1, 2012.

Fosse, N. 2016. "Replication Data for 'Power Posing: Brief Nonverbal Displays Affect Neuroendocrine Levels and Risk Tolerance' by Carney, Cuddy, Yap (2010)." *Harvard Dataverse* 3.

**202**  Frattaroli, J. 2006. "Experimental Disclosure and Its Moderators: A Meta-Analysis." *Psychological Bulletin* 132 (6): 823–65.

Froh, J., T. Kashdan, K. Ozimkowski, and N. Miller. 2009. "Who Benefits the Most from a Gratitude Intervention in Children and Adolescents? Examining Positive Affect as a Moderator." *Journal of Positive Psychology* 4 (5): 408–22.

Froh, J., W. Sefick, and R. Emmons. 2007. "Counting Blessings in Early Adolescents: An Experimental Study of Gratitude and Subjective Well-Being." *Journal of School Psychology* 46 (2008): 213–33.

Geary, J. 2011. *I as an Other: The Secret Life of Metaphor and How It Shapes the Way We See the World.* New York: HarperCollins.

Genovese, J. 2015. "Honing the Art of Observation, and Observing Art." *Stanford Medicine News Center*, March 6, 2015.

Gosselin, N., I. Peretz, E. Johnsen, and R. Adolphs. 2007. "Amygdala Damage Impairs Emotion Recognition from Music." *Neuropsychologia* 45 (2): 236–44.

Gottman, J. 1997. *Raising an Emotionally Intelligent Child.* New York: Simon and Schuster.

Grady, C., A. McIntosh, M. N. Rajah, and F. Craik. 1998. "Neural Correlates of the Episodic Encoding of Picture and Words." *Proceedings of the National Academy of Sciences of the United States of America* 95 (5): 2703–8.

Grape, C., M. Sandgren, L. Hansson, M. Ericson, and T. Theorell. 2003. "Does Singing Promote Well-Being? An Empirical Study of Professional and Amateur Singers during a Singing Lesson." *Integrative Physiological and Behavioral Science* 38 (1): 65–74.

Gridley, H., J. Astbury, J. Sharples, and C. Aguirre. 2011. *Benefits of Group Singing for Community Mental Health and Wellbeing.* Carlton, Australia: Victorian Health Promotion Foundation.

Grossman, P., L. Niemann, S. Schmidt, and H. Walach. 2004. "Mindfulness-Based Stress Reduction and Health Benefits: A Meta-Analysis." *Journal of Psychosomatic Research* 57 (1): 35–43.

Gruenfeld, D. 2013. "Power & Influence." *Stanford VMware Women's Leadership Innovation Lab.* Stanford University.

Gunderson, E. A., S. J. Gripshover, C. Romero, C. Dweck, S. Goldin-Meadow, and S. C. Levine. 2013. "Parent Praise to 1- to 3-Year-Olds Predicts Children's Motivational Framework 5 Years Later." *Child Development* 84 (5): 1526–41.

Gunderson, E. A., N. S. Sorhagen, S. J. Gripshover, C. S. Dweck, S. Goldin-Meadow, and S. C. Levine. 2018. "Parent Praise to Toddlers Predicts Fourth Grade Academic Achievement via Children's Incremental Mindsets." *Developmental Psychology* 54 (3): 397–409.

Hallman, S. 2014. *Evaluation of Apollo Music Projects.* London: Institute of Education, University of London.

Hambrick, E. P., T. W. Brawner, B. D. Perry, K. Brandt, C. Hofmeister, and J. Collins. 2018. "Beyond the ACE Score: Examining Relationships between Timing of Developmental Adversity, Relational Health and Developmental Outcomes in Children." *Archives of Psychiatric Nursing.* Article in press. Available at https://doi.org/10.1016/j.apnu.2018.11.001.

Hart, B., and T. R. Risley. 1995. *Meaningful Differences in the Everyday Experience of* **203** *Young American Children*. Baltimore, MD: Paul H. Brookes.

Hartling, L., A. S. Newton, Y. Liang, H. Jou, K. Hewson, T. P. Klassen, and S. Curtis. 2013. "Music to Reduce Pain and Distress in the Pediatric Emergency Department: A Randomized Clinical Trial." *Journal of the American Medical Association Pediatrics* 167 (9): 826–35.

Hemmeter, M. L., M. M. Ostrosky, K. M. Artman, and K. A. Kinder. 2008. "Moving Right Along: Planning Transitions to Prevent Challenging Behavior." *Young Children* 63 (3): 18–25.

Her Majesty's Government. 2018. "A Connected Society: A Strategy for Tackling Loneliness." Department for Digital, Culture, Media & Sport, October 15, 2018.

Hertenstein, M., and S. Weiss, eds. 2011. *The Handbook of Touch*. New York: Springer.

Ho, P., J. Tsao, L. Bloch, and L. Zeltzer. 2011. "The Impact of Group Drumming on Social-Emotional Behavior in Low-Income Children." *Evidence-Based Complementary and Alternative Medicine*: Article ID 250708.

Holt-Lunstad, J., T. Smith, and J. B. Layton. 2010. "Social Relationships and Mortality Risk: A Meta-analytic Review." *PLoS Medicine* 7 (7): e1000316.

Horst, J. S., K. L. Parsons, and N. M. Bryan. 2011. "Get the Story Straight: Contextual Repetition Promotes Word Learning from Storybooks." *Frontiers in Psychology* 2:17.

House, J. S. 2001. "Social Isolation Kills, but How and Why?" *Psychosomatic Medicine* 63 (2): 273–74.

Housen, A. 1999. "Eye of the Beholder: Research, Theory and Practice." Presented at the conference "Aesthetic and Art Education: A Transdisciplinary Approach," sponsored by the Calouste Gulbenkian Foundation, Service of Education, September 27–29, 1999, Lisbon, Portugal.

———. 2001–2. "Aesthetic Thought, Critical Thinking, and Transfer." *Arts and Learning Research Journal* 18 (1): 99–131.

Huang L., A. D. Galinsky, D. H. Gruenfeld, and L. D. Guillory. 2011. "Powerful Postures Versus Powerful Roles: Which Is the Proximate Correlate of Thought and Behavior?" *Psychological Science* 22 (1): 95–102.

Huebner, B., and J. Rossi. 2009. *"I Remember Better When I Paint."* Feature-length documentary film. French Connection Films.

Hutchins, P. 1989. *Don't Forget the Bacon*. New York: Greenwillow Books, HarperCollins.

Ji, J., S. B. Heyes, C. MacLeod, and E. Holmes. 2016. "Emotional Mental Imagery as Simulation of Reality: Fear and Beyond." *Behavior Therapy* 47 (5): 702–19.

Jiwen Song, L., G. Huang, K. Peng, K. Law, C. Wong, and Z. Chen. 2010. "The Differential Effects of General Mental Ability and Emotional Intelligence on Academic Performance and Social Interactions." *Intelligence* 38 (1): 137–43.

Jones, D., and K. Peart. 2009. "Class Helping Future Doctors Learn the Art of Observation." *Yale News*, April 10, 2009.

**204**   Jones, D. A., M. Greenberg, and M. Crowley. 2015. "Early Social-Emotional Functioning and Public Health: The Relationship Between Kindergarten Social Competence and Future Wellness." *American Journal of Public Health* 105 (11): 2283–90.

Jones, L., and G. Stuth. 1997. "The Uses of Mental Imagery in Athletics: An Overview." *Applied and Preventive Psychology* 6 (2): 101–15.

Kabat-Zinn, J. 2014. *Full Catastrophe Living*. New York: Bantam Books.

Kaimal, G., K. Ray, and J. Muiz. 2016. "Reduction of Cortisol Levels and Participants' Responses Following Art Making." *Art Therapy: Journal of the American Art Therapy Association* 33 (2): 74–80.

Kalyani, B., G. Venkatasubramanian, R. Arasappa, N. Rao, S. Kalmady, R. Behere, H. Rao, M. Vasudev, and B. Gangadhar. 2011. "Neurohemodynamic Correlates of 'Om' Chanting: A Pilot Functional Magnetic Resonance Imaging Study." *International Journal of Yoga* 4 (1): 3–6.

Kaschel, R., S. Sala, A. Cantagallo, A. Fahblöck, R. Laaksonen, and M. Kazen. 2010. "Imagery Mnemonics for the Rehabilitation of Memory: A Randomized Group Controlled Trial." *Neuropsychological Rehabilitation: An International Journal* 12 (2): 127–53.

Kashdan, T., and M. Steger. 2007. "Curiosity and Pathways to Well-Being and Meaning in Life: Traits, States, and Everyday Behaviors." *Motivation and Emotion* 31 (3): 159–73.

Kaufman, S. B., and C. Gregoire. 2015. *Wired to Create*. New York: Penguin Random House.

Keeley, T. 2014. "The Importance of Self-Identity and Ego Permeability in Foreign Culture Adaptation and Foreign Language Acquisition." *Keieigaku Ronshu* [Business Review] 25 (1): 65–104.

Keller, P. E. 2012. "Mental Imagery in Music Performance: Underlying Mechanisms and Potential Benefits." *Annals of the New York Academy of Sciences* 1252 (1): 206–13.

Kirschner, S., and M. Tomasello. 2000. "Joint Music Making Promotes Prosocial Behavior in 4-Year-Old Children." *Evolution and Human Behavior* 31:354–64.

Klassen, J. A., Y. Liang, L. Tjosvold, T. P. Klassen, and L. Hartling. 2008. "Music for Pain and Anxiety in Children Undergoing Medical Procedures: A Systematic Review of Randomized Controlled Trials." *Ambulatory Pediatrics Journal* 8 (2): 117–28.

Klemm, W. 2007. "What Good Is Learning If You Don't Remember It?" *Journal of Effective Teaching* 7 (1): 61–73.

Knight, C., and S. A. Haslam. 2010. "The Relative Merits of Lean, Enriched, and Empowered Offices: An Experimental Examination of the Impact of Workspace Management Strategies on Well-Being and Productivity." *Journal of Experimental Psychology* 16 (2): 158–72.

Kokal, I., A. Engle, S. Kirschner, and C. Keysers. 2011. "Synchronized Drumming Enhances Activity in the Caudate and Facilitates Prosocial Commitment—If the Rhythm Comes Easily." *PLoS ONE* 6 (11): e27272.

Korn, R. 2010. *Educational Research: The Art of Problem Solving*. New York: Solomon R. Guggenheim Museum Visitor Studies, Evaluation & Audience Research.

Kornblum, R. 2002. *Disarming the Playground: Violence Prevention through Movement & Pro-social Skills.* Oklahoma City: Wood and Barnes.

Kraemer, D. J., C. N. Macrae, A. E. Green, and W. M. Kelley. 2005. "Musical Imagery: Sound of Silence Activates Auditory Cortex." *Nature* 434 (7030): 158.

Kraft, T. L., and S. D. Pressman. 2012. "Grin and Bear It: The Influence of Manipulated Facial Expression on the Stress Response." *Psychological Science* 23 (11): 1372–78.

Lambert, N. M., M. S. Clark, J. Durtschi, F. Fincham, and S. M. Graham. 2010. "Benefits of Expressing Gratitude: Expressing Gratitude to a Partner Changes One's View of the Relationship." *Psychological Science* 21 (4): 574–80.

Landgarten, H. 1987. *Family Art Psychotherapy: A Clinical Guide and Casebook.* Levittown, PA: Brunner/Mazel.

Lengacher, C. A., M. P. Bennett, L. Gonzalez, D. Gilvary, C. E. Cox, A. Cantor, P. B. Jacobsen, C. Yang, and J. Djeu. 2008. "Immune Responses to Guided Imagery During Breast Cancer Treatment." *Biological Research for Nursing* 9 (3): 205–14.

Levine, P. 1997. *Waking the Tiger: Healing Trauma.* Berkeley, CA: North Atlantic Books.

———. 2010. *In an Unspoken Voice: How the Body Releases Trauma and Restores Goodness.* Berkeley, CA: North Atlantic Books.

Limb, C.J., and A. R. Braun. 2008. "Neural Substrates of Spontaneous Musical Performance: An fMRI Study of Jazz Improvisation." *PLoS ONE* 3 (2): e1679.

Lord, T. R., and J. E. Garner. 1993. "Effects of Music on Alzheimer Patients." *Perceptual and Motor Skills* 76 (2): 451–55.

Lowenfeld, V. 1947. *Creative and Mental Growth.* New York: Macmillan.

Macedonia, M., and K. Kriegstein. 2012. "Gestures Enhance Foreign Language Learning." *Biolinguistics* 6 (3-4): 393–416.

Maddison, R., H. Prapavessis, M. Clatworthy, C. Hall, L. Foley, T. Harper, D. Cupal, and B. Brewer. 2011. "Guided Imagery to Improve Functional Outcomes Post-Anterior Cruciate Ligament Repair: Randomized-Controlled Pilot Study." *Scandinavian Journal of Medicine and Science in Sports* 22 (6): 816–21.

Maguire, E., D. Gadian, I. Johnsrude, C. Good, J. Ashburner, R. Frackowiak, and C. Frith. 2000. "Navigation-Related Structural Change in the Hippocampi of Taxi Drivers." *Proceedings of the National Academy of Sciences* 97 (8): 4398–403.

Martin, L., R. Oepen, K. Bauer, A. Nottensteiner, K. Mergheim, H. Gruber, and S. C. Koch. 2018. "Creative Arts Interventions for Stress Management and Prevention—A Systematic Review." *Behavioral Sciences* 8 (2): 28.

Mehrabian, A. 1981. *Silent Messages: Implicit Communication of Emotions and Attitudes.* 2nd ed. Belmont, CA: Wadsworth.

Michel, D. E., and J. Pinson. 2005. *Music Therapy in Principle and Practice.* Springfield, IL: Charles C. Thomas.

Miller, J. F., M. Neufang, A. Solway, A. Brandt, M. Trippel, I. Mader, S. Hefft, M. Merkow, S. M. Polyn, J. Jacobs, M. J. Kahana, and A. Schulze-Bonhage. 2013. "Neural Activity in Human Hippocampal Formation Reveals the Spatial Context of Retrieved Memories." *Science* 342 (6162): 1111–14.

**206**     Miranda, L. 2016. "Hamilton: An American Musical." In *Hamilton: The Revolution*, ed. J. McCarter. New York: Grand Central Publishing.

Moser, J. S., H. S. Schroder, C. Heeter, T. P. Moran, and Y. H. Lee. 2011. "Mind Your Errors: Evidence for Neural Mechanism Linking Growth Mind-Set to Adaptive Posterror Adjustments." *Psychological Science* 22 (12): 1484–89.

Musu-Gillette, L., A. Zhang, K. Wang, J. Zhang, J. Kemp, M. Diliberti, and B. A. Oudekerk. 2018. "Indicators of School Crime and Safety: 2017." *National Center for Education Statistics*.

Naghshineh, S., J. Hafler, A. Miller, M. Blanco, S. Lipsitz, R. Dubroff, S. Khoshbin, and J. Katz. 2008. "Formal Art Observation Training Improves Medical Students' Visual Diagnostic Skills." *Journal of General Internal Medicine* 23 (7): 991–97.

National Crime Prevention Council. 2000. "Arts and Performances for Prevention." *Youth in Action*, no. 11 (January).

National Performing Arts Convention. 2012. "Useful Quotes for Arts Advocates." March 27, 2012.

Neff, K. 2011. *Self-Compassion: The Proven Power of Being Kind to Yourself*. New York: HarperCollins.

Nilsson, U. 2008. "The Anxiety and Pain-Reducing Effects of Music Interventions: A Systematic Review." *Association of Perioperative Registered Nurses Journal* 87 (4): 780–807.

Nobel, J. 2015. "The UnLonely Project Overview." Online video clip. *The Foundation for Art and Healing*.

Noice, H., and T. Noice. 2016. "What Studies of Actors and Acting Can Tell Us about Memory and Cognitive Functioning." *Current Directions in Psychological Sciences* 15 (1): 14–18.

Opezzo, M., and D. L. Schwartz. 2014. "Give Your Ideas Some Legs: The Positive Effect of Walking on Creative Thinking." *Journal of Experimental Psychology: Learning, Memory, and Cognition* 40 (4): 1142–52.

Orlick, T. 2016. *In Pursuit of Excellence: How to Win in Sport and Life through Mental Training*. Champaign, IL: Human Kinetics.

Pennebaker, J., J. Kiecolt-Glaser, and R. Glaser. 1988. "Disclosure of Traumas and Immune Function: Health Implications for Psychotherapy." *Journal of Clinical Consulting Psychology* 56:239–45.

Petty, R. E., and J. T. Cacioppo. 1986. *Communication and Persuasion: Central and Peripheral Routes to Attitude Change*. New York: Springer.

Pevtzow, L. 2013. "Teaching Compassion." *Chicago Tribune*, March 20, 2013.

Phelps, E. A. 2004. "Human Emotion and Memory: Interactions of the Amygdala and Hippocampal Complex." *Current Opinion in Neurobiology* 14 (2): 198–202.

Piferi, R., and K. A. Lawler. 2006. "Social Support and Ambulatory Blood Pressure: An Examination of Both Receiving and Giving." *International Journal of Psychophysiology* 62 (2): 328–36.

Pineda, J., ed. 2009. *Mirror Neuron Systems: The Role of Mirroring Processes in Social Cognition*. San Diego, CA: Springer.

Posner, M., and B. Patoine. 2009. "How Arts Training Improves Attention and Cognition." The Dana Foundation, September 14, 2009.

Pramanik, T., B. Pudasaini, and R. Prajapati. 2010. "Immediate Effect of a Slow Pace Breathing Exercise Bhramari Pranayama on Blood Pressure and Heart Rate." *Nepal Medical College* 12 (3): 154–57.

Pryor, J. H., S. Hurtado, L. DeAngelo, L. Palucki Blake, and S. Tran. 2010. *The American Freshman: National Norms Fall 2010*. Los Angeles, CA: Higher Education Research Institute, UCLA.

Puetz, T. W., C. A. Morley, and M. P. Herring. 2013. "Effects of Creative Arts Therapies on Psychological Symptoms and Quality of Life in Patients with Cancer." *JAMA Internal Medicine* 173 (11): 960–69.

Radaelli, A., R. Raco, P. Perfetti, A. Viola, A. Azzellino, M. Signorini, and A Ferrari. 2004. "Effects of Slow, Controlled Breathing on Baroreceptor Control of Heart Rate and Blood Pressure in Healthy Men." *Journal of Hypertension* 22 (7): 1361–70.

Ranehill, E., A. Dreber, M. Johannesson, S. Leiberg, S. Sul, and R. A. Weber. 2015. "Assessing the Robustness of Power Posing: No Effect on Hormones and Risk Tolerance in a Large Sample of Men and Women." *Psychological Science* 26 (5): 653–56.

Rauscher, F. H., G. L. Shaw, and C. N. Ky. 1993. "Music and Spatial Task Performance." *Nature* 365 (6447): 611.

Reddish, P., R. Fischer, and J. Bulbulia. 2013. "Let's Dance Together: Synchrony, Shared Intentionality and Cooperation." *PLoS ONE* 8 (8): e71182.

Reid-Searle, K., L. Quinney, T. Dwyer, L. Vieth, L. Nancarrow, and B. Walker. 2016. "Puppets in an Acute Pediatric Unit: Nurse's Experiences." *Collegian* 24 (4): 317–24.

Reynolds, P. 2004. *Ish*. London: Walker Books.

Richardson, M. P., B. A. Strange, and R. J. Dolan. 2004. "Encoding of Emotional Memories Depends on Amygdala and Hippocampus and Their Interactions." *Nature Neuroscience* 7 (3): 278–85.

Robinson, K. 2006. "Sir Ken Robinson: Do Schools Kill Creativity?" *TED Ideas Worth Spreading*.

———. 2011. *Out of Our Minds: Learning to Be Creative*. West Sussex, UK: Capstone.

Rosal, M., S. McCulloch-Vislisel, and S. Neece. 1997. "Keeping Students in School: An Art Therapy Program to Benefit Ninth-Grade Students." *Art Therapy: Journal of the American Art Therapy Association* 14 (1): 30–36.

Rowling, J. K. 1999. *Harry Potter and the Prisoner of Azkaban*. New York: Arthur A. Levine Books.

Rubin, D. 1995. *Memory in Oral Traditions: The Cognitive Psychology of Epic, Ballads, and Counting-Out Rhymes*. New York: Oxford University Press.

Sacks, O. 2008. *Musicophilia*. New York: Vintage Books.

Saltzberg, B. 2010. *Beautiful Oops*. New York: Workman Publishing.

Schellenberg, E. G., and S. Hallam. 2005. "Music Listening and Cognitive Abilities in 10- And 11-Year-Olds: The Blur Effect." *Annals of the New York Academy of Sciences* 1060:202–9.

Schore, A. 2016. *Affect Regulation and the Origin of the Self*. New York: Routledge.

**208**    Shapiro, F. 2012. *Getting Past Your Past*. New York: Rodale.

Shella, T. A. 2018. "Art Therapy Improves Mood, and Reduces Pain and Anxiety When Offered at Bedside during Acute Hospital Treatment." *The Arts in Psychotherapy* 57:59–64.

Siegel, D., and T. P. Bryson. 2012. *The Whole-Brain Child*. New York: Random House.

———. 2016. *No-Drama Discipline: The Whole-Brain Way to Calm the Chaos and Nurture Your Child's Developing Mind*. New York: Random House.

Simmons-Stern, N., A. Budson, and B. Ally. 2010. "Music as a Memory Enhancer in Patients with Alzheimer's Disease." *Neuropsychologia* 48 (10): 3164–67.

Simpson, B., and R. Willer. 2015. "Beyond Altruism: Sociological Foundations of Cooperation and Prosocial Behavior." *Annual Review of Sociology* 41:43–63.

Stallings, J. 2010. "Collage as a Therapeutic Modality for Reminiscence in Patients with Dementia." *Art Therapy: Journal of the American Art Therapy Association* 27 (3): 136–40.

Steers, M., R. Wickham, and L. Acitelli. 2014. "Seeing Everyone Else's Highlight Reels: How Facebook Usage Is Linked to Depressive Symptoms." *Journal of Social and Clinical Psychology* 33 (8): 701–31.

Stellar, J., N. John-Henderson, C. Anderson, A. Gordon, G. McNeil, and D. Keltner. 2015. "Positive Affect and Markers of Inflammation: Discrete Positive Emotions Predict Lower Levels of Inflammatory Cytokines." *Emotion* 15 (2): 129–33.

Stewart-Brown, S., L. Fletcher, and M. E. J. Wadsworth. 2005. "Parent-Child Relationships and Health Problems in Adulthood in Three UK National Birth Cohort Studies." *European Journal of Public Health* 15 (6): 640–46.

Stiffelman, S. 2012. *Parenting without Power Struggles*. New York: Simon and Schuster.

Stuckey, H., and J. Nobel. 2010. "The Connection between Art, Healing, and Public Health." *American Journal of Public Health* 100 (2): 254–63.

Suldo, S., and S. Huebner. 2004. "The Role of Life Satisfaction in the Relationship between Authoritative Parenting Dimensions and Adolescent Problem Behavior." *Social Indicators Research* 66 (1–2): 165–95.

Suresh, S., G. S. De Oliveira Jr., and S. Suresh. 2015. "The Effect of Audio Therapy to Treat Postoperative Pain in Children Undergoing Major Surgery: A Randomized Controlled Trial." *Pediatric Surgery International* 31 (2): 197–201.

Szalavitz, M., and B. Perry. 2010. *Born for Love*. New York: HarperCollins.

Tarr, B., J. Launay, E. Cohen, and R. Dunbar. 2015. "Synchrony and Exertion during Dance Independently Raise Pain Threshold and Encourage Social Bonding." *Biology Letters* 11 (10): 20150767.

Taruffi, L., and S. Koelsch. 2014. "The Paradox of Music-Evoked Sadness: An Online Survey." *PLoS ONE* 9 (10): e110490.

Thiessen, E. D. and J. R. Saffran. 2009. *How the Melody Facilitates the Message and Vice Versa in Infant Learning and Memory*. In S. Dalla Bella, N. Kraus, K. Overy, C. Pantev, J. S. Snyder, M. Tervaniemi, and G. Schlaug, eds. 2009. *The Neurosciences and Music III: Disorders and Plasticity* (Annals of the New York Academy of Sciences 1169). Boston: Blackwell/New York Academy of Sciences.

Torrisi, S. J., M. D. Lieberman, S. Y. Bookheimer, and L. L. Altshuler. 2013. "Advancing Understanding of Affect Labeling with Dynamic Causal Modeling." *NeuroImage* 82:481–88.

Toyota, H. 2002. "The Bizarre Effect and Individual Differences in Imaging Abilities." *Perceptual and Motor Skills* 94 (2): 533–40.

Tramo, M. J. 2001. "Biology and Music. Music of the Hemispheres." *Science* 291 (5501): 54–56.

Turkle, S. 2015. *Reclaiming Conversation: The Power of Talk in a Digital Age.* New York: Penguin.

Uchino, B. N. 2006. "Social Support and Health: A Review of Physiological Processes Underlying Links to Disease Outcomes." *Journal of Behavioral Medicine* 29 (4): 377–87.

Uhls, Y., M. Michikyan, J. Morris, D. Garcia, G. Small, E. Zgourou, and P. Greenfield. 2014. "Five Days at Outdoor Education Camp Without Screens Improves Preteen Skills with Nonverbal Emotion Cues." *Computers in Human Behavior* 39:387–92.

Ungerleider, S., and J. Golding. 1991. "Mental Practice among Olympic Athletes." *Perceptual and Motor Skills* 72 (3): 1007–17.

UNESCO International Bureau of Education. 2001. *World Data on Education: A Guide to the Structure of National Systems.* Geneva: UNESCO, International Bureau of Education.

UNICEF. 1994. *The Multigrade Teacher's Handbook.* Philippines: Bureau of Elementary Education, Department of Education, Culture, and Sports.

Valdesolo, P., and D. DeSteno. 2011. "Synchrony and the Social Tuning of Compassion." *Emotion* 11 (2): 262–66.

Valdesolo, P., J. Ouyang, and D. DeSteno. 2010. "The Rhythm of Joint Action: Synchrony Promotes Cooperative Ability." *Journal of Experimental Social Psychology* 46 (4): 693–95.

Van Baaren, R. B., R. W. Holland, B. Steenaert, and A. Van Knippenberg. 2003. "Mimicry for Money: Behavioral Consequences of Imitation." *Journal of Experimental Social Psychology* 39 (4): 393–98.

van der Kolk, B. 2014. *The Body Keeps the Score: Brain, Mind, and Body in the Healing of Trauma.* New York: Penguin.

van der Vennet, R., and S. Serice. 2012. "Can Coloring Mandalas Reduce Anxiety? A Replication Study." *Art Therapy: Journal of the American Art Therapy Association* 29 (2): 87–92.

van der Wal-Huisman, H., K.S.K. Dons, R. Smilde, E. Heineman, and B. L. van Leeuwen. 2018. "The Effect of Music on Postoperative Recovery in Older Patients: A Systematic Review." *Journal of Geriatric Oncology* 9 (6): 550–59.

Vickhoff, B., H. Malmgren, R. Aström, G. Nyberg, S. -R. Ekstrom, M. Engwall, J. Snygg, M. Nilsson, and R. Jörnsten. 2013. "Music Structure Determines Heart Rate Variability of Singers." *Frontiers in Psychology* 4:334.

Vogt, S., and S. Magnussen. 2007. "Expertise in Pictorial Perception: Eye-Movement Patterns and Visual Memory in Artists and Laymen." *Perception* 36 (1): 91–100.

**210**  Wammes, J., M. Meade, and M. Fernandes. 2016. "The Drawing Effect: Evidence for Reliable and Robust Memory Benefits in Free Recall." *Quarterly Journal of Experimental Psychology* 69 (9): 1752–76.

Watkins, P., K. Woodward, T. Stone, and R. L. Kolts. 2003. "Gratitude and Happiness: Development of a Measure of Gratitude, and Relationships with Subjective Well-Being." *Social Behavior and Personality* 31 (5): 431–52.

Weiss, N., and J. Raphael. 2013. *How to Make MeCards4Kids™*. Santa Cruz, CA: Hanford Mead.

Weissbourd, R., and S. Jones. 2014. *The Children We Mean to Raise: The Real Messages Adults Are Sending about Values*. Boston: Harvard Graduate School of Education.

Whalley, J. 2009. "The Arts as a Means of Increasing Emotional Intelligence in Teens." A Winston Churchill Memorial Trust Report.

Wilson, C., and B. Moulton. 2010. "Loneliness among Older Adults: A National Survey of 45+." Knowledge Networks and Insight Policy Research. Washington, DC: AARP.

Wolf, R. I. 2007. "Advances in Phototherapy Training." *The Arts in Psychotherapy* 34 (2): 124–33.

Wood, A. M., J. Froh, and A. Geraghty. 2010. "Gratitude and Well-Being: A Review and Theoretical Integration." *Clinical Psychology Review* 30 (7): 890–905.

Yang, Y. C., C. Boen, K. Gerken, T. Li, K. Schorpp, and K. M. Harris. 2015. "Social Relationships and Physiological Determinants of Longevity across the Human Life Span." *Proceedings of the National Academy of Sciences* 113 (3): 578–83.

Zatorre, R. and A. Halpern. 2005. "Mental Concerts: Musical Imagery and Auditory Cortex." *Neuron* 47 (1): 9–12.

Zeman, A., F. Milton, A. Smith, and R. Rylance. 2013. "By Heart: An fMRI Study of Brain Activation by Poetry and Prose." *Journal of Consciousness Studies* 20 (9–10): 132–58.

Zimmerman, F., D. Christakis, and A. Meltzoff. 2007. "Associations between Media Viewing and Language Development in Children Under Age 2 Years." *Journal of Pediatrics* 151 (4): 364–68.

# Index

academic performance: barriers to, 154–56; effect of art on, 5, 57, 130, 132, 138, 141; and social-emotional competence, 182

acceptance, 35, 142–43

activities: repetitive, 75; transitions in, 45–49

Altshuler, Ira, 168

Alzheimer's disease, 145

American Psychological Association Zero Tolerance Task Force, 31

Ames, Louise Bates, 99

anger: acknowledging, 39–40; addressing, 15, 23, 33, 86, 96–97; art as connector, 36, 37, 77, 88, 93; and destruction, 25–27, 31–33; as emotional visitor, 96–99; and music, 168

anxiety, 4, 9, 57, 99, 124, 127–28, 174

art: academic performance, effect on, 5, 57, 130, 132, 138, 141; apps, 91; commemoration in, 85–86; community, 86–87; for confronting fears, 124–29; as connector, 36, 37, 77, 88, 93; and creative thinking, 133–38; curriculum integration, 155–56; defined, 3; destruction in, 25–33; discomfort with, 9–10; as doorway to talking, 73–77; and empathy, 38; expressing feelings through, 32–33, 50, 63–70, 93–94, 105, 107–9, 123, 124, 156, 179–80; giving, 83–84; and identity exploration, 119–20; and internal needs, 2; interpretation of, 63–73; language of, 2–3, 63–64, 70–72, 94; limits vs. freedom of expression in, 12–20, 134; materials, properties of, 17–20; as messy, 11–12, 19, 23–25; metaphor in, 67–70; and mindfulness, 142–44; nonjudgmental observations of, 30, 33, 75–76, 83, 136; as nutritionally dense activity, 2, 130–32, 174, 175; and observation skills, 138–40; and problem solving, 141–42; and retention, 145–46; self-connection

activities, 112–15; and self-criticism, 174–75; for stress reduction, 121–23; and technology, 89–92; as unifying, 86–87; and values/beliefs, 116–18; and visual literacy, 54–56

attention-focusing. *See* paying attention

autism spectrum disorder (ASD), 17–18, 87–88

awe, 158–59

Baby Einstein DVD series, 131

behavior: vs. character development, 6; as communication, 49–53; curiosity about, 159–60; and frontal cortex, 103; and mental imagery, 164–65; qualities to encourage, 58; repetition of, 15, 44, 163; in synchrony, 78, 80–81; underlying reasons for, 15–16, 32, 51–53, 79, 99–100, 116, 156. *See also* containment

big feelings. *See under* feelings

bonds, 84–87

boredom, 49, 52, 112, 149–50

Bornstein, Ruth, 78

Bryson, Tina, 104

cameras and photos, 91, 180

celebrating, 179–80

Changing Education through the Arts (CETA), 155

clay, working with, 67, 73–74, 93, 101, 105, 151

Cohen, Lawrence, 2, 88

Colt, George Howe, 50

comprehension, 144–48

connecting/reconnecting, 37–40, 62–63, 72, 77–79, 87–92

containment, 14–17, 18, 102–3, 105–7

cozy place, 99, 101

creative thinking, 132–38, 149, 157–60, 161–62, 170, 178

critical thinking, 141–42